Adaptations of the Metropolitan Landscape in Delta Regions

Peter C. Bosselmann

Routledge
Taylor & Francis Group
NEW YORK AND LONDON

First published 2018
by Routledge
711 Third Avenue, New York, NY 10017

and by Routledge
2 Park Square, Milton Park, Abingdon, Oxon, OX14 4RN

Routledge is an imprint of the Taylor & Francis Group, an informa business

© 2018 Peter C. Bosselmann

The right of Peter C. Bosselmann to be identified as the author
of this work has been asserted by him in accordance with sections 77 and 78
of the Copyright, Designs and Patents Act 1988.

All rights reserved. No part of this book may be reprinted
or reproduced or utilised in any form or by any electronic, mechanical, or
other means, now known or hereafter invented, including photocopying
and recording, or in any information storage or retrieval system, without
permission in writing from
the publishers.

Trademark notice: Product or corporate names may be trademarks or
registered trademarks, and are used only for identification and explanation
without intent to infringe.

British Library Cataloguing in Publication Data
A catalogue record for this book is available from the British Library

Library of Congress Cataloging in Publication Data
Names: Bosselmann, Peter C., author.
Title: Adaptations of the metropolitan landscape in delta regions /
Peter C. Bosselmann.
Description: New York, NY : Routledge, 2018. | Includes bibliographical
references.
Identifiers: LCCN 2017035009| ISBN 9781138551916 (hardback) |
ISBN 9781138551961 (pbk.) | ISBN 9781315147871 (ebk)
Subjects: LCSH: Urban ecology (Sociology) | Coastal settlements. |
City planning—Environmental aspects. | Climatic changes. |
Urbanization—California—Delta Region. | Urbanization—China—Pearl River
Delta. | Urbanization—Netherlands. | Sustainable urban development. |
Deltas—Social aspects. | Water levels—Social aspects. | Coastal zone
management.
Classification: LCC HT241 .B67 2018 | DDC 307.1/216—dc23
LC record available at https://lccn.loc.gov/2017035009

ISBN: 978-1-138-55191-6 (hbk)
ISBN: 978-1-138-55196-1 (pbk)
ISBN: 978-1-315-14787-1 (ebk)

Typeset in Bembo
by Keystroke, Neville Lodge, Tettenhall, Wolverhampton

Contents

Foreword	vii
Acknowledgements	ix
Why this book?	1
Part I The San Francisco Estuary and Inland Delta	**7**
1 Water, Land and Places, the Origins of Urban Form in the San Francisco Bay Area	19
2 The Bay Area's Metropolitan Landscape, a Dispersed Metropolis	38
3 Causes and Consequences of Climate Change for the San Francisco Bay Area	56
Part II The Pearl River Delta	**73**
1 The Pearl River Delta as a Cultural Landscape – New Life for a Traditional Water Village	87
2 Whampoa Harbor	108
3 Jiangmen, a Historic City Remembers its Center and the Urban Expansion on Pazhou Island in Guangzhou	123
Part III The Dutch Delta	**145**
1 The Making of the Dutch Delta	149
2 An Archipelago of Cities – Five Delta Towns	158
3 Contemporary Examples and Strategies for the Future	184
Conclusion	201
Index	205

Foreword

This book comes at the right moment: the question of how cities can survive climate change has become acute. Already certain densely populated islands and parts of low-lying cities have to be evacuated because of sea level rise as they start to disappear in the floods! Even if this is still the exception, more than half of the global population lives in delta regions and many of these communities will have to find a way of life under the conditions of rising sea levels and rising rivers flooding their inhabited banks.

These days we talk about a new epoch in the world's natural history, the Anthropocene, an epoch in which we have to shoulder the responsibility of the environmental conditions and adaptations required for global survival. This book stimulates new ideas for coping with these responsibilities.

In the deltas, communities experience dependence on natural forces, most of them outside their control, in a most direct way: without a basic understanding of these natural forces, there will be no lasting solution! So, very appropriately, the discussion of each of the three cases – the metropolitan landscape of the San Francisco Estuary and Inland Delta, the Pearl River Delta, and the Dutch Delta – starts with a short natural history of its morphology and hydrology, demonstrating the embeddedness of humans in nature and their dependence on it.

Consequently, this natural history is, in each of the cases, complemented by a short history of humanity's answers to history in the form of special settlements, developed under these natural conditions. These answers form a body of valuable experiences.

But as this book is about the future and the contributions of urban design to mediate climate change, the focus is on the question of what could be an appropriate approach of urban design to adapt settlements to climate change and to achieve a coexistence, or better, a synergy of town and water. Imaginative answers in detail were developed and designed by students in their master's courses, working on typical examples. As the rich material of this successful international academic cooperation cannot be summarized, I restrict myself to two different examples of basic questions:

- What could be done to urbanize a typical Californian suburban development, and by that make it more resilient? Are there feasible means to gradually open the development to a mixed use, to higher residential densities, and to a community with fewer cars?
- What could be done to adapt a historic village in the Pearl River Delta surrounded by a much larger development and threatened by destruction? Could it be a feasible solution in the interest of the socio-economically weak inhabitants (mostly migrant workers) to preserve the basic historic pattern and to adapt it gradually to new, modern life?

In both cases the answers inform distinct urban design proposals that are both beautiful and stimulating. In short: they are promising!

The book closes with a fundamental dilemma, urgently discussed in Holland: will the solution of fighting the rising waters be found in ever more and bigger technical equipment? Or might a more feasible solution involve giving the water more space to expand and contract naturally? There is no definite answer yet, but it will be in this realm of strategic thoughts to develop answers that are both practically feasible and sustainable under the conditions of long-lasting climate change.

Tom Sieverts

Acknowledgements

Part I

I have a great number of collaborators to thank, first and foremost Sarah Moos, who as an urban design student in the dual degree program at the Departments of Landscape Architecture and Urban Planning at Berkeley helped me in preparing most illustrations related to part I on the San Francisco Bay Area. We jointly published an article for the journal *Built Environment* 40/2 edited by Han Meyer from TU Delft entitled 'Delta Urbanism: New Challenges for Planning and Design in Urbanized Deltas'. Geographic information science work for the San Francisco Bay Area 3D maps and transects was done by Amna Alruheili, Brian Chambers, John Doyle, Erik Jensen, Deepak Sohane, Justin Kearnan and Kushal Lachhawani. Hyun Young Kim prepared drawings to compare the urban block through history.

Student research on various subjects covered in part I included answers to the question, does urban infill near transit stations reduce people's use of private automobiles? Justin Kearnan, David Cooke, Yue Fu and Weining Cao; Yasir Hameed and David Amos; Andrew Toth, Sara Toufik Alharbali and Yueyue Wang answered that question in three parallel studies. Does the design of urban blocks with substantial tree growth at the core reduce the perception of density? That question was examined by Tani Elliot, Andrea Stoelzle and Chris Toocheck; HyunYoung Jin, Marta Gual, Sam Maurer, Alejandra Orellana and Justin Richardson; Lingyue Anne Chen, Daniel Collazos, Carlos Recarte and Gabriel Kaprielian in three parallel studies. Fernand Braudel's *Threshold Values of Urbanity* were tested by Rama Husamddine, Sonali Praharai, Arezoo Besharati and Irene Ho; Micaela Bazo, Stephanie Lin and Xiuxian Zhan in two parallel studies. Jeffrey Farrington and Crystal Ward researched the commute patterns of a new neighborhood at the urban fringe. Work done as a precursor of the 2017 Resilient by Design competition included Hasti Afkham, Niki Xenia Alygizou, Martin Galindez, Qingchung Li, Haonan Lu, Praveen Raj Ramanathan Mohanraj, Parisa Mir Sadeghi, Catherine Schiltz and Valentina Schmidt. Finally, the design proposal by David Cooke, Justin Kearnan and Daniel Church for San Francisco's Transbay Terminal Area illustrates the conclusion of part I.

Part II

Work on part II of the book started in October 2007 with a visit to the Pearl River Delta in China. I am very grateful to Liyan Yang, a former Berkeley student, who introduced me to Professors Wu and Feng at the Institute of Oriental Architecture and Culture in Guangzhou. There Professor Jiang Feng organized a trip on a river boat that took us through the branches of the Pearl River Delta near the city of Foshan. Together we visited the water village Dadun. That visit started our collaboration between the University of California at Berkeley and South China University of Technology in Guangzhou with yearly workshops that brought students and faculty from both schools together to work on a better understanding of rapid urbanization in the changing metropolitan landscape. Encouraged by Professor Qingzhou Wu, we focused on the water-system of the delta. Jiang Feng and I, together with my Berkeley colleague Mathias Kondolf, a fluvial geomorphologist, organized the work on Dadun that is covered in part II of this book. Initially we jointly authored an article for the *Urban Design Journal* 15/2 together with Zhimin Zhang, Mingxia Liu and Professor Geping Bao in 2010. In the years that followed, continued support for our work came from Professor Yimin Sun, Executive and Associate Dean of the School of Architecture and Planning, South China University of Technology. Francesca Frassoldati contributed to the writing of this book; we jointly published an article on Xinxi in *Territorio*, 2014. I am very grateful for the support from Francesca and from my Chinese colleagues, Professors Haohao Xu, Ping Su and Chunyang Zhang, who helped with various projects mentioned in the chapters about the Pearl River Delta. Their guidance and understanding of the context contributed greatly to this book.

The list of Berkeley College of Environmental Design students who worked with Chinese students on projects in the Pearl River Delta is long. On the future of Dadun the student team included: Nadine Soubotin, Kirsten Podolak, Jin Lei, Li Yue, Hu Lan, Li Boxie, Luo Yushan, Kirsten Johnson, Stacy McLean, Wang Ge, Li Wenxuan, Sui Xin, Li Xuesi, Chen Siyun, John Sugrue, Ye Bichen, Huang Xiaobel, Zhang Guojon, Andrea Gaffney, Xiong Xiangnan, Xu Diandian, Zhao Yiyun, Krishna Balakrishnan, Carrie Wallace, Guan Feifan, Zhang Yunyuan, Li Junjun, Hua Sha, Li Zheng, Chen Yipin, Gan Yile Chen Jingxiang, Peter Frankel, Sam Woodhans-Roberts, Lin Yuming, Lin Feng, Quan Xuewen, Chen Wei, Gun Xin. The redesign of Whampoo Harbor included Rebecca Finn, Dario Schoulund, Brinda Sengupta, Jassu Sigh, Supaneat Chananapfun, Jennifer Hughes, Patrick Race, Jessica Look, Robin Reed, Beth Harrington, Huang Qiaolun, Chen Qian, Liyue, Lin Yuming, Zhang Zhenhua, Xie Daibin, Zhang Lei, Cao Xibo, Zhang Yingyi, Liu Ping. Work for Jiang Men included Brian Chambers, Hugo Corro, Richard Crockett, Karlene Gullone, Leo Hammond, Kelly Janes, Se-Woong Kim, Qinbo Liu, Mohammed Momin, Sarah Moos and Deepak Sohane. Students who contributed designs to the Xinxi workshop included Alana Sanders, Hyun Young Kim, Miriam Aranoff, Benedict Han, Bin Cai, Kushal Modi, Ethan Paul Lavine, Erik Jensen, Benjamin Townsend Caldwell, Ruemel Sanchez Panglao, Tian Liang, Xi Hu, Rui Wang, Jianzhao Zheng, Jing Xu, Kuan He, Xinyu Liang. Wenji Ma, Fei Du, Xinjian Li, Xiaofei Xie, Xiaolan Zhou, Haoxiang Yang, Shibo Yin, Junmin Xiomg, Min Luo, Binsi Li, Shansi He. The last workshop covered in part II focused on Pazhou Island. Drawings by Patrick Webb, Rohit Tak, Wang Liwen, Zhu Xuewen, Zhu Jian and Wu Zhenxing have been reproduced in this book; drawings by Justin Kearnan, David Cooke, Huiyi Zhang, Chuwei Yang, Ying Ding, Haochen Yang, Xingling Cai are mentioned; so are drawings by a team that included Ken Hirose, Cacena Cambell, Yi Hu, Junxi Wu, Zeyue Yao, Yining Ying, Bilin Chen and Lolein Bergers. Lolein came as a visiting student from Belgium; Stephanie Brucart and Katrina Ortiz led a team that included Jiang Hewen, Li Chenxue, Shen Xinxin, Xu Xiang, Zhang Ao. The team also included Adam Molinski, Eden Ferry, Kaleen Juarez and Kevin Lenhart.

Part III

In January 2014, I started my sabbatical leave to write the first draft of the book manuscript. I was invited as a visiting professor to the Technical University at Delft by Han Meyer. In the Netherlands, I renewed my friendship with Martin van der Thoorn, who had visited us in Berkeley, where he had been a student in the 1970s. Martin and I cycled from Middleburg around Walcheren in Zealand, once an island between the Eastern and Western Scheldt, now connected to the mainland. I learned a lot from Martin about the landscape dynamics of the Netherlands. He introduced me to the TU Delft map archives and pointed me toward the literature that was coming into existence about the transformations of Dutch cities since medieval days. Irene Curuli, a friend from our initial 2005 efforts to define the understanding of the metropolitan landscape, was a frequent source of information. I gained much from my visits to Eindhoven where she teaches landscape architecture and urban design, and enjoyed having her as a frequent guest with us at Silodam, where my family and I lived during the six months of our stay in Amsterdam. I enjoyed my acquaintance with Frits Palmboom, who impressed me with his optimistic professionalism. He had just been appointed to serve as Van Eesteren Chair at the Delft school. Cornelis Van Eesteren had been responsible for the repair and expansion of Amsterdam after WWII; the new endowed chair was a fitting assignment for Frits Palmboom, who had been the designer for IJburg, one of Amsterdam's most recent extensions. Conversations during our cycle tour to IJburg have very much colored the conclusion of part III.

I need to acknowledge four students who have helped me in assembling the illustrations for the manuscript: they are Justin Kearnan, Adam Molinski, Sonali Praharei and Niki Xenia Alygizou. Funding for their work came from the UC Berkeley Committee on Research and from the Beatrix Farrand Fund in the Department of Landscape Architecture.

The book covers work from a ten-year period, largely done with students from the Master of Urban Design, the Master of Landscape Architecture and the Master of City Planning programs at Berkeley. Without the contributions from students in my studios and the research methods courses, this book would not have been written. Much gratitude goes to John Ellis, Jiang Feng and Martin van der Thoorn for reading and commenting on chapter drafts. Likewise, much thanks goes to our daughters, Thea and Sophia, for reading chapters, and to my wife, Dorit Fromm, for reading successive drafts of the entire manuscript and helping me with the formatting of the text.

Why this Book?

Adaptation is a concept borrowed from evolutionary biology. In this book, the term describes the adaptation of cities to become better fitted to survive accelerating climate change due to global warming. Like other biological concepts, adaptation can only be applied to cities with caution. Unlike a mutating cell, the agent of change is not the city structure itself, which is inanimate. Within cities, people are the agents of change. As we understand the far-reaching requirements of addressing both the cause and consequences of climate change, we also understand the consequences of failing to adapt.

The **causes**, with a high degree of certainty, are anthropogenic; the **consequences** consist of processes that naturally occur, but that will occur more frequently and with greater intensity, including rising sea levels and extended periods of extreme weather events, such as heat waves, cold spills, droughts, high winds and heavy precipitation.

Current predictions indicate that weather patterns in the northern hemisphere will depart from their norm. For example, by mid-century – sooner in the tropics – the calculation of a typical meteorological year for a given location will include a wider range of weather phenomena outside the historical variability (Mora, et al., 2013).

For urban designers to bring the **causes** of climate change towards a potential equilibrium requires the reduction of greenhouse gas emissions, chiefly carbon dioxide emission. Other forms of emissions contribute to the greenhouse effect, but among emissions, carbon dioxide emissions and their reduction are strongly influenced by the way we plan and design cities. For urban design to be most effective, a fundamental rethinking is needed about the use of land, the dimensions of space and access to land. A better integration of uses is required – as in the functions that land is designated for – as well as a less wasteful use of space – as in the dimensions of developable land, including its roads.

Access to land and its functions would need to be far less dependent on the consumption of fossil fuels than it has been for the past 50 years. Resilience to the **consequences** of climate change cannot be expected unless structural repair takes place that addresses the causes: a structural redesign of urban form that reduces dependency on carbon dioxide emissions. Climate scientists have warned that a rising of temperatures by 2 degrees Celsius (3.6 Fahrenheit) over the average global temperature during pre-industrial times would continue, if the carbon dioxide content in the atmosphere were to cross the 400ppm threshold.[1]

Skeptics say it might be too late, but what is the choice? Such repair chiefly has to include not just cities, but cities within their regions. For the professions shaping the physical world of cities and regions, the challenge is one not only of physical geometries but of social consequences. Urban form, as in the use, access and scale of urban structures, holds deeply social meaning.

This book reflects on the contribution that spatial planning and urban design can make to a complex discussion about how city form needs to adapt within metropolitan landscapes.

Metropolitan Landscapes

Metropolitan landscapes are associated with several distinct rhetorical approaches; *metropolitan* is an abstract concept describing large urbanized areas. *Landscape* evokes experiences of being outdoors in spaces that are defined by light, wind, vegetation and by landform with its hills, valleys and horizons. Yes, "landscape is the visible scene" but as the geographer Audrey Lambert reminds us:

> At the same time, landscape is the manifestation of all those elements, factors, influences – call them what you will – both physical and human, which give the surface of the earth its descriptive character at any given point of time. The study of the landscape cannot thus be merely descriptive, but must deal also in terms of origin and evolution.
>
> Lambert, 1985

Implied in Lambert's characterization of landscape is the need to take a long range view into the forces that shaped landscapes in the past as well as forces that will shape them in the future.

Joining the term *metropolitan* with *landscape* in its descriptive and evolutionary form acknowledges that significant portions of metropolitan areas evolved into settings that can neither be described as *country* nor as *urban*. Although they share characteristics with more densely populated urban areas, metropolitan landscapes do not have the concentration or vitality of city life nor the tranquility of the country. Labeling metropolitan areas as landscapes implies that cities have taken on a larger, more diluted character. Certainly, populations are still concentrated in places, but the large areas in between show much porosity. Metropolitan landscapes have become characteristic of contemporary life in cities, not only in the industrialized world, but also in the developing regions of Asia, South America, and beginning in Africa.

An appeal for a new creativity to deal with such a porous patchwork of urbanization was Thomas Sieverts' main argument in *Die Zwischenstadt* (1997), which was translated into *Cities without Cities* (2003, p. 28). Others, like Bernardo Secchi in *Centro, periferia, città diffusa* (2006) or Francois Ascher in *Métapolis* (1995, p. 36), described urban regions defined by mobility. Societies have become so heavily invested in transportation, infrastructure and private communication that life in cities has been transformed profoundly at all levels. It is no use denying that the dispersed city form and all aspects of dispersed living have become the prevailing urban condition.

The call for creativity in the shaping of the metropolitan landscape has taken on new importance as dispersed city form is highly responsible both for the causes of climate change and for the suffering from its consequences.

Threshold Values of Urbanity

The strategy of this book is to confront climate change with urbanity. Historians agree that *threshold values of urbanity* exist; the term was coined by the French environmental historian Fernand Braudel (1992, p. 484). He admits that it is impossible to reach agreement about where to place such thresholds, because they change over time and from place to place. It would be convenient if some firm and indisputable lower limit could mark what we so casually call *urban*, the threshold at which self-generating transactions between people occur.

Access to people, goods and services forms the basis of life in cities. This remains true in an age with vast amounts of information available. Human settlements are first and foremost social networks. Density of people is important, but density alone is not the only quantity that matters. Well-functioning public spaces that draw people together and offer opportunities to interact are just as important. It would also help a great deal if the various functions of city life were better integrated. Urban life only exists in relation to a form of life lower than its own.

Achieving threshold values of urbanity and responses to the causes of climate change are linked through the manner in which we utilize available space in cities: much more circumspect, and more space conserving than in current practice.

The Three Settings of the Book

In decades to come, climate change will affect cities everywhere, but nowhere have the effects of climate change already been felt as strongly as in low-lying coastal cities, cities located in large river deltas and near tidal estuaries.

Since the origins of life in cities, river deltas and tidal estuaries have attracted settlements as ideal locations where potentially large populations could sustain themselves on fertile alluvial soils. For the fluvial geomorphologist, estuaries and deltas are locations where the maritime influence of waves and the regular rhythm of tides meet the riverine influence of currents and sediments. For the biologist, an estuary is a dynamic ecosystem, a rich but fragile habitat that thrives with the mix of saline and freshwater through an abundance of aquatic and land-based species. For an urban morphologist, delta and estuary locations suggest a specific settlement form: a compact urban form that evolved over time in close proximity to waterways. City founders quickly realized that the land on which their cities emerged needed protection not only from adversaries but also from water. In future decades, the understanding of natural forces will become useful again when coastal cities confront the risk and consequences of climate change, a change that will produce inundation, requiring an upland migration of all species and their habitats, including humans and their settlement forms.

The scope of the subject is potentially very large. The list of delta cities is long; 60% of the world's population lives in cities near tidal estuaries or large river deltas (Ross, 1995). To keep the topic manageable, I will focus on urban form in three delta regions: the Pearl River Delta in Southern China; the Rhine, Maas, and Scheldt Deltas in the Netherlands; and the San Francisco Bay Area in Northern California. The regions differ greatly, but despite their different political systems, history, culture and locations in three different climate zones, all three will be forced to respond to similar issues that will trigger transformations and adaptations to their urban form within their metropolitan landscapes.

Upon the arrival of Europeans in Northern California, small settlements were placed along waterways, but in locations that must have appeared as the middle of nowhere. Towns were planted on the land largely in the form of colonial grids, some with the aspiration that they would grow into cities of stature; some did, but many did not. When these towns were started in the 19th century, villages as the next lowest settlement form were not intentionally planned. Instead, suburbs started to emerge quickly, as soon as interurban railroads made it possible to live outside cities. A highly dispersed region resulted that ranks fourth in the world with regard to energy consumption for travel in private automobiles (Newmann, 2006). The challenge here is to transform suburbs by increasing the potential for self-generating transformations through a better integration of land uses with the goal of reducing travel. At the same time, the low-lying cities in the region need to address their waterside edges with respect to rising tides and water discharge of a significantly large river system.

In China's Pearl River Delta, thousands of agricultural villages and some market towns connected by waterways supported relatively few large cities. This all changed with the rapid urbanization that started with the economic reforms of the late 1970s. Here the significant challenge is to protect low-lying land in a region that accommodates over one hundred million people. Public discussion has been relatively mute about the consequences of climate change that caused more frequent floods and inundation due to storm surges. Combined with a long-term geological subsidence of land, the consequences of climate change are very serious. High among the social challenges ranks the need to help the villages and market towns evolve as concentrations that support contemporary life and not only as dormitories for the millions of migrant workers who have relocated here from throughout rural China.

In the Dutch Delta, an archipelago of towns emerged in the 13th century. The term *archipelago* is telling, because water still connected all cities well into the age of railroads. Water also kept urban form compact, because all urbanized land had to be protected from inundation. Here the challenge is not to relax concentration. Dutch insights into management of urban form and water will be important for other low-lying coastal regions. Rising sea levels are a known phenomenon for the Dutch. They say it started at the end of the last ice age. Again and again land had to be protected from rising tides. Traditional engineering solutions to protect the coast of the Low Countries are now hotly debated in light of the fact that coastal barriers built between the 1930s and the 1970s are in need of major repair. Instead of repairing the barrier structures that closed off four of the five estuaries of the rivers Rhine (Ijssel), Maas and Scheldt, serious consideration has been given to opening the former estuaries again to tides and river discharge. Doing this in a country where sea and river water levels run well above significant portions of urbanized land will need much Dutch ingenuity.

In this book we define urban design broadly. Specifically, we focus on design as a decision making tool to communicate better spatial planning and design of urban form in stabilizing the detrimental effects of climate change. We acknowledge the difficult but important task to re-organize dispersed use of land; to reorganize those basic human activities specifically known to produce carbon dioxide emissions: travel, heating, cooling, and procuring food and disposal of waste.

Space, as in the use of land, is a form of capital. Like financial capital, its use needs to be understood for its investment potential. An investment in an urban future conscious of climate change starts with not wasting space.

"On all great subjects much remains to be said." John Stuart Mill's (1806–1873) quote also applies to the subject matter of this book.

Note

1   In May 2013, a long-feared milestone was crossed: for the first time since the Pliocene Epoch, the earth's atmosphere contained 400 parts per million (ppm) of CO2. Reported on May 10 by Neela Banerjee, *Los Angeles Times*, in reference to May 9 recordings by the Scripps Institution for Oceanography from its Mauna Loa Observatory in Hawaii. The daily average readings of carbon dioxide emissions in April/May are typically the highest during the course of the year. They are taken at a time prior to trees on the northern hemisphere leafing-out completely, a phenomenon that absorbs carbon emissions. By comparison, carbon content in 1958 measured at 318ppm, when recordings began at Mauna Loa.

References

Ascher, F., 1995. *Métapolis: Ou l'avenir des villes*. Paris: Odile Jacob.

Braudel, F., 1992. *Civilization and Capitalism, 15th–18th Century, Vol. I The Structures of Everyday Life*. Berkeley: University of California Press.

Lambert, A., 1985. *The Making of the Dutch Landscape, an Historical Geography of the Netherlands*. London and New York: Academic Press.

Mora, C. et al., 2013. The Projected Timing of Climate Departure from Recent Variability. *Nature*, 502, pp. 183–187.

Newmann, P., 2006. The environmental impact of cities. *Environment and Urbanization*, 18(2), pp. 275–295.

Ross, D., 1995. *Introduction to Oceanography*. New York: Harper Collins.

Secchi, B., 2006. *Centro, periferia, città diffusa: le disuguaglianze sul territorio*. Trento, relazione tenuta al Festival dell'Economia di Trento, pp. I–XXV.

Sieverts, T., 2003. *Cities without Cities: an Interpretation of the Zwischenstadt*. London: Spon Press.

Part I | The San Francisco Estuary and Inland Delta

With contributions by Sarah Moos

▲ Figure 1.1a

San Francisco Estuary and Inland Delta from satellite (source: Google Earth, October 2012).

▶ Figure 1.1b

The San Francisco Estuary (photo by Sarah Moos).

Most estuaries emerged 10,000 to 12,000 years ago, during the Holocene Period, when sea levels began to rise at the end of the last ice age. This is also partly true for the San Francisco Bay, an estuary of the Pacific Ocean and the inland delta formed by the Sacramento and San Joachim Rivers. But given the location of the Bay in a zone of great seismic activity, tidal and riverine dynamics were also shaped by tectonic forces. The two large tectonic plates, the North American and the Pacific Plates, slide past each other at a current speed of 2.5 cm per year (Stoffer & Gordon, 2001, pp. 61-86). The coastal ridges in Northern California started to uplift two to four million years ago when pressure along the North American Plate and the Pacific Plate increased along the plate boundaries. The valley between the two coastal ridges where the Bay resides began to form two to three million years ago. Geologists suspect that the lateral movement along the San Andreas Fault zone may be responsible for a major structural break in the western coastal ridge at the Golden Gate, causing a 130 degree clockwise rotation of the headlands.

This structural break created an opening. During the construction of the Golden Gate Bridge in the 1930s, borings revealed seven distinct estuarine periods over the last 500,000 years, and they correspond to interglacial periods. During glacial periods the bay floor became a valley where rivers created deep incisions, most notably the Sacramento River, which has its origins in the once glaciated mountains of the Northern Sierra Nevada. The river carved a deep gorge inside what is now the Golden Gate Strait. Approximately 8,000 years ago, ocean water again returned, for the seventh time in the estuary's 500,000-year history, to fill the Bay and to form the tidal estuary that we experience today (William, 2001). Figure 1.3 shows San Francisco Bay 125,000 years ago during the so-called Sangamonian (Hansel & McKay, 2014) interglacial period when the water table of the Bay was approximately 100 feet higher.

The Sacramento River with an annual discharge of 27 million cubic meters is joined by the San Joachim River to the east of San Francisco Bay, and the combined discharge amounts to 33 million cubic meters. Prior to the building of dams and water diversions for agriculture and urban use in 1914, the discharge would have been closer to 50 million cubic meters (Meko, et al., 2001). The two rivers and their tributaries drain the 1,000 kilometer long Sierra Nevada mountain range running north–south through all of Northern California. While the Sacramento–San Joachim River Delta is largely agricultural with few small towns, the two rivers are navigable by smaller ocean-going vessels to the major cities of Stockton and Sacramento.

Stream regulation through the delta started in the 1850s. Settling farmers hired Chinese laborers, largely from the Pearl River Delta, Guangdong Province, to reclaim marshland and

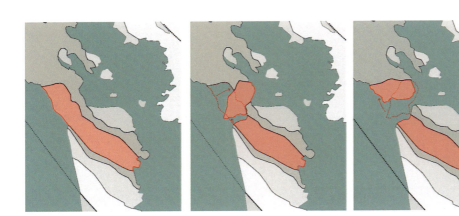

◀ Figure 1.2

The opening of the coastal ridge at the Golden Gate as a result of tectonic movement along the San Andreas Fault (maps drawn by author, assisted by Justin Kearnan).

▶ Figure 1.3

The Bay 125,000 years ago during the Sangamonian Interglacial Period, when the northern part of the San Francisco Peninsula was an island (map drawn by author, assisted by Justin Kearnan).

cultivate rich layers of peat soil. That is soil built up from decomposed tule reeds through millennia. Levees 1,800 kilometers long by 3 meters high by 9 meters wide were constructed by manual labor using a combination of peat and clay soil, a colossal undertaking.

Delta soil is oxygen rich and causes subsidence when cultivated. Like the waterways of the Pearl River Delta and the Dutch Delta, silting riverbeds caused the water level of rivers and sloughs to rise higher than adjacent land. Flooding at times of heavy rains and snow melt produced levee failure. Land subsidence, levee failure, the diversion of freshwater for urban use, and saltwater intrusion made the delta a highly contested landscape. Growers compete with urban users for a limited amount of freshwater, and environmental advocacy groups compete with both to ensure the survival of the delta ecosystem. The latter group advocates for marsh restoration, or conversion of low-lying farmland to constructed wetlands.

After the confluence, the two rivers form a tidal estuary, Suisun Bay, and discharge at the Carquinez Strait into San Pablo Bay, the northern portion of San Francisco Bay. Here an additional number of small rivers discharge directly into San Francisco Bay. At the time of Spanish discovery, the Bay water surface measured 1.295 km². In 1965, a surface area of 20,000 hectares had been reclaimed for urban use, railroads, highways, ports, an airport runway, military use and waste disposal.

The year 1965 is a critical date in the history of San Francisco Bay: a citizen-led campaign successfully stopped municipalities from additional land reclamation (Walker, 2007, p. 110). "For a century prior to 1965 no one thought twice about throwing anything and everything into the Bay. Canneries, rendering plants, tanneries discharged a river of effluvium; smelters, steel mills, and coal-gas plants spilled toxic ooze; and thousands of ships quietly voided their wastes into the water" wrote the political geographer Richard Walker (Walker, 2007, p. 112). A state chartered agency, the Bay Conservation and Development Commission, established in 1965, was created to prevent further bay fill and has reclaimed land for wetlands. Water quality of the Bay has improved significantly since 1965.

A current initiative will restore 15,100 acres of industrial salt ponds in the South Bay to wetlands. Understood as a soft edge approach, these wetlands will not only provide habitat

▼ Figure 1.4

San Francisco Bay, inundation of low-lying land due to sea level rise. Left: under current projections, inundation by the end of the 21st century. Right: in red, inundation of urbanized land. Approximately 9% of all urbanized land would be inundated unless protected.

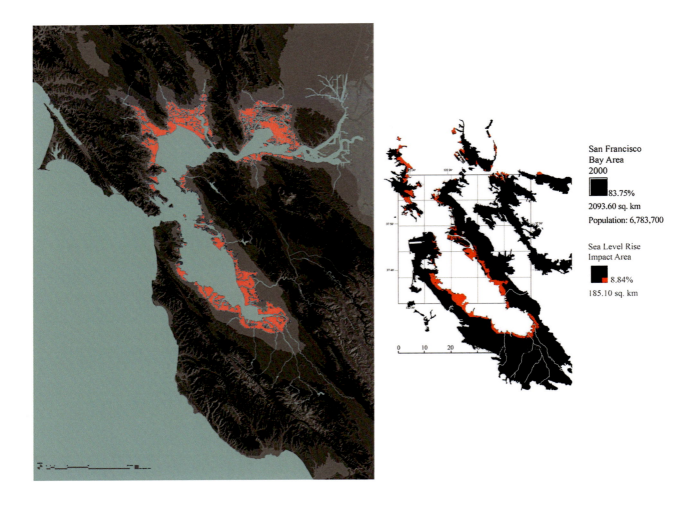

for bay species, but they will also serve as a horizontal levee combating sea level rise. Functioning as a large sponge, wetlands can absorb water when needed and serve as flood-control measures often less costly than reservoirs or dikes. Studies suggest that areas with 30% more wetland coverage decrease flood peaks by 60% to 80% (Novitzki, 1978). Wetlands also sequester approximately 250 g/m^2 carbon dioxide annually (Trulio, et al., 2007). Nearly all low-lying land along the Bay shoreline was once historic tidal marshland, making such land prone to subsidence. It is thus less valuable for development. Reverted to wetlands, these areas could become vegetated buffers between urban developments and the fluctuating tides (California Coastal Conservancy, 2015).

The San Francisco Bay water table has risen by 0.185 meters over the past century. By mid-century, a "one hundred year flood" is currently predicted to be 0.5 meters higher than today, and 1.4 meters higher by the end of the century (Heberger, et al., 2012). Unless protected by higher levees, sea level rise will inundate highway infrastructure, railroads, roadway and sewer treatment plants along the Bay, as well as industry in the southern and eastern portion of the Bay. Businesses in Silicon Valley, such as Oracle, CISCO, Facebook and Google, have all settled on or near former bay marshland and will all be at risk of inundation.

California Energy Commission predictions single out low-lying residential communities as the ones to be most affected. They emphasize that the 200,000 to 270,000 at-risk residents belong largely to minority and lower income communities. The commission concludes that sea level rise will have serious social justice implications.

Urbanization

Human settlements in the San Francisco Bay Area originated where Native Americans had settled in 126 small villages (Milliken, 2009).[1] The native population in the Bay area amounted to approximately 17,000 at the time of Spanish arrival in 1769. Due to Spain's policy of prohibiting foreign ships from entering ports on the west coast of the Americas, trade was limited, thus urbanization was virtually nonexistent in the rural areas around San Francisco Bay. Otto von Kotzebue (1787–1846) and fellow travelers on the Russian ship *Rurik* gave evidence. The ship under his command visited San Francisco Bay in October 1816. The historian A.C. Mahr (1932) suspected that the *Rurik* was on a spying mission. Russia, as a victorious nation in the Napoleonic wars, was keenly interested in the conditions along the Northern Californian coast, where it maintained colonies at Bodega Bay and Fort Ross in today's Sonoma County. Spain, in a forced union with France from 1808 to 1814, had left its colonies in the Americas without support. A Russian aristocrat, Nicolay Rumyantsev, who had served as imperial chancellor until 1812, had financed the *Rurik* expedition, officially to find the fabled waterway, Avian, or North-West Passage, but, as Mahr suspected, also on a spying mission. The arrival of the *Rurik* in San Francisco Bay in 1816, one year after the Congress of Vienna, where Napoleon's territorial conquests were redistributed, makes Mahr's suspicion plausible. However, the *Rurik* had on board the well-known naturalist and poet, Adelbert von Chamisso[2] (1781–1838) who served as Spanish interpreter. Chamisso's diary, *Tagebuch*, 1821, does not confirm Mahr's theory of a spying mission, but only attests to the scientific nature of the journey (Sterling, 2011). The Russian presence in the North Pacific had been an annoyance to Spain. So were the British interests in the fur trade that Russian hunters engaged in. The early Californian historian Robert Glass Cleland cites Adele Odgen: "men's desire for the fur of an animal led to the commercial opening of the Pacific coast" (Cleland, 1962).

As history showed, urbanization around San Francisco Bay was not guided by Russian influence; Russia gave up its colonies in California in 1842. Nor was it guided by Spain; Mexico started its war of independence in 1810 and seceded from Spain in 1821. The Monroe doctrine of December 1823 put an end to European speculation to establish an independent kingdom west of the Rocky Mountains and up to the Pacific coast. The doctrine addressed mainly Russia, which had formed a holy alliance with Prussia and Austria to re-establish monarchical rule in the former Spanish colonies: "The American continents are henceforth not to be considered as subjects for future colonization by any European power" (Cleland, 1962, p. 59). Urbanization only gained momentum with the occupation of San Francisco Bay by the United States in 1846.

Given the remoteness of the Bay Area, only accessible by sea, water transport remained the most important connection between emerging cities throughout the remainder of the 19th and well into the 20th century. The Bay connected San Francisco with all other destinations: travelers going east to Sacramento, by 1852 the state capital, and onwards to the gold mines, traveled via the delta by boat up the Sacramento River; to San Jose for fruits and agricultural supplies via a small port at Alviso; to the north for lumber via Sausalito; for livestock up the Petaluma river; or to the Napa Valley for grain. Thus small towns emerged along the routes of the river boats.

We show a number of towns that were laid out early in the history of the Bay Area's urbanization. Sausalito, 1838/1870, is a port city founded by the English sailor William Richardson, who was also instrumental in founding Yuerba Buena, the town that became San Francisco. We also show Sonoma, the northernmost of the Alta California missions established in 1823 under Mexican rule; Rio Vista, moved to its present location on the slope of the Montezuma Hills in 1862 after flooding at its former location in 1858; and Isleton, begun in 1874, only to be flooded in 1878, and again in 1881, 1890, 1907 and 1972; both river towns are located in the Sacramento River Delta. Dixon, from 1852, was a stopover on the route to the goldfields; as an agricultural town it was moved in 1868 to a crossing point of two section lines and the Central Pacific Railroad. Crockett–Velona, at the Carquinez Strait, was a company town from 1867 of the California Hawaiian Sugar Company; Half Moon Bay started in 1840 as a fishing town and center of the coastal agriculture along the Pacific Ocean. All plans drawn at the same scale show the same compactness: an urban form shaped by its location in response to landform, water and climate.

Railroad building connected cities in the 1860s, but it was not until bridges were built, starting in 1927, that highway-based transport replaced ferries.[3] When the Golden Gate Bridge opened in 1937, suburban neighborhoods sprang up to the north of San Francisco. Likewise, the San Francisco–Oakland Bay Bridge of 1936 extended urbanization opposite San Francisco to the East Bay. Suburban development continued with the Federal Highway Act of 1956; widespread use of automobiles made living outside of cities possible. Depending on the new interstate highway system to commute to downtown San Francisco for work, a young executive could decide to move the family to a new suburban home in the outlying counties 40 minutes away and drive in generally sunny weather at accelerated speed on freeways over bridges with sweeping vistas, directly into the podium of an office building in the new central business district. In all likelihood, such a building would stand on land reclaimed from the Bay. The lure of limitless space was irresistible. As long as unlimited space was available, society expected to benefit from it.

Two types of limits to space will be forced upon Bay Area cities. As in all delta cities located near tidal estuaries and large river systems, rising water will set limits on the use of low-lying land. The process of rising tides is slow, but communities are starting to take note of it. A second, less noticed, limit is the danger of flooding to land near the mouths of rivers and creeks. When water discharge from rivers is delayed due to rising tides, rivers will flood the land near their natural discharge area and even further upstream. This is especially true

▶ Figure 1.5

Sausalito, below left as shown on a USGS survey of 1919; below right in 2000; above: the idea of a town, shown as a 3D model with the initial grid superimposed in grey. The model shows topography and bathymetry in fivefold exaggeration of the vertical axis. (Maps by author and Sarah Moos.)

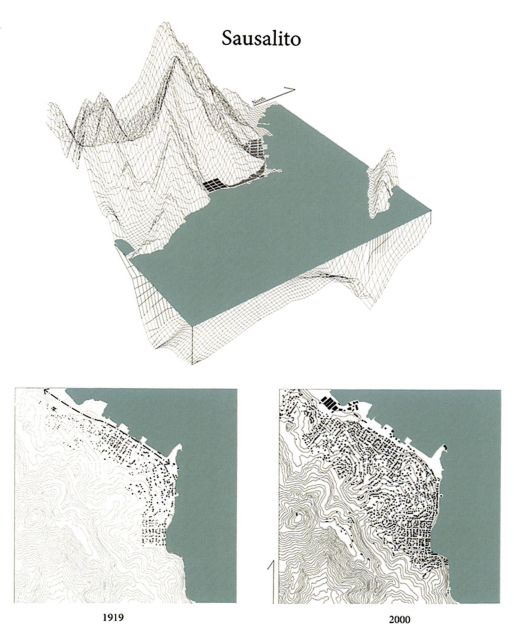

1919

2000

along all rivers that are channelized, and where land in the river's natural flood plains has been urbanized. As we will see in the final part of the book, in the Netherlands the limitation on the use of land near rivers has been recognized as equally serious an issue as the further strengthening of coastal defenses against storm tides.

A third type of limitation to the use of space goes much further as it cuts more deeply into the seemingly unlimited supply of land. Any serious attempt to curtail the risks and consequences of global warming will result in limits on any urban expansions that cannot be supported by public transportation. Urbanization has expanded because of the seemingly unlimited mobility

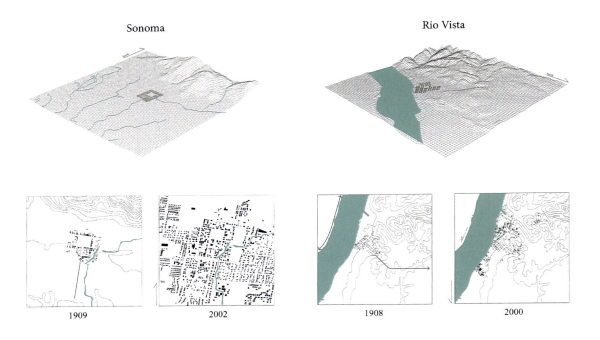
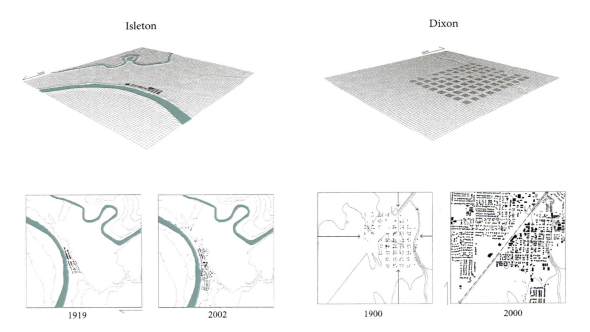

▲ Figure 1.6a

Sonoma, Rio Vista, Isleton, Dixon. Below left: towns are shown on USGS surveys from the early 20th century; below right: in 2000/02; above: the idea of a town, shown as a 3D model with the initial grid super imposed in grey. Model shows topography in fivefold exaggeration of the vertical axis. (Maps by author and Sarah Moos.)

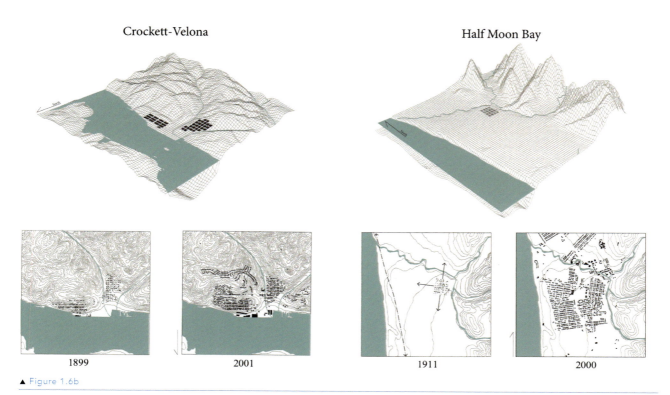

▲ Figure 1.6b

Crockett–Velona, Half Moon Bay. Below left: towns are shown on USGS surveys from the early 20th century; below right: in 2000/02; above: the idea of a town, shown as a 3D model with the initial grid superimposed in grey. Model shows topography in fivefold exaggeration of the vertical axis. (Maps by author and Sarah Moos.)

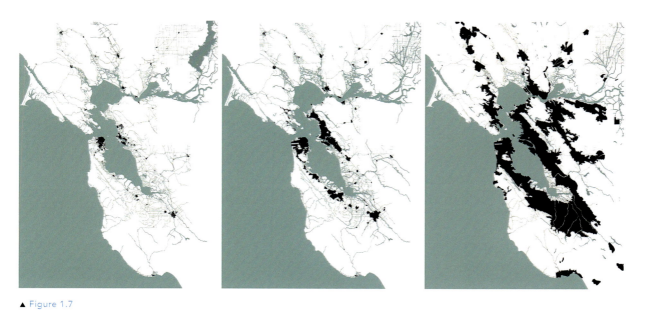

▲ Figure 1.7

Urbanization of the San Francisco Bay Area. Left: at the time of the Great Earthquake in 1906, population: 925,708 (1910). Middle: 1947, population: 2,681,322 (1950). Right: 2010, population: 7,150,739 (2010).

PART I The San Francisco Estuary and Inland Delta

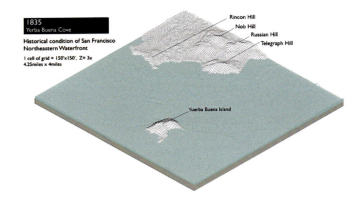

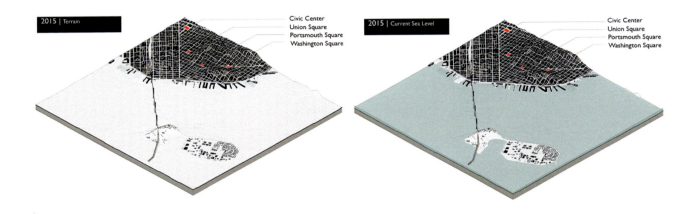

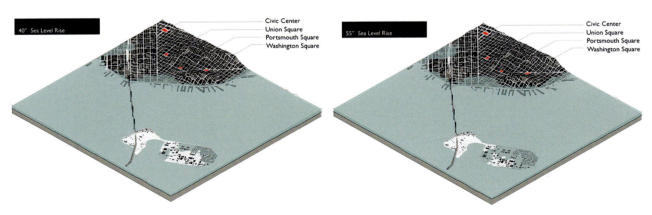

▲ Figure 1.8

Top: original landform; middle left: 2015 terrain and bathymetry; middle right: 2015 current sea level; below left: 40" sea level rise; below right: 55" sea level rise (maps by the author assisted by Justin Kearnan and Kushal Lachhawani). Source: Radke, et al., 2017.

that society has enjoyed since the mid-20th century. Not everyone will agree, but we hope that technology will help us out. For some it will. It is more likely that access to financial resources will make a difference. It would be tragic for society as a whole if only individuals with access to resources could live sustainably. Those of lower income would be pushed to the periphery of the region, depending on long commutes, because the locations where the structures of everyday life are sustainable have also become unaffordable.

Notes

1 Ethno-geographer Randal Milliken identifies 126 settlement locations by name. He refers to most settlements as watershed villages because of their location near the confluence of creeks or waterways leading to coastal wetlands.
2 Chamisso (1954) is best known for his allegorical fairy tale about Peter Schlemihl, who sells his shadow to the devil. The piece has been translated into all European languages.
3 The last car ferry ceased operation in 1954.

References

California Coastal Conservancy, 2015. *The Baylands and Climate Change*. [Online] Available at: www.baylandsgoals.org [Accessed 25 April 2017].

Chamisso, A., 1954. *The Wonderful History of Peter Schlemihl*. London: Rodale.

Cleland, R., 1962. *From Wilderness to Empire, a History of California*. New York: Alfred Knopf.

Hansel, A. K. & McKay, E. D., 2014. Quaternary Period. In: D. R. Kolata, ed., *The Geology of Illinois*. Urbana: Illinois State Geological Survey.

Heberger, M., Cooley, H. & Moore, E., 2012. *The Impact of Sea Level Rise on the San Francisco Bay*. CEC 500-2012-014 ed. Sacramento: California Energy Commission.

Mahr, A., 1932. *The Visit of the Rurik in San Francisco, 1816*. Stanford: Stanford University Press.

Meko, D., Therrell, M., Baisan, C. & Hughes, M. K., 2001. Sacramento river flow reconstructed to AD 869 from tree rings. *Journal of the American Water Resources Association*, Nov, 37(4), pp. 1029–1039.

Milliken, R., 2009. *A Time of Little Choice: Disintegration of Tribal Culture in the San Francisco Bay Area 1789–1810*. Santa Barbara: Balena Press.

Novitzki, R., 1978. Hydrology of the Nevin Wetland near Madison, Wisconsin. U.S. Geological Survey Water-Resources Investigations, 78(48), p. 25.

Radke, J. D. et al., 2017. *An assessment of climate change vulnerability of the natural gas transmission infrastructure for the San Francisco Bay Area, Sacramento-San-Joaquin Delta, and Coastal California*. [Online] Available at: www.energy.ca.gov/2017publications/CEC-500-2017-008/CEC-500-2017-008.pdf [Accessed 25 April 2017].

Sterling, P., 2011. A historic 1816 Russian voyage to San Francisco. *Argonaut, Journal of the San Francisco Museum and Historical Society*, 22(22).

Stoffer, P. W. & Gordon, L. C., 2001. Geology and Natural History of the San Francisco Bay: A field trip guidebook. *US Geological Survey Bulletin 2188*.

Trulio, L., Crooks, S. & Callaway, J., 2007. *White Paper on Carbon Sequestration and Tidal Salt Marsh Restoration*. [Online] Available at: www.southbayrestoration.org/pdf_files/Carbon%20Sequestration%20Dec%20%2007.pdf

Walker, R., 2007. *The Country in the City: The Greening of the San Francisco Bay Area*. Seattle: University of Washington Press.

William, E. P., 2001. *Geology of the Golden Gate Headlands*. [Online] Available at: www.nps.gov/goga/learn/education/upload/geology%20of%20the%20golden%20gate%20headlands%20field%20guide.pdf [Accessed 4 April 2017].

Chapter 1

Water, Land and Places, the Origins of Urban Form in the San Francisco Bay Area

The oldest cities around San Francisco Bay are barely 200 years old. Urbanization has changed natural systems, but to a far lesser extent than in the settlements of the Dutch Delta with their origins in the Middle Ages, or the nearly one thousand years that shaped the villages and towns in the water landscape of the Pearl River Delta.

As in other delta city locations, the origins of compact urban form can be traced to maritime concerns. The exact location for the city of San Francisco was decided by a British sailor, William A. Richardson, who had arrived as second mate on a British whaling ship in April 1822. A month prior to his arrival, news of Mexican independence from Spain in 1821 had finally reached the furthest northern outpost of the former Spanish Empire at San

▶ Figure 1.1.1

San Francisco in 1846–7. Engraving by W. F. Swasey, presumably done in the 1860s. (Source: Bancroft Library University of California, Berkeley.)

CHAPTER 1 Water, Land and Places

19

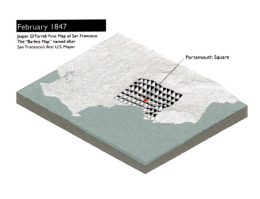
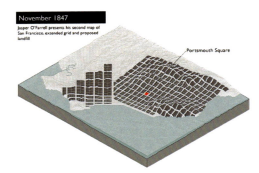
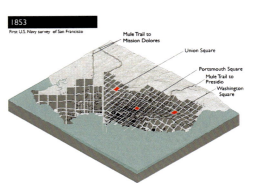

◀ Figure 1.1.2

The Origins of San Francisco. Redrawn as a three-dimensional model using the topographic coast survey from 1853 (drawn by the author, assisted by Justin Kearnan and Kushal Lachhwani).

Top left: (Oct. 1835) William A. Richardson drew a line on the land to mark Calle de la Fundacion. The map shows the first three homesteads and mule trails to the Presidio and to the Mission Dolores.

Top right: (Oct. 1839) first plan of Verba Buena re-drawn after a map made by Jean Jacques Vioget.

Middle left: sketch indicates the survey method used by O'Farrell to create an orthogonal grid by squaring its cardinal directions to the peaks of Telegraph Hill and Nob Hill. Section lines indicate the lines of sight that O'Farrell must have used in laying out the city on top of the location's hilly topography.

Middle right: (Feb. 1847) Jasper O'Farrell's first map, "the Bartlett" map named after San Francisco's first US military appointed mayor. (Drawn in a graphic convention similar to the maps of San Francisco by Florence Lipsky in her 1999 book "San Francisco, la grille sur les collines / the grid meets the hill", Marseille.)

Below left: (Nov.1847) Jasper O'Farrell's second map of San Francisco from the same year showing an extended grid and proposed landfill of Yerba Buena Cove, the first land reclamation of San Francisco Bay. The map also shows the beginning of Market Street and the South of Market grid.

Below right: (1853) US Navy coastal survey shows San Francisco, its streets, blocks and buildings after California's 1850 annexation by the United States.

Francisco Bay. Richardson was sent ashore to secure provision at the Presidio, but instead of returning to his ship he joined a fiesta, met Maria Martinez, the daughter of the commandant at the Presidio and decided to stay. He went to see the governor, Pablo Vicente de Solá, the last governor to rule Alta California as a colony of Spain. Richardson became a Mexican citizen and converted to Catholicism. Governors after de Solá rescinded Spain's long-held blockade of its Pacific ports for non-Spanish ships. To improve trade and to maintain the outlying territory, a formal port at the Golden Gate had to be established. As a person educated in navigation, Richardson was appointed port captain and in 1835 was charged with improving a natural harbor with the design for a town. The chosen location had already provided anchorage for occasional ships visiting San Francisco Bay.[1]

For protected anchorage, Richardson selected a cove opposite Yerba Buena Island as the site for the new town. Sailing vessels driven by generally strong westerly or northwesterly winds sailed through the Golden Gate, were recognized by soldiers at the Presidio, held to starboard, and, once past Telegraph Hill, reefed their sails to glide into anchorage in the small cove protected from wind by Telegraph Hill. Richardson laid out the town's first street, Calle de la Fundacion (Scott, 1985), more or less parallel to the shoreline. The new street demarked, on the Bay side, government property down to the high waterline and on the land side, property available for private acquisition through land grants or later through purchase. There, on the land side of Calle Fundacion, where it would have crossed today's Washington Street, Richardson staked out the first homestead for his family.

In 1846, towards the end of the Mexican American War,[2] a US naval force occupied Yerba Buena and renamed the port San Francisco. Jasper O'Farrell (1817–1875), an Irish civil engineer who had arrived in California via Chile in 1843, was commissioned to draw the first official map of San Francisco. Approved in February 1847, the map has become known as the Bartlett map, named after San Francisco's first US appointed mayor (Figure 1.1.2, middle right).

The San Francisco Urban Blocks

The map in Figure 1.1.2 middle left was made to better understand how those who laid out the city struggled with the concept of a regular grid on an irregular topography. Despite the obvious obstacles, the process of platting the land with a grid had surprising longevity. San Franciscans after O'Farrell extended his design westwards and to the south, applying a total of 27 grids, until the entire peninsula was covered by the middle of the 20th century. To this day, designers modify, add and transform the modular order of properties within the grid of streets and blocks. Buildings are added and transformed, but the concept of urban blocks remains valid because of its inbuilt flexibility. Its characteristics are made up of buildings constructed in rows, where all four rows face the perimeter streets in almost equal measure.

San Francisco's urban form came about as a result of 19th century land platting practices influenced by Spanish colonial traditions made more complex by siting a town in a hilly location at the water's edge. O'Farrell must have set his tripod with an eyeglass at the edge of the cove, a location 100 varas[3] from the high waterline at an elevation 3 meters above sea level. He aimed his transit, as we would refer to his surveying instrument today, towards the 130 meter (380 feet) high top of the nearest hill to the west, now Nob Hill. He would then swivel the transit 90 degrees to aim at the 67 meter (220 feet) high top of the nearest hill to the north, Telegraph Hill. If necessary, he would correct the location of his transit to ensure that both sight lines were at a 90 degree angle. The exact point – marked with an "o" on Figure 1.1.2 middle left – falls in the middle of Montgomery Street, at the center of the block between Clay and Washington Streets. Today, Merchant Street meets Montgomery in this location. The point marks the beginning of O'Farrell's new axis for San Francisco. He then walked 100 varas westwards, along the center line, to a location where the second, 85 meter (280 feet) high peak of Telegraph Hill came into view. He set up his transit again aiming at Nob Hill, axial to his design, and again swiveled the instrument around by 90 degrees to aim at Telegraph Hill's second peak. He must have done so to verify the bearing angle of his center line to ensure that his resulting map maintained a perfect orthographic projection.

It is highly unlikely that O'Farrell had been trained in the ancient Chinese practice of Feng Shui, but what he did was very much akin to bringing wind, land and water into harmony. If geomancy was not on his mind, it was the exactness of his survey; the resulting map was intended as a legal document to be used by government to issue title to land. O'Farrell had to concern himself with exactness because his predecessor, Jean Jacques Vioget, a Swiss newcomer who initially surveyed the settlement for Mexican authorities in 1839, had mistakenly laid out trapezoidal blocks with angles off by 2.5 degrees from right angles (Figure 1.1.2 top right). Also, Vioget had oriented the grid not according to cardinal directions, but eleven degrees west of north, a decision O'Farrell could not correct without changing the legal titles to properties already granted. In 1839, in Vioget's time, these mistakes had been of little concern in a small village of 50 inhabitants at what seemed to be the edge of the world. Who could have anticipated that only 10 years later, in 1849, thousands of newcomers would arrive, lured by the riches of gold? We know that in 1847, when O'Farrell made his map, San Francisco had 800 residents (Lipsky, 1999, p. 25). By 1850, San Francisco's population had grown to 37,776 inhabitants (Moudon, 1989, p. 26). The changing political situation and later the discovery of gold had attracted a growing population of settlers, who saw the purchase of property as a tradable investment. San Francisco's location still seemed remote, but an orderly grid with clear titles to property mattered greatly.

Spanish colonial towns traditionally laid out a plaza consistent with directives codified in 1573 by the "Law of the Indies" (Crouch, et al., 1982). The explicit directives drew from the writings of Vitruvius, who wrote about the layout of colonial towns at the time of Emperor Augustus. The laws indicated the width and directions of streets to avoid – or take advantage of – winds for a comfortable micro climate. The laws also addressed the dimensions of a plaza sufficient in size to assemble all anticipated residents. In San Francisco, the *Plaza* measured 100 by 100 varas. In O'Farrell's design, the plaza, which became known as Portsmouth Square, was rectified, but kept one block away from the shoreline. It remained in its location and served as the center of San Francisco until the 1880s. At that time the center of the city shifted westwards and the square became the center of the city's Chinatown.

Historians recorded the discussion about the "folly" of a regular grid on a steep topography (Lipsky, 1999, p. 51).[4] O'Farrell's February 1847 map followed an ancient tradition of colonial settlement form. The same year he was put under pressure to revise his map, and these revisions are important in the context of our discussion. In November 1847, eight months after the initial survey, O'Farrell had to make more room for the new city by designing extensions. Importantly he extended the city onto reclaimed land, land taken from the San Francisco Bay that in the 21st century will be subject to inundation. He was forced to make this second map (Figure 1.1.2, bottom left) because newcomers were arriving faster than anticipated.

In a highly pragmatic move, he delineated three rows of city blocks on what was not land but shallow water. Properties on such blocks would become the most valuable real estate in the city, because the newly gained land, once reclaimed, would bring the city closer to navigable water. Sailing ships would no longer have to anchor off shore as shown in the W. F. Swasey engraving, but could tie up on soon to be built wharfs. Seven such wharfs show up on the 1853 survey of actual conditions made six years after O'Farrell's November 1847 map. Eventually, even the water between those wharfs would be filled. All reclaimed land to the north-east of Montgomery Street between the foot of Telegraph Hill and Rincon Hill would become San Francisco's financial district. These blocks, built on low-lying land, will also be subject to inundation due to sea level rise unless protected.

O'Farrell for his second map made another pragmatic move. He must have realized that San Francisco, if it were to expand in its hilly location, needed a level street that would become the central spine of commerce, transportation and cultural life. He surveyed the land to the south of his original map, an area of knolls and hollows, mostly muddy because of poor drainage and proximity to tidal marshes. This is where Market Street began. O'Farrell sited Market Street 40 varas wide at a 45 degree angle to his earlier grid. Again, he aimed the new street towards a set of hills: the Twin Peaks. The new street became a divider between two grids. On its northern side, Market Street formed irregular intersections with the established grid. On the southern side, O'Farrell was free to establish a new grid with larger block dimensions. In years to come, warehousing and port-related industries settled here, but also neighborhoods for newly arriving immigrants. Traces of these early neighborhoods south of Market Street are now largely gone. St. Patrick Church of 1851 on Mission Street, between 3rd and 4th Streets, was once the center of an Irish neighborhood. The community was erased by urban renewal in the 1960s.

Urban Blocks and the Threshold Values of Urbanity

The reader might wonder about the relevance of historic information for today's decision making. It is only now that the siting of urban form in relation to landform provides a new lesson as we address the consequences of climate change.

Not by coincidence, urban blocks are found in cities around the world, not just from one period in history, but whenever it was necessary to concentrate people and their activities on limited amounts of land in proximity to water. Space along valuable street frontages is used at an optimum. The front of buildings face towards public streets. Their entrances, windows and commercial frontage define streets as a positive space that fosters interaction. Thus streets are well defined as channels of movements and conduits of public life in cities. The best perimeter blocks have a fine grain parcel size; eight meter frontage length, as in San Francisco, is still ideal for low to midrise construction. With parcel sizes at such dimensions, there are frequent entrances, which in turn results in frequent encounters with people who live or work there. The compact form yields a moderately high density, allowing for an integration of diverse activities. Or, using Fernand Braudel's phrase from his book *The Structures of Everyday Life* (Braudel, 1992, p. 484), streets and blocks create an environment that crosses the threshold from non-urban to urban. Implied in Braudel's threshold is the presence of people as a key ingredient of urbanity. The thresholds mark levels at which self-generated transformations are possible;[5] a sufficient number of people live in one location to enable economic transactions that sustain services, including public transportation.

More subtle, but equally important, is the orientation of dwellings to the rear, meaning the center of the block. Implied in the configuration of a block is the fact that there needs to be space behind buildings that is open to the sky to allow for daylight to reach the rear facades. While the front of buildings orients towards the street, the rear orients towards a common airspace, not necessarily in the form of a shared space like a common courtyard, although it can be. The space is more likely divided into private rear yards. Such yards are used for various activities, sometimes for lower structures that contain workspaces, gardens or storage. The urban block design is actually highly contemporary in its use. Paola Viganò (2016, p. 150) presents drawings of perimeter blocks in the port city of Antwerp, ideally suited for young families who need to combine child friendly homes with gardens and with the advantages of workplace proximity and low automobile dependency. Ideally, a resident of a perimeter block has a view onto a public city street in the front and onto a private space in the rear. The majority of San Francisco row houses offer such a dual orientation. Inside most blocks the space is large enough for trees to grow. Once trees have reached the height of the third or fourth floor, or higher, the view towards the rear windows brings nature into the domestic realm. Through the presence of light, residents become aware of seasons and climate. Other block configurations produce similar effects, but none does it in as concentrated a manner as the urban block where buildings form the perimeter.

Trees taller than buildings can grow inside perimeter blocks and that brings to mind the uniformity of building heights on San Francisco's typical blocks. The uniform three to four story building heights were not produced by building codes or planning regulations but by the technical limitation of the customary wood frame construction. The world over, wood construction efficiently spans 4 meters between walls. Given the 10 varas, or 8-meter wide lot dimensions, two structural bays resulted inside each row house. Building up to a maximum height of four floors required no special knowledge of applied mathematics. In the mid to late 19th century, confident craftsmen could easily construct row upon row of such buildings. Later, the allowable building heights were codified to protect residents from fire hazards, but initially the height limitations were solely imposed by the method of construction. Wood was readily available in areas to the north and south of San Francisco. Huge trunks of redwood trees were felled. Entire forests were cut, dragged and floated across the Bay to their new location to be transformed into a city.

Living Inside Perimeter Blocks

Urban designers in California are easily pressed into the defensive when talking publicly about the benefits of moderately high density. Density is associated with crowding, compromised privacy, or lack of parking. These are the polite concerns. There are other, more confrontational concerns that citizens of a multicultural society do not easily talk about. These concerns involve race and income, lifestyle and the integration of immigrants. Objection to density is not as much about living at close quarters, but living together with others who are perceived to behave differently. Amos Rapoport (1975) called for a redefinition of density that not only expressed density as a measure of people or homes per unit of land area, but added perceptional qualities that add or subtract from judgments about crowding. He suspected that monotony of built form would be associated with higher density, as would visual clutter, but presence of greenery and individual expression of built form would lower the perception of density. He concluded that observers pass judgment about density based upon clues they associate with the behavior and social standing of the occupants.

A question that remains of interest to urban designers, who want to address the causes of climate change through designs that accommodate people at moderately high residential density and a form that conserves space is: in what form is a moderately high density acceptable to residents? This question takes on new importance in a region like the San Francisco Bay Area, where the compact form of housing in rows is largely confined to San Francisco neighborhoods, but where freestanding single family homes predominate in all surrounding cities.

Affordability will become a prime reason to advocate for higher densities. A society of single home dwellers for several generations might very likely be forced into dwellings of stacked flats for reasons of greater affordability. However, the choices for apartment living are currently limited to double loaded corridor buildings in the form of slabs or towers, where neighbors share a central corridor on all floors and occupy apartments with a single orientation to one side of a building or the other. In response to the causes of climate change and for reasons of affordability designers will need to demonstrate that an urban form can be designed that mitigates people's negative perception of density. The San Francisco perimeter blocks serve as an excellent example. How does such a design counteract the feeling of being crowded? In consecutive studies we put this question to a test.

The Haight-Ashbury district in San Francisco is known for its counterculture movement of the 1960s. Fifty years later, with less room for social experiments, rising housing costs and harder economic realities, two or more stable wage earners are required in order to rent or own a flat in this district. The median household income for San Francisco residents in 2010 was $60,700 per year. With rising rental costs, the amount spent on rent or mortgage could easily approach 50% of household income. During a first round of studies (Elliott, et al., 2012), we selected five blocks of similar residential density, with an average of 30 flats per acre (27 to 33). The blocks varied in size, thus in population. In the five chosen blocks, the largest block housed 388 residents, the smallest block 131. When asked to estimate the number of people living in the block where the respondent lived, residents in units with dual orientation towards fronting streets and to rear yards consistently underestimated the total population of their block. Residents did so regardless of block size. Residents with a single orientation towards the street and no backyard orientation consistently overestimated the total population of the block they lived in. We concluded that direct and visual access to the inner block lowers residents' perceived density. That finding remained true when we looked at resident responses from units with only a rear yard orientation. These residents also underestimated the actual population size.

One year later, we refined our questions and repeated the survey (Jin, et al., 2013) in the same neighborhood, but in a comparison that kept the block size and population size the same, around 300 residents per block. The second study confirmed that residents with direct access to private backyards perceived their block to be of a lower density than residents with shared access or no access. The difference was large and statistically significant. Survey respondents with access to private yards estimated the population of their blocks to be 30% lower, on average, than other respondents. All respondents lived in similar sized units. Similarly, residents with a full view of backyards, but no direct access, estimated the population of their block to be 25% lower than residents without such a view. We concluded that access to a private yard, or a full view of the backyard space reduces the perceived presence of others living on a block to a lower number.

In both study rounds we asked residents to describe the views from their windows. When asked to choose from a list of 54 positive and negative adjectives, residents described the view out front towards the streets most frequently as *active and busy*. Somewhat less frequently, residents checked adjectives like *leafy, light, lively, loud and pleasant*; also checked, but less frequently were adjectives like *bright, sunny and noisy*. The choice of adjectives did not vary much by block. Indeed, residents look out onto very similar street scenes. Views into the rear of blocks varied more substantially, depending on tree canopy, presence of rear buildings and the maintenance of gardens. However, in the first round of studies we found that residents, regardless of block size and amount of greenery, associate similar attributes with their rear view. In the first round, residents of the largest block with over 300 residents and a tree canopy of 28% surface area, agreed on *bright, green, leafy, calm and light*. These are the same adjectives that were marked by residents of a smaller block with 251 residents and a tree canopy of 52%

surface area. Likewise, residents of the smallest block with 131 residents and a tree canopy of 38% surface area checked the same adjectives. With blocks of the same density, 30 units per acre, the presence of greenery in the rear of a block matters greatly, but the amount of greenery and block size seem to matter less in people's perception of the qualities inside perimeter blocks.

In the San Francisco urban block study, we were curious whether a tighter, narrower block may feel less private because the proximity between rear facades is reduced. At the narrowest block in our study, the space between rear facades measured 50 feet. The conditions there reminded us of Hitchcock's film *Rear Window* set in the perimeter of a Manhattan

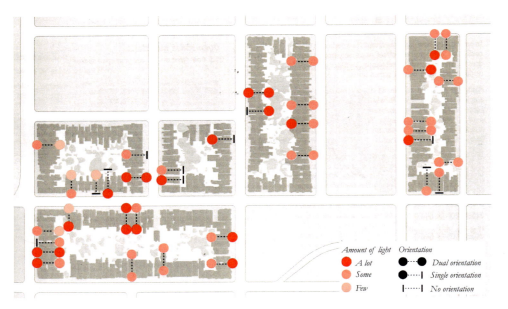

◀ Figure 1.1.3

Above: Haight Ashbury perimeter blocks (source: Google Earth 2010)

Below: Haight Ashbury perimeter blocks. Map view shows the five blocks selected for a survey of residents and their perception of density. The map indicates the location of participating survey residents, the amount of light they receive and the orientation of their apartments to the front, to the rear, or in both directions. (Drawn by Tani Elliott, Andrea Stoelzle and Chris Toocheck.)

block. Asking residents whether they thought their neighbors could see inside their homes, we found that the concern for intrusion into privacy was more common in units with a single orientation towards the street.

For designers, dimensions are important. Density can be measured in a number of ways. We measured the land area of each block between the center lines of the surrounding streets. In absolute numbers, the resulting rectangles contained between 3.6 hectares for the largest block and 2 hectares for the smallest in our first round of studies. These are gross density measurements. Expressed as a ratio, the amount of street space, including sidewalks, measured between 31% for the largest block and 41% for the smallest block. The

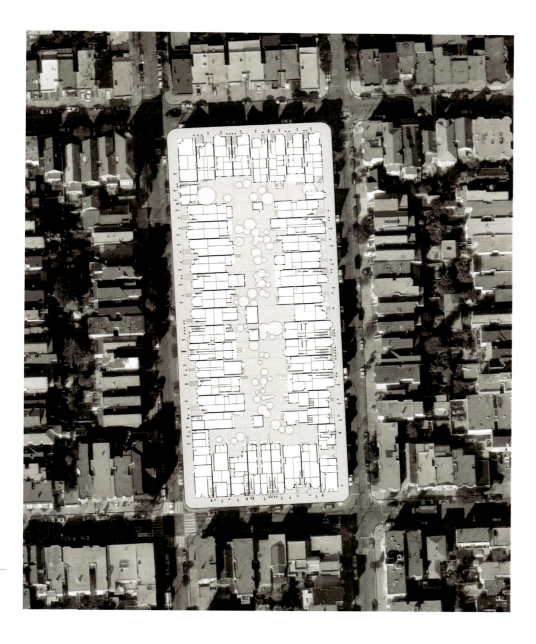

▶ Figure 1.1.4

San Francisco Mission Area block (drawn by Anne Lingye Chen).

CHAPTER 1 Water, Land and Places

amount of land covered by buildings varied between 37% and 46%. The amount of yard space varied between 19% and 29%. In the second round of studies, we selected blocks of the same size, just over 2.6 hectares each, with 50% of land covered by buildings, about 26% dedicated to streets and sidewalks and 20% given to yard space in the center of each block. A 2.6-hectare block seems to produce an efficient distribution of land assigned to buildings, private open space and the public realm of streets and sidewalks.

As residents recorded favorably the orientation of windows to light and greenery, we wanted to learn more about the advantages of different block orientations. San Francisco

Matrix Based On Orientation and Shape

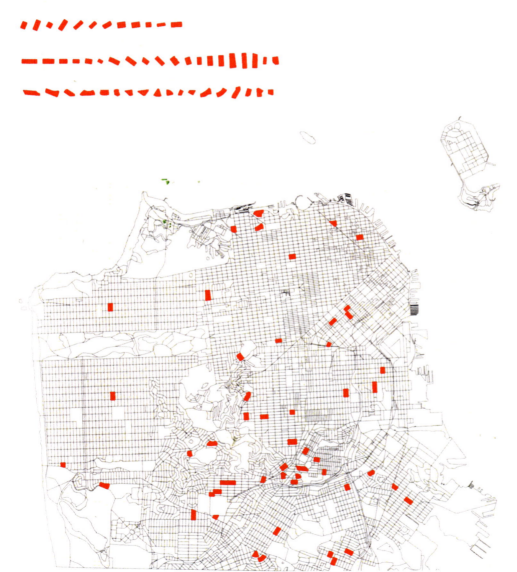

◀ Figure 1.1.5

The orientation of San Francisco blocks (drawn by A. Chen, D. Collaros, R. Recarte and G. Kabrialian).

28   PART I The San Francisco Estuary and Inland Delta

has a total of 5,808 perimeter blocks. Most follow the cardinal directions. As discussed earlier in this chapter, Jasper O'Farrell was largely responsible for correcting Richardson's earlier diagonal street design into an orderly grid of north–south and east–west running streets. In his grid, the east–west streets are longer, thus more windows face north or south than east or west on a given block. As grids grew, a bias for blocks with longer north–south streets was introduced, thus increasing the number of east–west facing flats. Bay windows with their angled window panes compensate to some extent by orienting flats to the missing light directions in the front and back of flats.

In part to confirm earlier research on ideal block orientation, as in the work by Ralph Knowles, or by Victor Olgyay (Knowles, 1981),[6] a third team (Chen, et al., 2012) went out to sample San Francisco perimeter blocks with regard to physiological comfort. Equipped with instruments to measure sun exposure, temperature, light intensity, color, temperature, wind and humidity we sampled climate data around the perimeter of the three block types: north–south, east–west, and a block angled on a 45-degree diagonal to the cardinal directions. The measurements confirm that a block angled by 45 degrees received higher values in solar radiation and luminance than the other two block types for morning and afternoon readings. As expected, values at midday were similar for all three block types. In the team's climate and luminance modeling, east–west blocks ranked second in receiving solar radiation, north–south blocks ranked third. These findings are not new, but do residents living in flats on blocks with a diagonal orientation perceive the availability of sun and light as predicted by field measurements and modeling? The answer was yes. When asked how much sunlight does your home receive, on a 5 point scale from *none* to *extremely high*, residents on the 45-degree angled block checked *high* more than residents from the other two types of blocks. When asked to rate their satisfaction with the amount of sunlight their home receives, diagonal block residents marked *very satisfied* more frequently than residents from the other two block types.

Urban Blocks in History

There is an irony in professionals talking about the benefits of light, air and greenery in the context of urban blocks, when the same argument for more light and air was made by CIAM[7] participants, who advocated the abandonment of urban blocks in favor of freestanding buildings surrounded by open space, frequently undesignated space. Philippe Panerai reminds us that urban designers seem to be going in circles around the advantages and disadvantages of urban blocks. Professionals allied with the CIAM movement attributed urban ills to the 19th century crowded conditions of urban blocks in European cities and favored freestanding towers in parklike settings (Panerai, et al., 2004). Not only European cities condemned perimeter blocks; Catherine Bauer labeled New York's 1879 Housing Act "possibly the worst legalized building form in the world" (Bauer, 1934). The law allowed 80% land coverage for stacked flats in dumbbell tenements. Throughout history, land speculation was fueled by large influxes of population into cities from rural areas or from abroad. Lax building laws brought the urban block into a state of discredit.

It is worthwhile looking at the urban block throughout history. The 1975 French book, *Formes Urbaines*, translated with much delay as *Urban Forms: The Death and Life of the Urban Block*, is important in this context. So is the introduction by one of its authors, Philippe Panerai, to the next important book: *Atlas of the Dutch Urban Block* (Komossa, et al., 2005), a compendium spanning three centuries of Dutch urban block design. Even more recently, the London architect Bob Allies agrees, in *The Fabric of Place* (Allies & Haigh, 2014, p. 138), that density has been seen as a threat to established notions of scale, privacy and character. But the urban block with increased density is becoming a prerequisite for sustainable urban form. Like the established notion of a carbon footprint, Allies argues for a reasonable residential footprint. If in the past a typical three-story London terraced house on a perimeter block, occupied by a family of five, with a small front yard and 10-meter deep backyard, computed to around 30 square meters per person, current urban block designs by his firm reduce the residential footprint to half that amount or less. The renewed interest in moderately high, yet livable density provides evidence that there is a new relevance for the urban block in a society that will have to come to grips with reduced available space in its response to the causes of climate change and the need to build affordably. In the following nine examples of perimeter blocks in history, I have followed Bob Allies' computational method in calculating residential footprints.[8] Figures 1.1.6A, 1.1.6B and 1.1.6C show the urban block in port cities from Pompeii to Malmö, drawn to the same scale (footprint maps drawn by Hyun Young Kim).

Essential for the response to the causes of climate change are housing designs that attract new residents to live in urban blocks, and this is best done by addressing the need for privacy and inclusion of nature. At the same time, housing needs to be affordable and this requires, especially in the San Francisco Bay Area, moderately high density and small unit sizes. Reducing the institutional character is accomplished by giving residents access to the status of a dwelling with individuality. While the selection of urban blocks shown in Figures 1.1.6A, 1.1.6B and 1.1.6C is of historic interest, the historic de Klerk blocks (Sherwood, 2002) in Amsterdam provide a strong identity (Komossa, et al., 2005, p. 63). Likewise, the Potato Rows in Copenhagen (Ørum-Nielsen, 1996, pp. 146-151) and the Haight Ashbury blocks in San Francisco counter the sense of feeling crowded by giving units a dual orientation to nature in the rear and city life in the front. These urban block designs with their vegetative cover at the center of the block also contribute to a cooling effect, important as temperatures in cities rise. Despite their moderately high density, units in these blocks offer a high degree of privacy. The new Malmö (Rose, 2005) blocks at the former Western Harbor perform like the two new San Francisco blocks in Figure 10.1.6C. Inside the last three, growing tall trees in the center of blocks is curtailed by the parking podium that extends below the block. Currently, it sounds idealistic to say that block dimensions should not be determined by parking configurations below ground, but by the ability to free up the ground to bring nature into the

▶ Figure 1.1.6a (opposite)

Top: urban blocks in Pompeii, 79 AD are included here because such blocks are typical in cities with courtyard houses. The chosen block in the center of the frame has a land coverage of 79%. The block size is small with 2,880m² net. The chosen block has seven parcels, two large homes with stores facing a major street. The five remaining parcels are of medium or small dimensions and face minor streets. Given the different household sizes, we assumed an average occupancy of five residents per single story courtyard house, the residential footprint resulting in 66m² per resident. The occupancy per house would have included an extended family and servants.

Middle: block between Herengracht and Keizersgracht in Amsterdam, 1616 to 1658. The block has a land coverage of 61.6%. The bylaws, Keur in Dutch, intentionally prescribed an "Arcadian" quality for the block interior and prohibited tenements, alleyways and craftsmen shops of "injurious and pernicious trades" in the center of the block (Komossa, et al., 2005). The block size is large with net 16,275m². We count 71 parcels on this chosen block with an average of four story buildings fronting the canals and cross streets. In addition, the parcels facing the canals accommodate a second structure to the rear connected by a courtyard. In its historic condition, the residential footprint computes to 11m² per resident, assuming an average of eight family members and live-in employees per merchant household. To arrive at a residential footprint, we subtracted 40%, or the equivalent of two floors per structure containing offices and storage in a typical merchant household. (Today the block contains mainly offices and institutions.)

Bottom: Bloomsbury Block near Russell Square, London, 1776. The row houses have an intentionally uniform character "to suit every family with a certain income" as Steen Eiler Rasmussen (1974, p. 200) observed. The block has a low land coverage of 43% and a block size of 15,900m². We count the equivalent of 60 row houses. The estimated residential footprint computes to 19m² per resident, assuming that eight persons including live-in servants occupied a four story row house. Originally this Bloomsbury Block contained mews that were removed and given over to a public yard shared by some of the hotels that occupy the block today.

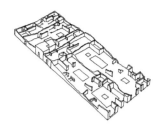

66 m² footprint per resident

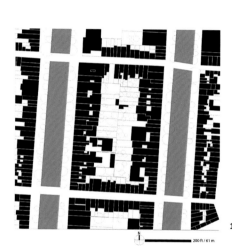
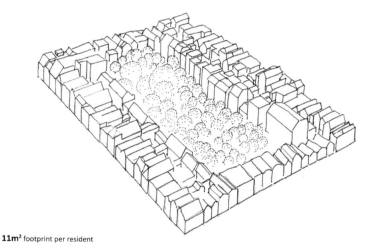

11m² footprint per resident

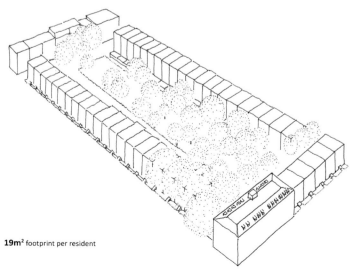

19m² footprint per resident

CHAPTER 1 Water, Land and Places

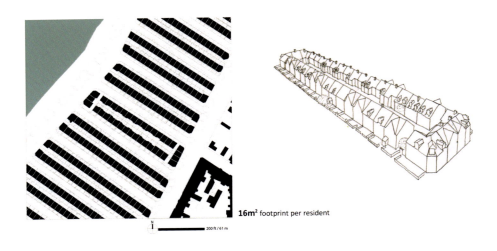

16m² footprint per resident

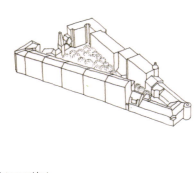

14m² footprint per resident

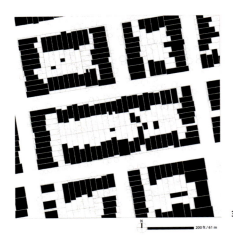
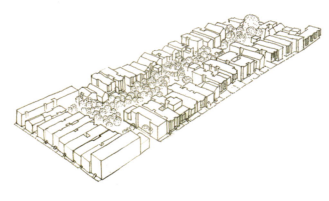

30m² footprint per resident

PART I The San Francisco Estuary and Inland Delta

◀ Figure 1.1.6b (opposite)

Top: Copenhagen, Potato Rows, 1873 to 1889. Today, the neighborhood is one of the most sought-after locations in the inner parts of Copenhagen. The small row houses are highly prized. The irony of the cooperative building society movement is that the urban blocks offered low-income housing only for a short period of time. The original owners sold their property relatively quickly because of the increase in value (Ørum-Nielsen, 1996). The land coverage on a typical block is low, with 49%. The block size is also small, with 3,961m^2. The chosen block consists of 40 predominantly two-story single family row houses with attics. The current residential footprint for three people per household computes to 16m^2 per resident.

Middle: "Het Ship", the triangular block which includes a school and a post office, now a museum. The block was designed by Michel De Klerk in 1919. Ownership was retained by a cooperative; newly renovated in 1968, the blocks appear in excellent condition, having provided housing for moderate-income residents for 100 years. The triangular block has a land coverage of 49%; it has 102 stacked flats in mostly four-story buildings on one continuously owned parcel of land, or an area of 7,311m^2 gross. When the land area for the school and post office is subtracted, the net residential site area amounts to 3,334m^2. The residential footprint results in 14m^2, assuming three residents per household.

Bottom: Haight Ashbury blocks, San Francisco,1913–20. The block in the middle of the frame has a land coverage of 55.3% on a net land area of 19,572m^2, with 62 multifamily row house properties. Census block data shows 388 residents. The residential footprint computes to 30m^2 per resident.

interior of blocks. That would make multifamily housing more palatable to individuals and families who would otherwise not consider urban blocks as a way of life.

Searching for examples of recent infill housing in San Francisco, we wondered under what conditions we could find new housing where residents live at moderately high densities and do not use their cars on a daily basis, thus requiring less parking. We compared six new urban infill projects in San Francisco, plus one in Oakland and one in a smaller town north of Oakland. Yes, such residential infill with lower car use exists. Having access to frequent public transit alone does not reduce vehicle miles traveled. Crucial is access on foot to shops, services and primary schools for households with small children. If such access is available, the car stays in the garage. We asked residents who had recently moved into new infill housing to tell us how many weekly trips they made to each of the following seven activities: work, grocery shopping, recreation, school, eating out, socializing, and occasional shopping for clothing and bigger items. We then asked them to tell us how many trips they made to the same activities at the location of their previous residence.

In one location with frequent transit service residents reduced their vehicle miles drastically. But this location also offered many amenities and services within walking distance. Train services every 3 to 5 minutes to downtown employment within a 20-minute commute distance entirely eliminated work-related trips by car. At the previous residence, cars had been used 67% of the time to commute to work. Also, trips to the grocery store, recreation and shopping trips took place not by car, but on foot, bicycle and public transit. Only trips to socialize and to eat out required the use of cars, and that number of trips by car increased (Kearnan, et al., 2014). The location of the 2010 infill project included a grocery store at the ground level of the infill project. The neighborhood offered coffee shops, restaurants, a hardware store, bookshop, public library, banks, beauty shops and a primary school all within 5 minutes' walking distance. We compared this infill location with a second infill project that is located near a new light rail stop with service to downtown San Francisco, but in a location where none of the above amenities existed. Car use did not decrease. Even work-related trips were still predominantly done by car. It appears from the commute distances that residents had moved to new loft housing in the inner city from suburban locations, but continued to commute to their workplaces in the suburbs of Silicon Valley. At a third location in San Francisco near the commuter train station to Silicon Valley, work-related trips remained split, 35% by transit compared to 35% by car at the previous residence, now 30% and 30% at the new location. More residents walked to work. But, again judging from the distances traveled, many residents maintained their employment in Silicon Valley. Trips on foot for grocery shopping increased from 50% to 83%. There was no noticeable increase or decrease of vehicle miles traveled by car for any of the other trips.

CHAPTER 1 Water, Land and Places

22m² footprint per resident

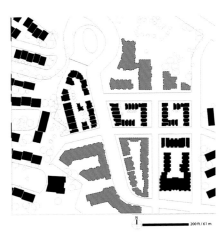

8m² footprint per resident

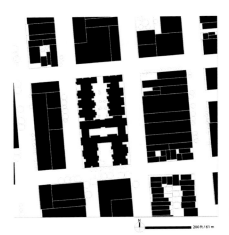
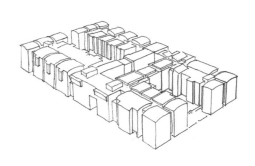

16m² footprint per resident

◀ Figure 1.1.6c (opposite)

Top: West Harbor, Malmø 2001, urban design by Klas Tham. A critique of the project was published by the *Guardian* (Rose, 2005). A typical block in the middle of the frame has a land coverage of 65.7% on a land area of 1,750m^2 net (the smallest block in the sample). The u-shaped block in the center contains ten single family row houses with two floors on ten parcels, plus one parcel with nine flats in a three-story structure. The residential footprint amounts to 22m^2 per resident.

Middle: Hunters View, San Francisco, was designed by Paulett Taggart Architects in 2008. The block to the right in the middle of the frame has a land coverage of 70% on a net land area of 2,052m^2. The block contains 60 stacked flats on a single parcel of land. The residential footprint amounts to 10m^2 per resident, the highest per person density in the sample.

Bottom: Mosaica, design by Daniel Solomon, Mithun/Solomon Design Partners in 2010. The block in the center of the frame has a land coverage of 80% on a single parcel of land that measures 7,405m^2 net. The four-story structures contain 151 units or a residential footprint of 13m^2 per resident.

From this round of studies we learned about the many variables that influence car use by those who have moved to new housing in the inner city. We also learned how to ask more detailed questions about the residents who share these households. In the following year we examined three additional infill projects in San Francisco. Again, all three infill projects were located in close proximity to transit. Residents owned cars, but did not use them for daily trips (Toth, et al., 2015). We also selected two infill locations near rapid transit stops in Oakland and El Cerrito, a city to the north-east of San Francisco. The results confirmed that car use increases in locations with a lack of amenities, in this case downtown Oakland, and decreases in a largely suburban location, but within walking distance to grocery shopping and other amenities. Both locations had equally good access to public transit.

Information about households revealed that residents attracted to infill projects belong predominantly to the age group of 25 to 35 year olds plus some single, retired people above 65 years of age, but virtually no families (Amos & Hameed, 2015). That of course is not only related to the small unit sizes, but primarily to the lack of reputable schools. One could argue for multi-bedroom units in vain, if access to schools was lacking. Therefore, studio apartments and one-bedroom apartments predominate, the latter for $2,500 monthly rent, but there were two and three-bedroom apartments available in Oakland for $2,900 (2015); in El Cerrito, two-bedroom apartments rented at the same cost. It is more common that unrelated adults occupy a multi-bedroom unit than families. Unit sizes are the same for the San Francisco infill projects, but the rental/purchase cost is higher: the rent for a one-bedroom flat was $3,400 to $3,700 per month in 2015.

The studies instill hope that a lower daily use of cars can be expected in infill projects that are as well connected to amenities as they are to frequent transit services. In the future, lower automobile use could result in the use of more car sharing services and lower parking ratios imposed by city government. Freeing up the center of urban blocks from building garages to provide private and shared open space would also attract more families. The convenience of car sharing services showed up in the interviews with residents. Taxi or ride-call services were mentioned as the selected option to go grocery shopping by young professionals. Will young professionals stay accustomed to the urban way of life once they decide to start their families? Unless there is more public investment in schools and services, the argument remains circular.

Reducing parking ratios, encouraging multi-bedroom units, maintaining a regulatory framework that supports well-balanced land coverage ratios and density requirements, as well as investing in schools in inner-city neighborhoods are all initiatives that are only partly driven by market forces. They remain the responsibility of the public sector.

Notes

1 Prior to the visit of the *Rurik* in 1816, among the non-Spanish ships, George Vancouver explored the bay in 1792 and the Russian ship *Juno* in 1806.
2 The Mexican American War ended in 1848 with the treaty of Guadalupe Hidalgo.
3 A vara is a pre Napoleonic Spanish unit of measurement. One hundred varas equal 84 meters.
4 Florence Lipsky summarizes the discussion about grid and topography using various sources.
5 Braudel credits the German economist and statistician Ernst Wagemann (1952).
6 See also *Design with Climate* (Olgyay & Olgyay, 1963).
7 Congrès internationaux d'architecture moderne (CIAM) founded in 1928, generally associated with the modern movement in architecture representing many of the famous architects in Europe of that time.
8 Bob Allies together with Paul Eaton in their essay "Density and its virtues: what is our residential footprint?" (Allies & Haigh, 2014, pp. 138-139) define residential footprint, f = (a-b) c : 100d, where a = total site area, b = site area dedicated to public use, c = the percentage of the land area dedicated to residential use, d = number of occupants.

References

Allies, B. & Haigh, D., 2014. *The Fabric of Place*. London: Artifice Books on Architecture.

Amos, D. & Hameed, Y., 2015. *Urban Infill & VMT [Unpublished student research report]*, Berkeley: Department of City and Regional Planning, University of California, Berkeley.

Bauer, C., 1934. *Modern Housing*. Boston: Harvard University Press.

Braudel, F., 1992. *The Structures of Everyday Life: The Limits of the Possible*. Berkeley: University of California Press.

Chen, L., Collazos, A. D., Recarte, C. & Kaprielian, G., 2012. *Investigating Solar Comfort in San Francisco Perimeter Blocks [Unpublished report]*, Berkeley: College of Environmental Design, UC Berkeley.

Crouch, D., Garr, D. & Mundigo, A., 1982. *City Planning Ordinances of the Law of the Indies in Spanish City Planning in North America*. Cambridge, MA: MIT Press.

Elliott, T., Stoelzle, A. & Toocheck, C., 2012. *The Qualitative Effects of Perimeter Block Configurations [unpublished report]*, Berkeley: Department of City and Regional Planning, UC Berkeley.

Jin, H.-Y. et al., 2013. *Perception of Density in Haight-Ashbury Perimeter Blocks [unpublished report]*, Berkeley: College of Environmental Design, UC Berkeley.

Kearnan, J., Cooke, D., Fue, Y. & Cao, W., 2014. *Urban Infill, The VMT Success and Failure of California Senate Bill 375 [Unpublished student report]*, s.l.: UC Berkeley.

Knowles, R. L., 1981. *Sun, Rhythm and Form*. Cambridge, MA: MIT Press.

Komossa, S. et al., 2005. The Scale of the Urban Block. In: *Atlas of the Dutch Urban Block*. Bussum: Thoth Publishers, pp. 11–14.

Lipsky, F., 1999. *San Francisco, la grille sur les collines / the grid meets the hill (English and French edition)*. Marseille: Editions Parenthèses.

Moudon, A. V., 1989. *Built for Change, Neighborhood Architecture in San Francisco*. Cambridge, MA: MIT Press.

Olgyay, V. & Olgyay, A., 1963. *Design with Climate: Bioclimatic Approach to Architectural Regionalism*. Princeton: Princeton University Press.

Ørum-Nielsen, J., 1996. *Dwelling: At Home – In Community – on Earth: The Significance of Tradition in Contemporary Housing*. Copenhagen: Danish Architectural Press.

Panerai, P., Castex, J., Depaule, J. C. & Samuels, I., 2004. *Urban Forms, The Death and Life of the Urban Block*. Oxford: Elsevier Architectural Press.

Rapoport, A., 1975. Towards a Redefinition of Density. *Environment and Behavior, 7*(2), pp. 133–158.

Rasmussen, S., 1974. *London: the Unique City*. Cambridge, MA: MIT Press.

Rose, S., 2005. *Ecological City of Tomorrow 8-29-05*. London: Guardian.

Scott, M., 1985. *The San Francisco Bay Area, A Metropolis in Perspective*. Berkeley: University of California Press.

Sherwood, R., 2002. *Housing Prototypes.Org.* [Online] Available at: http://housingprototypes.org/project?File_No=NETH002 [Accessed 20 September 2014].

Toth, A., Alharbali, S. & Wang, Y., 2015. *Urban Infill Development and the Effect on VMT in San Francisco [Unpublished Student Report],* Berkeley: Department of City and Regional Planning, UC Berkeley.

Viganò, P., 2016. *Territories of Urbanism: The Project as Knowledge Producer.* New York: EPFL Press/Routledge.

Wagemann, E., 1952. *Economia Mundial.* Santiago: Editorial Juridica de Chile.

Chapter 2

The Bay Area's Metropolitan Landscape, a Dispersed Metropolis

Our concern is the design of future urban form that responds to the causes and consequences of climate change. Located rather precisely at third points on a circumference around the globe, a global comparison between the three delta regions covered in this book goes beyond the obvious similarities that are implied by a region's relationship to ocean tides, river deltas and estuaries. True, water in its various forms and with its complex dynamics will have a much greater influence on urban form in the future. With a greater respect to water, designers in all three regions will have to address the consumption of buildable land. The argument sounds banal, when land is of seemingly unlimited supply. To demonstrate that the consumption of land is not a trivial matter, we included Randstad Holland in the third part of this book. Here, the long history of building on land that needed protection from water serves as a reminder of how low-lying land is used, not just in history, but presently and in the future.

In part II of the book we confirm that land was seemingly in endless supply in the Pearl River Delta in 1979, when the policies of economic development opened the region to foreign investment and triggered a process of dispersed urbanization of staggering proportion. Dispersed urbanization prevailed in the San Francisco Bay Area after bridges and highways made it possible to live in communities far removed from the historic concentration of work places. That process started in the late 1930s and continued into the 1970s. The trend of seemingly unlimited land consumption accelerated in the mid 1980s when an exodus of downtown workplaces into suburban office parks accelerated. As the structure of the larger region can be held responsible for the causes of climate change, it is important to remember how such structures emerged.

In 1984, California's largest corporation, Chevron, vacated two 40-story office towers in downtown San Francisco and relocated to a low-rise office park at the former rural fringe of the San Francisco Bay Area. The company was not alone; the nation's largest telecommunications company made the same move to a neighboring site, as did the regional headquarters of a foreign car manufacturer. These companies were not trendsetters; suburban office parks have a longer history (Mozingo, 2011). Also, such corporate exodus was not confined to suburban Northern California; similar relocations took place in most metropolitan regions in North America. The reasons companies moved from downtown locations to the suburban fringe were associated with the automation of corporate office operations that took place in the 1980s. Data processing could happen in locations with lower real estate values; no longer was it necessary for corporations to maintain a significant presence in publicly accessible locations; members of the public would no longer come in person, but communication had taken the form of electronic file transfers that needed analysis and storage. The decision

38   PART I The San Francisco Estuary and Inland Delta

about exactly where to move was made by senior management and corporate board members, who preferred locations in the vicinity of their homes in semi-rural settings, locations where management already lived and where they sent their children to reputable suburban schools (Fishman, 1987).

The 4,500 Chevron office workers had to follow. No longer would they travel to work by regional transit, which in downtown San Francisco functions like a subway with direct pedestrian connections to high-rise office towers. At the new location, the small former rural community of San Ramon, office workers had no choice but to drive and leave their car in the office park's vast parking lots for the remainder of the day. Here, Chevron and a number of companies had located on a former ranch. The landowners notified the county that they were taking steps towards incorporating as an independent municipality and applied to convert additional agricultural land for residential use of predominantly single family homes. The argument was made that more land was needed to provide housing for the new working population.

The process described here repeated itself not only in one geographic location; it radiated outwards from the historic handful of employment centers of San Francisco, San Jose and Oakland, plus a few smaller ones to produce a polycentric metropolitan region of fifteen such centers.

An early critique of North America's predominant vision for large metropolitan areas was written by Anthony Downs (Downs, 1989).[1] In his analysis, Downs did not use the term *unsustainable* to characterize the current vision for large metropolitan areas in North America. The term was not commonly applied to land-use decision making in the 1980s. Nor did he point to the inefficient use of energy or the high carbon emissions that make the move from high-rise office towers to low-rise office parks unsustainable in our current assessment. But

▶ Figure 1.2.1

Concentration of high-rise office towers in San Francisco (photo by Judith Stilgenbauer).

▲ Figure 1.2.2

San Ramon Bishop Ranch Office park (source: Microsoft BING, TerraServer). The map shows the center of Bishop Ranch at Bollinger Canyon Road, east of Interstate 680. The Chevron campus is visible on the lower left, AT&T is located in the north-western corner, and an empty block is slated to house the future San Ramon city center. Running diagonally through the frame center is the "Iron Horse Trail", abandoned as a railroad in 1977.

both factors are implicit in his critique about the major flaws of the North American vision for dispersed regions.

According to Downs, the first major flaw of the typical American vision was that it produced excessive travel; the second that it had no housing provision for a broader range of income groups including lower paid workers who are essential for the functioning of any economy; the third that there was no consensus on how to finance infrastructure fairly; and the fourth that there was no mechanism for resolving inevitable conflicts between the welfare of society as a whole and the welfare of geographically small parts of society.

Remedies necessary for the repair of the metropolitan vision called for at least moderately high density, especially of housing but also for workplaces, together with a better integration of land use, thus the encouragement to live nearer to where people work. His new vision preserved local authority, but within a framework that compels local government to act responsibly to meet regional needs, and his vision contains incentives that encourage individuals and their households to take a more realistic account of the collective costs of their behavioral choices.

Downs did not extend the collective cost of behavioral choices to corporations, but should have. An employment center in downtown San Francisco high-rise towers is clearly more sustainable than the low-rise suburban office park alternatives. Certainly this observation holds true if all costs are taken into consideration, including the cost of highway infrastructure to support a polycentric regional configuration, the cost of housing for lower paid workers, the cost of energy consumed by the individual driver, and the costs associated with increased carbon emissions. However, since none of these costs are entered onto the balance sheet for companies like Chevron, the move from high-rise towers to low-rise office parks has proven to be highly sustainable for the company's finances over the last 30 years.

Senior management at Chevron from the 1980s has now retired. We can only speculate what new senior management will decide about Chevron's future location. For example, the office park in San Ramon would go up for sale if Chevron were to move. I am not saying that it should or will make such a move, but what is illustrated by the Chevron example is the fact that the work performed there is not tied to a specific location.

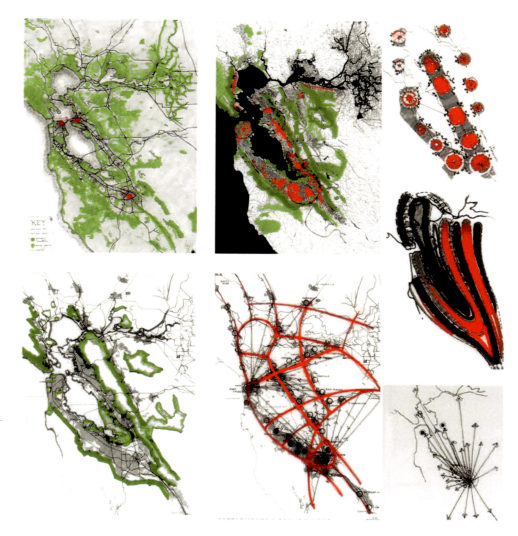

▶ Figure 1.2.3

Diagrams depicting a polycentric region. Greenbelts, workplace concentrations, controls to sprawl, and major connectors define the structure of the region. (Drawn by Ashish Karode, top left by Stefan Pellegrini.)

CHAPTER 2 The Bay Area's Metropolitan Landscape

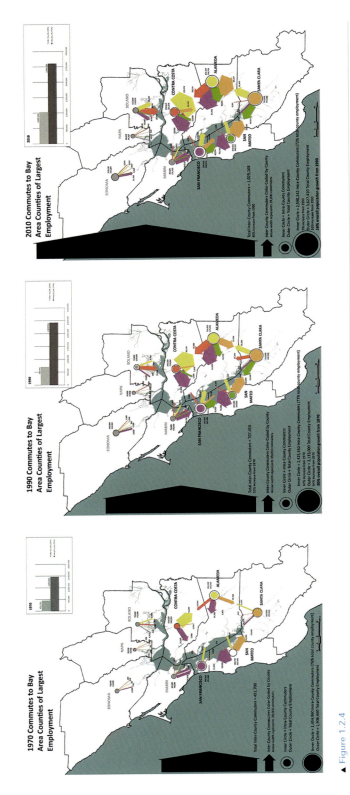

▲ Figure 1.2.4

Commute patterns between Bay Area counties from 1970, 1990 and 2010. Daily commute patterns intensified when corporations left downtown locations in the early 1980s to settle in suburban office parks. The figure explains the intensity of Bay Area commute patterns between major employment centers in the nine-county San Francisco Bay Area. (Diagrams by the author, assisted by John Doyle.)

The example also illustrates that the Chevron case is not unique to North America. Societies so heavily invested in transportation infrastructure and private communication have transformed urban regions profoundly at all levels (Ascher, 1995).

As a whole, the Bay Area has an extremely low intensity of land use. Urbanization has spread as if there are no limits to space and no regard for differences in location. However, examples of compact urban form exist, largely in a historic context. Living in the inner parts of San Francisco, or in a number of smaller compact Bay Area cities, offers residents a way of life that reduces their dependency on cars. Here properties have risen in value and remain much in demand. San Franciscans, more so than residents in any major west coast city, make over 50 percent of all trips to work not by driving alone, but by transit, walking, cycling or carpooling (SF Municipal Transportation Agency, 2015). It is therefore important to take a careful look at compact urban form, where it still exists. That is what Reid Ewing and Robert Cervero concluded when they compared 50 empirical studies on the potential to moderate travel demand through changes of settlement form (Ewing & Cervero, 2001).

Clearly, compact urban form conserves non-renewable energy, thus addressing the causes of climate change. The question is how to achieve a more compact form when a highly dispersed urban form prevails.

Through legislation, the State of California has been a forerunner in linking the importance of improved air quality to urbanization. Not only has the state been a trendsetter, legislating stricter vehicle emission standards (such as 2011 State Senate Bill 375) than in other states, California has provided incentives to reduce vehicular travel by encouraging the type of moderately high density infill development near public transit stations that we discussed in the previous chapter (Barbour & Deakin, 2012). But as an incentive the Senate Bill does not have sufficient force to bring about a better integration of uses, moderately higher densities and a lower dependency on automobiles. The authority over land-use decisions remains at the municipal level.

> Virtually every American problem, real, imagined or socio-psychopathic, was solved by physical isolation and segregation, whether race, illness, illegal behavior or undesired contact with persons of lower income, spatial segregation was the answer.
>
> L.C. Gerckens (1994, p. 10)

Living at the Edge

A first encounter with the Chevron office park at Bishop Ranch in San Ramon and the residential community that emerged in Dougherty Valley dates back to the fall of 2000. I visited the site on the eastern edge of the San Francisco Bay Area because I was curious to see first-hand what a metropolitan edge looks like. I had produced maps of 50 metropolitan regions worldwide and had assumed that unless a body of water or a sudden rise in topography limits urbanization, a clearly demarked edge does not exist, but rather a zone where urban conditions transform gradually to nonurban conditions, whatever the exact definitions of these two conditions might imply (Bosselmann, 2008, p. 11). I was wrong; in this case the edge of urbanization in the San Francisco Bay Area was clearly and recently demarked as a line drawn by large earthmoving equipment. I took visitors to Dougherty Valley, chiefly foreigners who were fascinated to see cattle grazing on hillsides and large bulldozers carving away at the bottom of the same hills. The machines created level pads, where neighborhoods would be built. On consecutive visits I saw machinery that came to grade new streets. The drivers were equipped with global positioning devices that directed the plows to shape curb lines and cul-de-sacs. I timed the operation; it took an operator 15 minutes to delineate a cul-de-sac on the ground where none had been. Shortly afterwards, crews arrived to form concrete edges. I watched an industrialized process of production that eventually resulted in 11,000 homes for 36,000 new residents.

For a large project like Dougherty Valley, a battery of earthmoving machines was necessary. Prior to the November rains, for obvious reasons, the machinery needs to be moved. It gets loaded onto large wheeled carriages and pulled by trucks over the interstate highway system, where it travels on lanes with a minimum standard width of 12 feet or 3.6 meters (Federal Highway Administration, 2014). The lane width dimension determines the width of the carriages, the width of the earthmoving equipment; thus the freeway lane width also becomes a design determinant for the layout of local road dimensions inside the subdivision. A more reasonable lane width on local streets can be as narrow as 10 feet; even 9 feet (2.7m) is possible. The 3 foot (0.9m) difference does not appear to make much of a difference, but when multiplying the difference in width over a large area with many streets, the difference becomes very significant.

Interestingly, the arterial roads were completed first, even prior to the construction of homes. These roads were brought to a finished state with asphalt and concrete curbs. Even trees were planted and bicycle lanes striped. For sale signs went up prior to the construction of homes. Selling homes and building roads went hand in hand. Future residents were encouraged during the construction phase to drive on the new arterial roads to view the emerging neighborhoods. What they saw were wide roads with generous landscaping. They saw sound-walls even prior to home construction. A resident, considering moving to Dougherty Valley, was helped to see an image of what it would be like to drive home, looking over hills that appeared golden in the afternoon sun. What visitors saw was an image of luxury based on spaciousness and remoteness, but somewhat unreal, especially so if the driver became mindful of the contrast between the finished new roads and the memory of open grazing land.

To expose future residents to the finished designs of tree-lined roads was part of risk management. A project of this size had to be organized in phases. For each phase, a sufficient number of interested buyers had to be committed in order to justify the capital layout for roads and services for the next phase.

The arterial streets in Dougherty Valley function as limited access roads and do not provide access to homes, not even those that are located adjacent to such streets. It is important to dwell on this observation for a moment. Current land development practice calls for a type of street that optimizes mobility and prohibits direct access to properties that line such streets. To facilitate a high level of mobility, intersections are permitted, but only at a minimum of a quarter mile separation. To access homes, drivers turn off at intersections onto neighborhood streets from where drivers turn into private or collective driveways between clusters of homes.

Both types of streets, the local neighborhood streets as well as the arterial limited access roads, are very wide, one could easily say too wide. The main arterial street in Dougherty Valley, Bollinger Canyon Road, measures 250 feet or 86 meters in width, that is 3 meters wider than the Champs Élysées in Paris (Jacobs, 1993) or twice as wide as Market Street, San Francisco's main street.

On my early visits, when only a few homes had been completed, the more than generous allocation of road space was hard to understand. Why would it ever be necessary to build two parallel left turn lanes? Why would travel lanes on local roads measure as wide as freeway lanes. Why such extensive median strips? Apparently, professionals predicted the

▶ Figure 1.2.5 (opposite)

The common practice of land development at the urban edge: all vegetation is removed by large earthmoving equipment; level pads are carved onto the land; the scraping of a cul-de-sac; constructing roads; framing of a single family home; idle earthmoving machinery; loading equipment onto wheeled carriages; transporting equipment away from the site; and finally, completed neighborhoods.

roadway capacity and calculated that car traffic at peak hours would demand that much space. Apparently, these calculations were never challenged by the permitting authority. The generous dimensions have a direct consequence on the daily life of residents. In a survey, residents report that they use their cars for even the shortest trips, like taking a child to a friend's home in an adjacent neighborhood. Residents agree, walking is not convenient; even a fast walking pedestrian cannot cross the 250-feet wide Bollinger Canyon Road during a single green light phase. A person in need of a carton of milk will predictably start up the car for a short, but circuitous drive to the market, a destination easily reachable by walking or cycling, if such direct connections were to exist. However benign the added lane width might appear in detail, cumulatively these dimensions add up, they increase the distance between places where people live and work and therefore the distance they need to travel.

The spacing of homes appears equally generous, but that observation is only true when measured across the street from front entrance to front entrance. Regardless of income group, front façade to front façade cross-sections measure between 84 and 90 feet, occasionally up to 116 feet.[2] All other separating dimensions between homes are much tighter: the rear façade to rear façade distance adds up to 42 feet, leaving each family a 21-foot deep rear yard and side yards between homes typically measure less than 12 feet. Most homes are too closely spaced to afford views of the scenic hillsides.

The homes are grouped by size. As a result, the population is stratified by mortgage payments. Again, risk management is responsible for the separating of homes by value. A prospective homeowner will assume that the value of a large home is best protected if it is built in a neighborhood of similarly large homes. The largest homes are found on the highest elevation. Even very sizable homes of 4,500 square feet are placed on relatively small lots. Homes that are somewhat lower in elevation measure around 3,000 square feet and are built on even smaller lots. In 2010, these homes were selling for just under $1 million (Windemere, 2010).[3] On the next lowest level, 2,500 square foot homes are arranged in four-plexes with shared driveways and a shared access walkway. The same home size also exists in six-plexes, followed by multifamily homes of 2,000 square feet built attached in rows along shared walks with shared parking at the rear of the structure. Finally, three-story multifamily structures complete the array of the housing production; they are placed in parking lots with the first floor dedicated to parked cars. Thus the entire array of homes includes a composition of six basic unit types with some minor variation in style.

The layout of Dougherty Valley conforms to the latest thinking of master planned communities. Rene Davids commented on the "ordinariness" of Dougherty Valley in his article on the identity of this new suburban metropolis (Davids, 2008). The development incorporates themes of neo-traditional design, such as verandas and porches with columns that the residents we interviewed never use, nor see their neighbors use.

Apart from a critique of the development character, fundamental concerns about the suitability of the location were raised early (Farooq, 2005). Permitting development in a valley without groundwater or natural springs is not new in California. The hills of Dougherty Valley are covered with a deep layer of clay, which forms a barrier to rainwater. The already low annual precipitation of less than 20 inches runs off quickly. With no capacity to store rainwater or to tap groundwater, Dougherty Valley had to purchase water rights. Such rights were found in Kern County in Southern California. Here the Berrenda Mesa water district had rights to water from the Feather River in Northern California. The farmers in this part of Kern County could not use their water allotment because of poor soil conditions and decided to offer their water rights up for sale. In a three-way agreement that involved the City of Livermore, a portion of the Kern County water allocation is now channeled to

▶ Figure 1.2.6

Dougherty Valley, San Ramon 2015 (source: Microsoft Bing TerraServer).

Dougherty Valley without ever reaching Southern California. Livermore's participation was necessary, because Livermore holds membership in the state water system and is privileged to receive Feather River water. The city of San Ramon is too young to benefit from such membership; a convoluted practice but not uncommon in California.

The Forces of the Large Industrialized Development Complex

Water politics were not the only reason why regional planners objected to Dougherty Valley. From a regional perspective, planners questioned the wisdom of decentralizing the Bay Area's employment concentrations. While the trends that caused dispersion of workplaces and population were discussed with much intensity in the 1980s by regional open space advocates (Greenbelt Alliance, 1988), drastic shifts in policy came gradually; it is fair to say that the debate about the consequences of a dispersed region had little influence on regional policy at the time. To counter the trends of dispersed workplaces in the 1980s, the City of San Francisco approved a 1985 plan to set aside land for 11 million square feet for downtown office space.[4] Only 10% of new office space was built in downtown San Francisco's high-rise office district prior to the year 2000, while at San Ramon, during the same time, on the former Bishop Ranch 9 million square feet of office space came into use (Bishop Ranch, 2014).

Twenty-five years later, when the discussion about the consequences of decentralization focused on energy consumption and greenhouse gas emissions, changes in policy emerged because, among climate scientists, the discourse about vehicle emissions and their contribution to the "greenhouse effect" transformed from debatable theory to verifiable facts (Weart, 2017). Not until the passage of Plan Bay Area on July 18, 2013 would the Metropolitan Transportation Commission make an attempt to implement a regional policy framework.

Californians are most prolific emitters of greenhouse gasses. As elsewhere, an estimated 42% of all greenhouse gasses are the result of fossil fuel combustion caused by passenger vehicles and small trucks. A 1990 baseline emissions inventory conducted for the State of California resulted in the State Assembly Bill, AB 32, a state law passed with the purpose of establishing targets for the reduction of greenhouse gas emissions levels to be reached by 2020. [5] In the years that followed, public debate focused on methods to achieve such targets. State law, Senate Bill 375, provided the mechanism for the necessary reductions; it requires that the Metropolitan Transit Authorities[6] of each region include a sustainable community strategy in their regional transportation plans for the purpose of better "aligning transportation and housing", which means to reduce the miles residents habitually travel as a result of the distance between home, workplace and services.[7]

In one Dougherty Valley neighborhood, where homes are priced somewhat below the $1 million mark, residents commute an average of 22.9 miles; a commute far beyond the 3-mile distance to the employment center at Bishop Ranch, and well beyond three employment centers in the 8 to 15 mile range, which also includes stations of the regional rapid transit system (8 miles). Only one third of residents interviewed commute to destinations relatively close by, within the 2 to 15 mile range. Another third, the far distance commuters, said that they can reach San Francisco within 40 minutes by car and Silicon Valley in 45 minutes (overly optimistic, I found. It took me well over one hour to reach San Francisco from San Ramon). The remaining third of residents in the middle of the commute distance range of 20 to 30 miles reach various East Bay commute destinations. Interesting was the comparison with the commute pattern of residents in the next highest income neighborhood of well above $1 million homes. Here residents commute shorter distances, an average of 17.5 miles. Half of them are less than 15 miles from the three nearest employment centers, including the nearest rapid transit station; the other half travels between 18 and 25 miles (Farrington & Ward, 2009).[8]

Admittedly, I am reporting on a small sample, but those we talked to confirm Downs' (1989) observation that American homeowners do not necessarily select a place of residence in close proximity to their place of work and this might very well no longer be a matter of choice but affordability. In retrospect though, when asked where residents would ideally like to live, the far distance commuters in the neighborhood with less than $1 million homes preferred places of residence near workplace concentrations like San Francisco and Silicon Valley. The same response could not be found among residents in the freestanding above $1 million category of homes; here the majority have "found their ideal home".

To better align transportation and housing with the aim of reducing the causes of global warming will be a major challenge in the Bay Area's dispersed region. To introduce the drawings that follow in the next chapter as illustrations of a community brought into compliance with Senate Bill 375 is not entirely correct. The law, the first of its kind in the nation and lauded as blueprint for similar laws in the United States, does not regulate the use of land

and does not diminish the authority of cities and counties to entitle property owners within their jurisdiction. Instead, the state law offers to negotiate: local government is required to use travel demand forecasting prior to permitting. If local government cannot demonstrate that it is possible to reduce vehicle miles and greenhouse gas emissions, the law provides a fallback. If on the other hand local government can demonstrate how to better align housing with transportation, the state law offers incentives in the form of a streamlined environmental review (Darakjian, 2009).

Transects as a Tool towards Understanding the Whole Prior to Restructuring its Parts

Urban design is still a relatively new field. The graphic methods used to gain an understanding of location and its contexts originated in the architecture and engineering professions. The conditions these methods describe are static, frozen in time and place; the structures that result from such representations follow the same predicament. When concerned about the design of the region, more dynamic forms of representation are needed. Here the design professions can learn from the geographic information sciences how to deal with morphological descriptions. A single method will not necessarily reform the knowledge base of an entire field, but an important lesson is the discovery of how dynamic processes reveal interconnectedness. More so than a single structure like a building or a road, the structure of a metropolitan landscape is shaped by a chain of causes and effects.

▼ Figure 1.2.7

The diagram is entitled, "A Painting of Nature (Naturgemälde) based on Observations and Measurements between 10th Degree Northern Latitude and 10th Degree Southern Latitude taken between 1799 to 1803 by Alexander von Humboldt and A.G. Bonpland". The painting was created as an attachment to "Essay on the Geography of Plants" simultaneously published in Paris and Tübingen, Germany, in 1807. (Source: Bancroft Library, UC Berkeley.)

CHAPTER 2 The Bay Area's Metropolitan Landscape

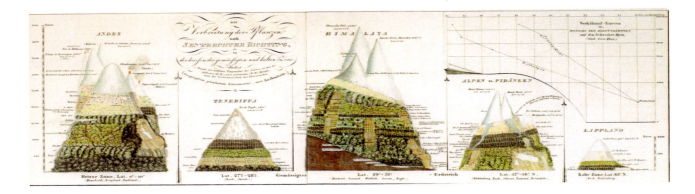

▲ Figure 1.2.8

Table illustrating transects through the plant geography of the Andes, Tenerife, Himalaya and the Alps/Pyrenees. The table is entitled: "The Distribution of Plants According to Vertical Elevation and Climate Zones." Statistics of Noble Plant Families and Groups by A. von Humboldt. (Source: Berghaus, 2004)

In the natural sciences, the methods used to record interconnectedness are generally attributed to Alexander von Humboldt (1769–1859), who in 1802, together with Aime Bonpland, surveyed vegetation along a steep gradient in the Venezuelan Andes. There are two reasons why Humboldt is relevant to this book: he is the first scientist to comment on the danger of climate change due to human causes, and second, he moved away from taxonomic mapping of land use to dynamic descriptions.

Humboldt, on his journey to the Americas, stopped in Tenerife and climbed the Pic de Tide Volcano (Berghaus, 2004). He was surprised by the rich diversity and size of the vegetative cover at high altitudes despite severely cold nighttime temperatures. He knew that at comparable elevations in Europe only very sparse vegetation was found. On the ascent of the Venezuelan Andes, Humboldt took twice-daily measurements of altitude and climate conditions in addition to taking a survey of trees and other major plant communities. The climb resembled a journey from the Equator to the Poles; it revealed interconnected plant worlds layered on top of each other, from tropical palms to lichens near the snow-line.

Humboldt experimented with a graphic representation of his observations and measurements. Upon his return to Paris, he worked with an artist to publish what he called "Naturgemälde". There is no good translation of this German term: an artwork, a painting of nature that shows how nothing in nature develops in isolation, but is connected and interrelated as a whole.

The outcome of Humboldt's survey established vegetation zones and bioclimatic belts in relation to elevation. As a sampling method, observations along transects clarified the importance of photosynthesis on plant variety and growth, a process that is stronger in the equatorial zone and weaker in the Alps located at 46° northern latitude. Thus the transect method improved the scientific understanding of gradients within biological communities. In the history of the natural sciences, Humboldt's work stands between static taxonomy and dynamic historical description, a concept that influenced Charles Darwin (1859) in his theory of evolution, and Ernst Haeckel (1866);[9] thus in the early 19th century Humboldt's transect gave birth to the new field of biogeography.[10]

When nature is understood as a web of interrelated causes and effects, its vulnerability also becomes evident. Humboldt saw the devastating environmental effects of colonial plantations on deforestation and wrote about human-induced climate change (Wulf, 2015, p. 6). The large-scale loss of vegetative cover reduced moisture in the atmosphere, and thus the cooling effect, as well as the retention of water and the protection of soil against erosion.

Humboldt's work influenced Patrick Geddes, who provided the important precedent for transects in the urban context with his Valley Section (Geddes, 1947). Geddes, trained as a biologist and professor of botany when he published *Cities in Evolution* (1915), used transects to describe the human habitat conditions from highland to valley floor.[11] The transect was and still is widely used as a descriptive tool, chiefly in biogeography, where a sample strip of land is used to monitor plant distribution and animal population within a given area. Biologists, foresters, geographers and geologists use transects as a sampling method with reduced dimensionality to survey large geographic areas.

Humboldt's influence on Geddes continued in the writings of fellow Scotsman Ian McHarg's *Design with Nature* (1971) and more recently Anne Whiston Spirn (1984) and Michael Hough (Hough, 1995), an approach to urban design now referred to as ecological or landscape urbanism.

Likewise in urban design, transects are useful as a descriptive tool. They give the designer a large canvas, large enough to keep an eye on the whole when working on parts of the metropolitan landscape.

In recent decades, the transect method was used to defend a normative planning strategy promoted in the United States by the Congress of New Urbanism (Duany, 2002).[12] Here transects delineate a desired urban to rural gradient. While such a gradient frequently existed in history, it is questionable that it can be imposed at the scale of a region. Urban form did not emerge in a gradated fashion in the San Francisco Bay Area. We are dealing with a metropolitan landscape that resembles a patchwork. Repairs or transformations of patches require incremental

▼ Figure 1.2.9

Transects of the San Francisco Bay Area with station points every 5 miles. As shown here, land coverage is computed for each station point, but a multitude of other environmental dimensions can also be computed and shown graphically, such as population density, demographics, permeability of ground surfaces, vegetative cover, climate variables and presence of water.

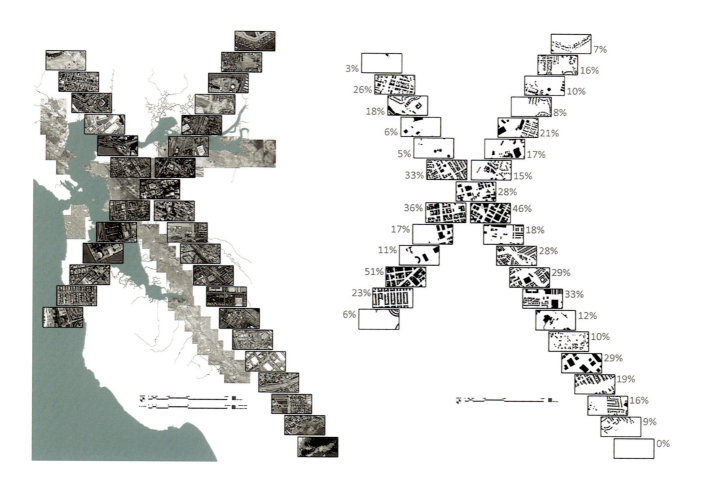

CHAPTER 2 The Bay Area's Metropolitan Landscape

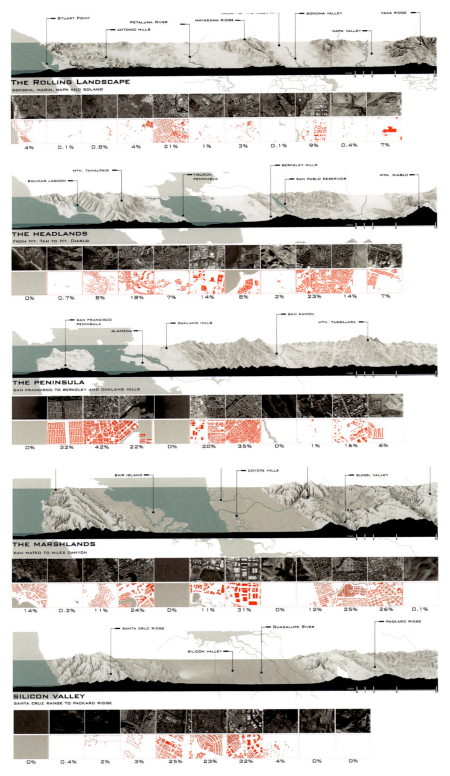

◀ Figure 1.2.10

Five cross sections through the San Francisco Bay Area. The building footprint tiles associated with each section show the amount of land covered by urban development. On average, the utilization of land is extremely low. (Modeled by the author, assisted by John Doyle and Erick Jensen.)

52 PART I The San Francisco Estuary and Inland Delta

change in a highly localized approach, simply due to the decision making power given to local municipalities.

Not as a normative planning tool, but as a description of patches, transects were made by teams of students who described the urbanization of the San Francisco Bay Area. Students traveled from a point of origin, the Campanile on the Berkeley campus, to the extreme edges of the urbanized region. Students were asked to stop every 5 miles and record the conditions around them. In the years that followed, graphic conventions evolved. Like Humboldt, students experimented with vertical exaggeration to emphasize topography and bathymetry along east–west cross-sections of the San Francisco Bay Area. Figure 1.2.10 shows a fivefold exaggeration on the vertical axis. The more sections the better, but five such cross-sections sufficed to represent the San Francisco Bay Area.

The cross sections improve our understanding of landform in relation to settlement form. The compelling graphics in a book by Clemens Steenberger and Wouter Reh illustrate how important it is to see the famous block and street patterns of Rome, London, New York, Berlin and other cities in their three dimensional setting of hills, plains and near water bodies. These graphic representations open the reader's mind to the evolution of urban form over time (Steenberger & Wouter, 2011).

We began this chapter with an observation about the forces that shape urban form. Such forces reveal to some extent the values of their inhabitants at a certain time in history, but more strongly they reveal market forces. This chapter also revealed the astonishing amount of underused space. In California, and not only there, spaciousness has been a reflection of the inhabitants' value system, but much underused land has resulted. In 1912, Raymond Unwin claimed: "Nothing gained by overcrowding" (Unwin, 1912). One hundred years later that sentiment is still with us. Overcrowding is not what we will talk about in the next chapter. We will address how wasted land in a highly dispersed metropolitan landscape like the San Francisco Bay Area can be used more sustainably. There is simply no other choice, if we are to address the causes of climate change. While sustainable urban form might be increasingly unaffordable in the center city locations of San Francisco and selected other cities, it ought to be possible to reform places to support a sustainable and affordable way of life in the urbanized metropolitan landscape of the region.

Notes

1 A study commissioned by Solomon Brothers.
2 These cross-section dimensions are somewhat wider than the 1936 FHA standards and much wider than the road standards for Laguna West, a 1991 neo-traditional community in California (Southworth & Ben Joseph, 2003).
3 For updated housing prices see neighborhoods.com (2017).
4 City of San Francisco, Downtown Development, adopted as part of the general plan, 1985.
5 The California Global Warming Solutions Act of 2006, signed by Governor Schwarzenegger on July 27, 2006.
6 Plan Bay Area approved by the Association of Bay Area Governments and the Metropolitan Transportation Commission, July 18, 2013. The Plan established *Sustainable Community Strategies* and *Priority Development Areas* designated for accommodating a population increase from seven million to nine million Bay Area residents by 2040 in places well served by public transit.
7 For an analysis of SB375 see the Institute for Local Government website: http://www.ca-ilg.org/ (2015).
8 The interviews were carried out by two graduate students. In a pilot project they interviewed a total of 22 households in two *Dougherty Valley* neighborhoods.
9 See Robert J. Richards (Richards, 2008) for more on Haeckel and the endeavors over evolutionary thought.

10 Humboldt traveled to America from 1799 to 1804. His essay on the geography of plants, *Essai sur la géographie des plantes* (Humboldt, 1807), was simultaneously published in Paris and Germany. Humboldt started publishing his life work, *Kosmos*, in 1845 and the fifth volume appeared in 1862; Humboldt's *Kosmos* has been republished (2004).

11 An elaborate aerial perspective of a typical Valley Section was reproduced for the 1910 Urban Exhibit in India, but was lost at sea when the ship that carried the exhibition sunk. The 1947 new and revised edition of *Cities in Evolution published* by Williams and Norgate shows a reproduction of the exhibit and the Valley Section.

12 See also: Emily Talen (2002).

References

Ascher, F., 1995. *Métapolis: Ou l'avenir des villes*. Paris: Odile Jacob.

Barbour, E. & Deakin, E., 2012. Smart Growth Planning for Climate Protection: Evaluating California's Senate Bill 375. *Journal of the American Planning Association*, 78(1), pp. 70–86.

Berghaus, H., 2004. *Physicalischer Atlas, Sammlungen von Karten, auf denen die hautsächlischten Erscheinungen der anorganischen und organischen Natur nach ihrer geographischen Verbreitung und Verteilung bildlich dargestellt sind. Zu Alexander von Humboldt, KOSMOS*. Frankfurt am Main: Eichborn Verlag.

Bishop Ranch, 2014. *Bishop Ranch*. [Online] Available at: www.bishopranch.com/ [Accessed 26 April 2017].

Bosselmann, P., 2008. *Urban Transformation: Understanding City Design and Form*. Washington: Island Press.

Darakjian, J., 2009. SB 375 Promise, compromise and the new urban landscape. *UCLA Journal of Environmental Law & Policy*, 27(2), pp. 372–404.

Darwin, C., 1859. *On the Origin of Species by Means of Natural Selection, Or, the Preservation of Favoured Races in the Struggle for Life*. London: J. Murray.

Davids, R., 2008. Development, topography and identity: Dougherty Valley and the new suburban metropolis. *Places*, 20(3), pp. 58–64.

Downs, A., 1989. *The Need for a New Vision for the Development of Large US Metropolitan Areas*. Washington DC: Brookings Institution.

Duany, A., 2002. The Transect. *Journal of Urban Design*, 7(3), pp. 251–260.

Ewing, R. & Cervero, R., 2001. Travel and the built environment: A synthesis. *Transportation Research Record*, 1780, pp. 87–114.

Farooq, S., 2005. Water Politics Shape Dry Valley's Development. *Oakland Tribune*, 12 Aug.

Farrington, J. & Ward, C., 2009. *Neighborhood Design and Automobile Dependency [Unpublished student report]*, Berkeley: Department of City and Regional Planning, UC Berkeley.

Federal Highway Administration, 2014. *Lane Width*. [Online] Available at: https://safety.fhwa.dot.gov/geometric/pubs/mitigationstrategies/chapter3/3_lanewidth.cfm [Accessed 27 April 2017].

Fishman, R., 1987. *Bourgeois Utopias: The Rise and Fall of Suburbia*. New York: Basic Books.

Geddes, P., 1915. *Cities in Evolution: An Introduction to the Town Planning Movement and to the Study of Civics*. London: Williams & Norgate.

Geddes, P., 1947. *Cities in Evolution*. London: Williams & Norgate.

Gerckens, L. C., 1994. American zoning and the physical isolation of uses. *Planning Commissioners Journal*, 15, p. 10.

Greenbelt Alliance, 1988. *Reviving the Sustainable Metropolis*. San Francisco: Greenbelt Alliance.

Haeckel, E., 1866. *Generelle Morphologie der Organismen*. Vol. 2: *Allgemeine Entwicklungsgeschichte*. Berlin: G. Reimer.

Hough, M., 1995. *Cities and Natural Process*. London: Elsevier Science.

Humboldt, A. v., 1807. *Essai sur la géographie des plantes: accompagné d'un tableau physique des régions équinoxiales*. Strasbourg: Levrault.

Humboldt, A. v., 2004. *Kosmos, Entwurf einer physischen Weltbeschreibung*. Frankfurt: Eichborn Verlag.

Institute for Local Government, 2015. *The Basics of SB 375*. [Online] Available at: www.ca-ilg.org/post/basics-sb-375 [Accessed April 2017].

Jacobs, A. B., 1993. *Great Streets*. Cambridge, MA: MIT Press.

McHarg, I., 1971. *Design with Nature*. New York: Published for the American Museum of Natural History.

Mozingo, L., 2011. *Pastoral Capitalism, a History of Suburban Corporate Landscapes*. Cambridge, MA: MIT Press.

Neighborhoods.com, 2017. *Windemere*. [Online] Available at: www.neighborhoods.com/windemere-san-ramon-ca [Accessed 28 April 2017].

Richards, R. J., 2008. *The Tragic Sense of Life: Ernst Haeckel and the Struggle Over Evolutionary Thought*. Chicago: University of Chicago Press.

SF Municipal Transportation Agency, 2015. *Board of Directors' Workshop Presentation (PDF)*. [Online] Available at: www.sfmta.com/calendar/meetings/board-directors-meeting-february-3-2015 [Accessed 26 April 2017].

Southworth, M. & Ben Joseph, E., 2003. *Streets and the Shaping of Towns and Cities*. Washington: Island Press.

Spirn, A., 1984. *The Granite Garden: Urban Nature and Human Design*. New York: Basic Books.

Steenberger, C. & Wouter, R., 2011. *Metropolitan Landscape Architecture*. Bussum: Thoth Publishers.

Talen, E., 2002. Help for urban planning: the transect strategy. *Journal of Urban Design*, 7(3), pp. 293–312.

Unwin, R., 1912. *Nothing Gained by Overcrowding: How the Garden City Type of Development may Benefit Both Owner and Occupier*. London: P.S. King & Company.

Weart, S., 2017. *The Discovery of Global Warming*. [Online] Available at: http://history.aip.org/climate/index.htm [Accessed 26 April 2017].

Windemere, 2010. *Windemere*. [Online] Available at: www.visitwindemere.com [Accessed 9 January 2010].

Wulf, A., 2015. *The Invention of Nature: Alexander Von Humboldt's New World*. New York: Vintage Books.

Chapter 3

Causes and Consequences of Climate Change for the San Francisco Bay Area

Urban designers chiefly take responsibility for setting dimensions. They set the dimensions of streets and lanes, blocks and parcels, building setbacks, entrances and driveways, building heights, the separation between buildings, the size of building footprints and the amount of land each building is allowed to cover in relation to the available land area. The result of these decisions determines the scale of a city. The designer's decisions also determine human experience: the length of a walk, the likelihood of human encounter, the amount of light that is received, protection from wind, exposure to noise, what is available to the eyes, when we feel a sense of closeness, when we are participants on a civic stage. In short, city scale determines many aspects of human experience, including the energy needed for transport and the energy needed to heat or cool dwellings and commercial places.

Designers of master planned communities would not only need strategies to include proximity to transit; they would also need strategies to address the parcelization of land that reduces distances and avoids wasted land, combined with a mixing of building types that serves a range of activities, providing workplaces and homes for diverse income and age groups, including the less mobile. Such rules would include improvement to "the state of the art". Roads would generally be narrower than currently prescribed. They would be shared between multiple types of users and with greater connectivity, so residents do not depend on just one arterial street with its intersections spaced at currently quarter mile distances. As these concepts suffer from less than clear interpretations and sometimes sound outright vague, drawings are needed. Best suited are measured drawings that compare alternative geometries, adjacencies, spatial quantities and the human experiences that are influenced by such geometries.

For the following illustrations I have zoomed in on a 64-acre (26ha) square of San Ramon's Dougherty Valley neighborhoods from the previous chapter. I show existing conditions on the top and proposed changes side by side. The first pair of maps, Figure 1.3.1B, shows the "public right of way", in grey. This is the space currently designated for roadways and roadside landscaping, as well as median strips between roadways. In this case, the grey area contains all land not privately owned by residents; it is the land that converted back to the City of San Ramon for public ownership and maintenance. In total, it amounts to a high 40% of the land area within such a 64-acre square. In the second frame, I have reduced the "public right of way", but maintained an equivalent number of traffic lanes, plus I have designed additional new road connections to increase connectivity between neighborhoods. The new roads are shown in red. As a consequence, I have reduced the acreage set aside for "right of ways" by 10 acres and I have added 6 additional acres for new roads. The gain in land to be built on is still substantial.

▶ Figure 1.3.1a

Alternative Geometries. The map shows a plan view of Dougherty Valley, centered on Bollinger Canyon Road, near a shopping center. A red line defines a square of 8 by 8 acres, 64 acres total. Such a large square equals 1,624 by 1,624 feet, or 490 meters along each of its sides. (Source: Microsoft Bing TerraServer.)

The second map pair shows in red additional buildings that I have constructed on public land. These structures would be built along Bollinger Canyon Road on land that was occupied by the roadway and along adjacent arterial streets. I have also constructed additional office buildings in the parking lot of the retail area. Those buildings could function as satellite offices of the Bishop Ranch Office Park or serve local tenants.

Towards Threshold Values of Urbanity

There is no agreement on a precise number of people needed to cross the threshold values of urbanity (Braudel, 1992, p. 482). Also, a higher density alone is not the only criteria for urbanity. A design is needed that fosters interaction between people so that spontaneous transactions and transformations become possible. An architecture not necessarily found in suburbia needs to be developed. I call this the architecture of *urban hybrids*, because the architecture in the rear of properties is suburban in scale, but the architecture that faces the arterial street has an urban character with a four-story high façade. In Figure 1.3.2,

SAN RAMON CA.
Right of Way

SAN RAMON CA.
Roads and footprints

SAN RAMON CA. 64 acres area
Density

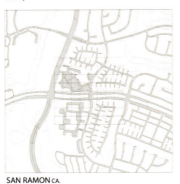

SAN RAMON CA.
Proposed roads connections

◀ Figure 1.3.1b
Top row: streets become a reservoir for density. Left: existing. Right: the width of the public "right of way" is reduced without reducing the number of available traffic lanes.

Second row: additional build-able land. Left: existing. Right: map shows potential building footprints.

Third row: density computation. Left: the number in each square indicated current density. Right: potential future density per acre resulting in an increase in density by 40%.

Bottom row: circulation. The map on the right shows additional cycle routes and pedestrian paths in red.

(Drawings by the author, assisted by Dario Schoulund.)

▲ Figure 1.3.2

Urban hybrids. A new building type relates in the rear to the scale of the existing suburban neighborhood but creates an urban frontage on Bollinger Canyon Road.

four of six units share a garden court which is located on top of a garage. The garden court gives access to the two rear units and the two upstairs units facing Bollinger Canyon Road. All units have private open space. The two units in the rear have additional garden space. Walkways connect Bollinger Canyon Road in between each group of six units to the shared walkways or driveways in the existing neighborhood. Architects or builders could give various interpretations to green building articulation such as vegetated roofs, naturally ventilated units, or solar panels mounted on roofs to capture energy. In the drawings, I have emphasized a roof design that captures rainwater and stores water in cisterns for use in irrigation and, where possible, for use in household appliances such as laundry machines.

A second building type, Figure 1.3.3, envisioned at the corners of Bollinger Canyon Road and arterial roads, does not currently exist in suburbs. Like the architecture of the garden court, the corner buildings respond to the changed intersection design, which is pedestrian friendly. The entrance to the building is an urban portal on Bollinger Canyon Road; it signifies the importance of the newly re-configured Bollinger Canyon Road. Upon entry, the building opens and a walkway links via a curving ramp to the suburban homes in the neighborhood above. Residents from the neighborhood are invited to follow the reverse route on their walk down through the building to the bus stop. The building offers a critique of the stratified housing conditions. Residents from all income groups could eventually live here, if they are interested in downsizing their households. I am thinking primarily of older residents, who might give up their spacious homes once their children have grown up and left, or people who have become single. On the ground floor, the corner building

◀ Figure 1.3.3

A corner building accommodates mixed functions without being antagonistic to its context.

could house a clinic or local health services. Would a family-run neighborhood restaurant be feasible? At the beginning of the ramp there is a daycare center, near the olive tree grove that is cared for by students from the nearby high school. (The reader will accuse me of dreaming, but bear with me.)

For the building design, I have adopted an O. M. Ungers (1982) design, because, first, he was a mentor and his rational architecture has inspired me since the beginning of my career and second, I was looking for an architectural expression that is not antagonistic towards its neighbors but has elements of a mutual interdependence. The expectation is that over time the architecture of the neighborhood and the architecture of the urban block could adapt to reaffirm each other.

Why No-one Would Build What I Have Drawn

I harbor no illusions: substantial opposition will meet my drawings. First, the argument will be made that the current practice of road design does not allow the conversion of limited access roads to roads that allow driveways to individual homes or clusters of homes. That argument is relatively easy to counter. The current practices, though codified in ordinances, came about at a time when subdivision standards focused on mobility for vehicular traffic. There is support for re-examining such standards and focusing instead on improved access for all modes of movements, especially non-motorized.

A second argument against what I have drawn proves more stubborn: market forces do not support the construction of buildings and roads shown in this chapter. An argument like that cannot be ignored. Even if all the new roads built as part of the planned unit development reverted back to public ownership, the opposition would still argue that current market practices generated the existing neighborhood pattern. Thus the opposition is consistent with the current dynamics of housing production and marketing and with the current methods of financing.

While the argument about conformity to market forces and its rebuttal needs further depth that can only be found by stressing affordability of housing by residents in need of housing and by acknowledging the obligation of municipalities to house their citizens in a way they can afford, a third, more complex, argument awaits us, made not by land economists but by regional planners and environmental advocates. My designs – many would argue – perpetuate a type of development that was unsustainable at the time of its conception and will continue to be unsustainable. The latter argument was articulated a long time ago, even before the word sustainable became so widely used. I fully agree with the thrust of this third argument because it questions the wisdom of providing infrastructural support for the production of housing and commercial spaces with low-use intensity. The same argument also questions the wisdom of establishing polycentric regions; meaning permitting employment centers not served by frequent public transport. The matter has been actively debated over the decades.[1] Opponents to polycentric urban regions rightly pointed to the fact that once a region embarks on a polycentric concept, there is no way to keep the number of centers from proliferating. The critics of a polycentric region anticipated population dispersion and challenges to available resources. These arguments, however, have become largely academic. Office parks and neighborhoods within the former Bishop Ranch have proliferated in the Bay Area, and neighborhoods like Dougherty Valley exist in large numbers. Society is not likely to abandon them.

Since my designs propose changes not only to physical but also social conditions, a fourth type of opposition will be heard that starts with the observation that neighborhoods once built change very little. This is less true for neighborhoods built prior to the 1920s and 1930s. We observe conversions and densification there, but neighborhoods that were built three or four decades ago have not accommodated higher residential densities, overlapping uses and activities. They have stayed largely the same; the original residents have passed on and new residents have moved in, but the roads and buildings remain in their original form. The observation is largely true, therefore I expect the most severe opposition to my drawings to come from the current residents, who – in the case of Dougherty Valley – only recently decided to move there, residents who are very likely to identify with their new homes, streets and neighborhoods, who have formed attachments, financial dependencies and for whom the homes and streets provide a sense of place. Current homeowners will use all political influence to maintain the value of their investment.

To counter the four types of opposition and to bring the necessary relevance to my proposal, I request that the reader take a mental leap: imagine 30 years from now what will happen to a neighborhood like this one mid-century, let's say the year 2050, when today's residents who moved here while in their thirties and forties will face, or will have chosen, retirement, when today's small children will have moved through their education, ready to form careers of their own.

The beauty of this argument is that nobody knows how we will live 30 years from now. But today's justifiable answers bring into better focus the improvements to metropolitan landscapes that would need to be made to deal with diminishing resources, chiefly water, energy and land, including land coverage by vegetation, and the combined influence of all the above on air quality and climate. If for a moment we could imagine a future when today's edge of a metropolitan area is still the edge, because the edge has not moved further, when growth that would have extended the edge was reduced because it was accommodated through infill in areas that were formerly leapt over by urbanization, when people drive less because workplaces are located closer to homes, and when the emission of greenhouse gasses is curtailed.

After reading this list, a fifth type of opposition to my drawing is gaining strength. I am met with a shrugging of shoulders. Today, nobody can imagine an authority that would have the power to regulate such a metropolitan landscape into existence, and if such power were to exist, could the process possibly be respectful of the aspirations and desires of each community? The answer to this last question leaves us in the same a state of quandary as the answer to solutions to so many larger environmental issues. Will changes be forced on us, or will we have time to deal with change creatively? In other words, the next 30 years might not be like the three decades that just passed. The pace of change will increase, leaving us no choice but to adapt places like Dougherty Valley to a more sustainable future.

Strategies for the Future

In the San Francisco Bay Area the causes of climate change were addressed in the 2013 Plan Bay Area. The plan was established in collaboration with cities and counties; it accommodates growth, and promotes housing and transportation choices through a transportation plan that aims to make improvement with a time horizon up to the year 2040. One such improvement is the designation of Priority Development Areas. These are neighborhoods within walking distance to frequent public transit, offering a wide range of housing choices, amenities and community services. Thus, the plan encourages the design of areas that meet what we have called the threshold values of urbanity.

What the plan does not do is to prohibit residential developments in locations like Dougherty Valley or workplace concentrations like those at Bishop Ranch. Nor does it encourage the adaptation of such developments to a form that is more consistent with the sustainable community strategies. The reason for that is that land-use decision making authority remains at the level of local government. Local government might still permit developments like Dougherty Valley. The consequences would be a more stringent environmental review, a process that the state law promises to relax for developments that are supported by existing public transit infrastructure.

The "carrot and stick" approach to the **causes** of climate change is the only process that could find broad political support.

The response to the **consequences** of climate change such as sea level rise is not addressed by Plan Bay Area 2040. Here the municipalities and counties still follow a "wait and see" approach. The Bay Conservation and Development Commission (State of California, 2015) has been charged with the task of carrying out detailed analysis of existing shoreline conditions and publishing maps that delineate areas likely to experience inundation by mid-century and by the end of the 21st century under assumptions agreed upon at the time when the analysis is carried out.

We ended the last chapter with reflections on the power of city government, or the lack thereof, over what is largely an unregulated market. Important here is the scale of developments that need to be evaluated and approved. Adaptations to the consequences of climate change, like sea level rise, in all likelihood trigger large scale interventions. This is especially true if cities delay their responses until major action is necessary. Likewise, responses to the causes, as in building or repairing neighborhoods to be consistent with sustainable community strategies, is made significantly more difficult if such projects involve very large tracts of land. My concern here is the potentially large size of development and the associated power of private enterprise that would make itself available to provide the expected results. The power of private development would be reduced if the size of developments were smaller. When municipalities issue permits for large units of land, their power to manage development is reduced. The opposite is true if permits are issued for smaller increments of development. Thus, the performance of development can be better monitored and checked to comply with long-range goals.

Indeed, the dynamics of large-scale developments is a concern. Hand in hand with all development projects goes the perception of risk, something that always needs to be calculated and is reflected in costs and profits. Large-scale projects are associated with higher risks; they also drive industry standards. Take, for example, the assumed best practices for building roads in master planned communities. Practices of road building have changed over time and can continue to change. It is not an absolute truth that intersections with left turn options on arterial roads should be spaced at a minimum of a quarter mile apart. That just concentrates traffic into channels of movement, channels that are not very good for much else but driving, often fast. In large projects, these standards are never questioned; they are frozen at the time when permits are issued. A finer grain of access is the answer, not the current concentration on few roads with high mobility.

Size, amounts and absorption of housing units drives much decision making. Again, the flexibility to adjust to demand is greater in smaller increments of development. Leave alone the goal to better integrate different functions within a single development, like living and working. A developer that would take on a project with mixed functions is rare because of the different financing methods and different absorption rates. A finer parcelization of land and separate permitting processes would help to address a better integration of land uses.

There is another concern in the power equation. The playing field is not level between city government and private enterprise when projects are large. The public representatives fight an uphill battle against lawyers, vested industry interests, threats of liability and access to direct political influence via elected officials. The conclusion is to keep developments small and manageable. A larger pool of developers will bid on smaller projects than the very few who currently bid on large projects.

Designs to Address the Causes of Climate Change

In San Francisco, the 1992 removal of the Embarcadero Freeway, damaged in the 1989 Loma Pieta earthquake, made available ten acres or 4.3 hectares of inner city land adjacent to the financial district and a major transit hub that will provide the terminus for California's high speed train to Los Angeles. Plans to redevelop the publicly owned land were approved in 2005 and a bidding process started in 2014/15. Developers interested in developing properties on twelve city blocks started to submit bids. These bids would be for entire blocks or for as much land as available on a given city block. A number of blocks will house high-rise towers of 400 feet; a total of twelve residential towers were permitted under the 2005 plan. The spacing of towers is determined by sun access rules that guarantee direct sunlight to new open spaces during midday hours for six months of the year.

City government also imposed a rule that sets 35% of units aside for households with incomes that would not qualify for current market rate flats or apartments. Developers submitting bids declare in their documentation where and how they intend to accommodate such units. The rules state that such units need to be incorporated within the project and cannot be constructed somewhere else in the city. Developers generally place such units in the lower portions of towers or in podium structures that occupy midrise portions of blocks.

Interested in testing the merits of smaller projects versus the projects that take on an entire city block, our studio experimented with parcel sizes, allowable building heights and desired densities. We also made sure to understand the housing needs of San Franciscans.

The model on the left of Figure 1.3.4. represents the outcome of the current bidding process. Here a city block is considered as a single parcel of land. The lobby of the high-rise tower will determine the location of the main residential entrance. Additional building

▼ Figure 1.3.4

Alternative futures. The diagram compares two development models for urban blocks in downtown San Francisco.

Current Approach

Building Types: Tower over Podium
Townhomes
Modified Type III
Total Population: 806
Density (Per Acre): 448 people per acre
FAR: 7.95
Total Units (Per Acre): 424 (235)
Total Cost: $277,278,000
Cost per Unit: $654,000

1 Bedroom	255	60%
2 Bedroom	125	30%
3 Bedroom	44	10%

VS

Proposed Approach

Building Types: Stacked Flats
Townhomes
Skip Stop
Total Population: 601
Density (Per Acre): 334 people per acre
FAR: 3.31
Total Units (Per Acre): 241 (134)
Total Cost: $86,078,000
Cost per Unit: $357,000

1 Bedroom	81	34%
2 Bedroom	41	17%
3 Bedroom	119	49%

▶ Figure 1.3.5

Sense of community. The infrastructure needed to create a downtown community.

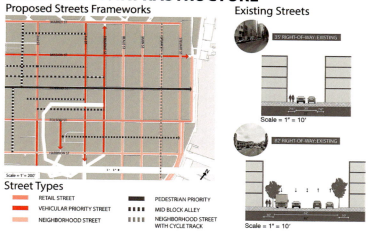

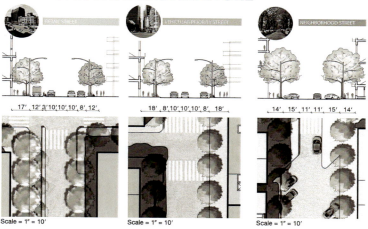

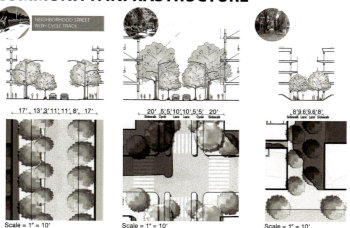

entrances will be needed to access the lower, podium structure. The project will have a total of five residential entrances per block. The housing unit mix is heavily in favor of single bedroom units. In the preferred alternative, on the right, this mix of unit sizes is reversed to satisfy the current housing need for multifamily housing. Instead of twelve projects on twelve city blocks, the alternative approach would result in 73 parcels and 94 buildings.

The preferred alternative is consistent with official policy. But in order for developers of twelve large projects to bid on the available land, city government is making allowances that reflect what developers prefer to build: single bedroom units in tower flats that are not only attractive to wealthy San Franciscans, but also as investment property for a global market. The planners responsible also responded by saying that the staff necessary to review 94 building projects is currently not available. Under the current bidding arrangements, the city will get 35% of the units below market rate and some of them will be multifamily units. That, the planners in the mayor's office say, is the best solution that can be expected.

Granted, under the alternative more staff would be needed to review projects because the city would issue 73 permits instead of 12. But if bids for smaller parcels would be accepted, additional developers would submit bids that are financially not qualified to bid on large projects under current conditions. Again, the pool of developers will be greater and city government can monitor the development process more carefully to check if stated goals are met: to house San Franciscans according to their needs.

The increase in multifamily units would require a school. There is room for one on a less traveled street. The result of our experiment is a downtown community of 8,000 new residents within walking distance of regional and local transit. These residents will live in a community that is integrated with existing workplaces. They will live in proximity to the waterfront; they will have a school within walking distance. Such a development will have

COMMUNITY: PROPOSED DEVELOPMENT

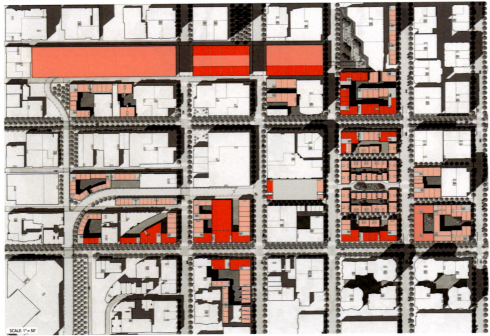

◀ Figure 1.3.6

Preferred development to satisfy the need for housing by people with a range of household incomes.

OUR COMMUNITY

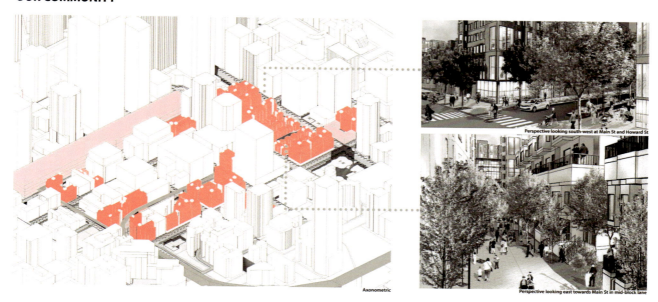

▲ Figure 1.3.7

An integrated downtown community. Drawings 1.3.4 to 1.3.7 by David Cooke, Justin Kearnan and Daniel Church.

reached the threshold values of urbanity, because the urban form proposed here increases the likelihood of transactions between people. There are simply more places of contact for people on foot. On a daily basis, a private automobile would not be needed. It would be an adaptation of the inner city that addresses the causes of climate change.

Designs to Address the Consequences of Climate Change

The direct consequences of climate change in the form of sea level rise need to be addressed at the scale of the region. Figure 1.3.8 shows a transect of shoreline conditions around San Francisco Bay. Initially, our studio selected shoreline sites every 5 miles by closing a circle around the entire Bay. The placement of the sites was adjusted to center the chosen frames on a location where a creek or river entered the Bay. The modeling method combined LYDAR data to represent the topography of the land and SONAR data to represent the bathymetry of the below water surfaces. The tidal action was modeled following the current assumption of sea level rise and augmented with data of a past storm event for which sufficient data was available. This was done to realistically simulate how water levels would rise given combined tidal and storm conditions. Essential support for this type of modeling came from my colleague John Radke and his team at the Geographic Information Science Center in our college (Radke, et al., 2017). We compared modeling with consideration of bathymetry data and without. The comparison showed that the combined topography and bathymetry data resulted in more extensive inundation along shorelines near deep water and less extensive along shorelines near shallow water.

In an exercise our studio called *adaptation by design*, we then modified the urban form in ten Bay Area locations in response to rising water levels. The guiding principle for such design work was to orient urban form towards water and not against it. Water will always hold attraction if managed with respect to its dynamics. In some instances it meant to find land within the existing urban fabric where some retreat was possible; to design ponds and

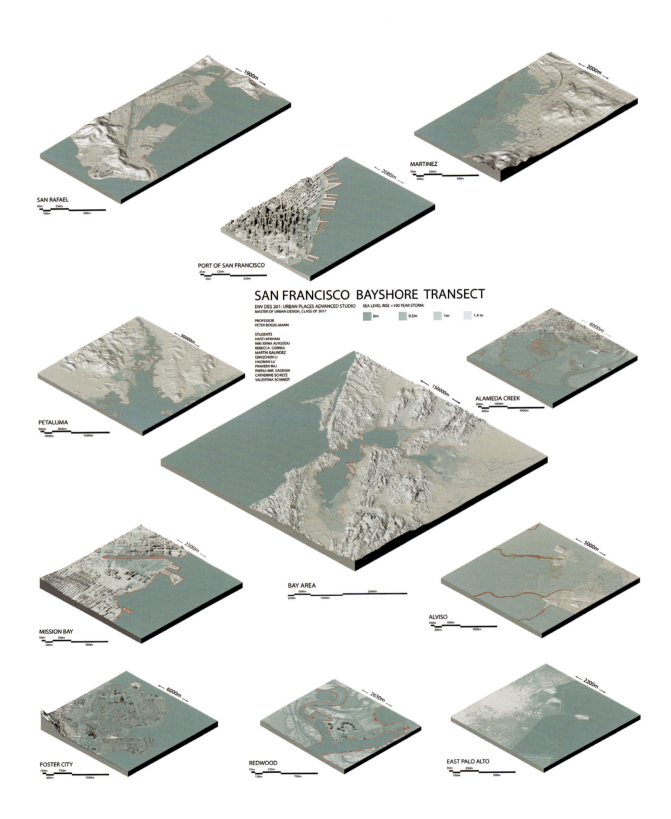

68 PART I The San Francisco Estuary and Inland Delta

◀ Figure 1.3.8 (opposite)

A transect in the form of a loop was laid around San Francisco Bay with 0.4, 1.0 and 1.4 meter inundation projections of shoreline conditions. (Maps and drawings of the following figures were made by Hasti Afkham, Niki Xenia Alygizou, Martin Galindez, Rebecca Leigh Correa, Qingchun Li, Haonan Lyu, Praveen Raj Ramanathan Monhanraj, Parisa Mir Sadeghi, Catherine Schiltz and Valentina Schmidt.)

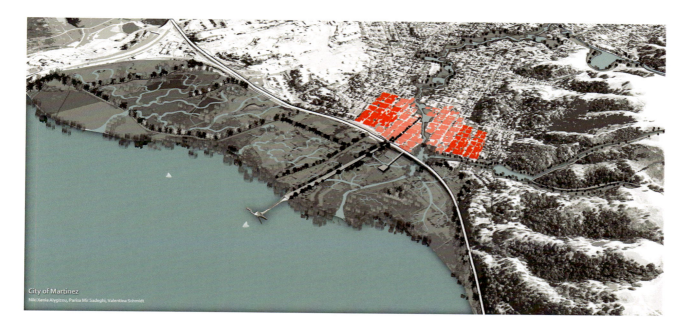

▲ Figure 1.3.9a

The town of Martinez. We increased the density on vacant sites, but created more floodable space for Alhambra Creek as it flows through town. We also increased the tidal channels through the marsh to improve creek discharge at low tide and to store more water on days with coastal flooding due to spring tides. (Drawings by Niki Xenia Alygizou, Parisa Mir Sadeghi and Valentina Schmidt Escobar.)

CHAPTER 3 Causes and Consequences of Climate Change

▲ Figure 1.3.9b

East San Rafael. The Canal District is shown to the north. Here a low income neighborhood is threatened by inundation from the San Rafael Creek. The creek is channelized through reclaimed land that historically functioned as an estuary. Some displacement of homes built on reclaimed land will become unavoidable when levees along the creek need to be raised. We found infill sites in the adjacent areas. To address combined tidal and seasonal fluvial flooding, we proposed to elevate the freeway onto a causeway and store water in a bypass below the freeway during flood conditions. (Drawings by Hasti Afkham and Catherine Schiltz.)

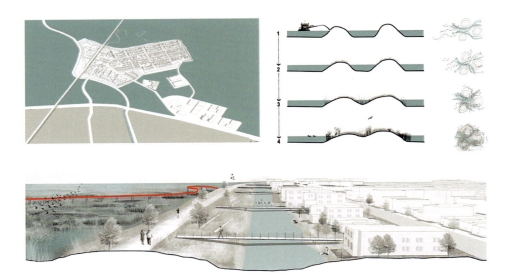

▲ Figure 1.3.9c

Alviso Archipelago. Drawings show the small historic town of Alviso in the southern tip of the bay. Once a harbor for the transport of agricultural produce, the waterways have silted in. Here an archipelago of islands can emerge to be reached by causeways. The levees would need to be raised. Sediments are dredged and deposited along sloughs and waterways. This will create a floodable water landscape where over time a vegetative cover will emerge on elevated land. In this large vertical landscape a fresh green line will form the horizon above the darker waterlogged grey-green of the tidal marsh and against the silhouette of the hills in the distance. (Drawings by Niki Xenia Alygizou, Parisa Mir Sadeghi and Valentina Schmidt.)

 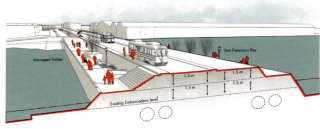

▲ Figure 1.3.9d

The Embarcadero in San Francisco. The roadway was built in the early 20th century on a seawall well in front of the historic shoreline. This brought the city closer to the navigable deep water channel. The low-lying reclaimed land became the financial district of the city, some of the most valuable real estate on the West Coast. Sea level rise of 1.4 meters would flood the district up to the historic shoreline unless the seawall at the Embarcadero is raised. The drawings show an incremental transformation of the land currently occupied by the Embarcadero Roadway. They also show a system of canals on existing streets that are designed to store run-off. (Drawings by Praveen Raj Ramanathan Monhanraj.)

canals that are capable of storing water when needed, but that are attractive when water has drained away and a vegetated cover remains. In other cases, key design concepts rest on redundancy, not in the sense of unnecessary duplication, but as a safety measure when one line of protection fails. It was important to demonstrate an approach that can be implemented incrementally and can be repaired if necessary. While these concepts are reasonably clear, the implementations are challenging. I am showing four responses here to demonstrate that highly location-specific approaches are needed.

Note

1 In the context of the San Francisco Bay Area, the *Greenbelt Alliance* and its forerunner *People for Open Space* are primarily associated with their advocacy for regional open space in the form of greenbelts. The organization in their various reports persuasively asserts that all of the growth in housing and jobs expected by 2035 around the bay can be absorbed within existing cities, without annexing an acre of open land (Greenbelt Alliance, 2017).

References

Braudel, F., 1992. *The Structures of Everyday Life: The Limits of the Possible*. Berkeley: University of California Press.

Greenbelt Alliance, 2017. *Greenbelt Alliance*. [Online] Available at: www.greenbelt.org [Accessed 27 April 2017].

Radke, J. D. et al., 2017. *An Assessment of Climate Change Vulnerability of the Natural Gas Transmission Infrastructure for the San Francisco Bay Area, Sacramento-San-Joaquin Delta, and Coastal California*. [Online] Available at: www.energy.ca.gov/2017publications/CEC-500-2017-008/CEC-500-2017-008.pdf [Accessed 25 April 2017].

State of California, 2015. *The San Francisco Bay Conservation and Development Commission (BCDC)*. [Online] Available at: www.bcdc.ca.gov/ [Accessed 27 April 2017].

Ungers, O. M., 1982. *Architettura come Tema*. Milan/New York: Lotus Documents, Electra/ Rizzoli.

Part II | The Pearl River Delta

With contributions by Mathias Kondolf and Francesca Frassoldati

> "I have quite often contemplated the beautiful views of Rhine and Maas in Europe," wrote Michel of Brabant in 1753, "but these two together are not a quarter of what the rivers of Canton alone offers for admiration."

Fernand Braudel (1992) included this quote by the Dutch traveller in his *Structures of Everyday Life* and adds: "Perhaps no site anywhere in the world was more privileged for short and long distance trade than Canton. The town was thirty leagues from the sea (120 km from Hong Kong), but still felt the throb of the tide on its numerous stretches of water. Sea vessels, junks, or three masters from Europe could therefore link up with small crafts, the sampans, which reached all or nearly the entire Chinese interior using canals."

Canton was the name given to the seaport by Portuguese sailors in 1514. The name in Portuguese, *Cantão*, was probably an auditory interpretation of the Chinese *Guangdong*, the name of the province with Guangzhou as its capital. The first Chinese name for the location was *Panyu*, first mentioned in 206 BC, now used to refer to a location south of Guangzhou's historic center.

Briefly expelled from the region, Portuguese traders established Macao, the first European colony in China in 1557. Among the Europeans, the Portuguese held a monopoly on trade with China until the arrival of Dutch ships in the early 17th century, but for a much longer time the port at Guangzhou was a regular destination for ships on the maritime silk route from the Middle East and India. From the Chinese perspective, Guangzhou and the ports of the Pearl River Delta are China's most southern ports; they owed their fortunes to the Manchu empire's[1] desire to keep the European influence with its trade as far to the south as possible. Finally, from the perspective of the local population: "the heaven is high, the emperor is far away", an attitude towards central authority that is characteristic to the present day.

More than people from other parts of China, the Cantonese migrated to places all over the world, to the Americas but also to Malaysia and Singapore, where industrial development started earlier than in China. When China's leaders announced economic reforms in the late 1970s, it was the Cantonese people's intensive global network that brought industrial development to the Pearl River Delta region. Because of Canton's history as a gateway into China, its location near Hong Kong and the political decisions to designate Shenzhen and Zhuhai, later the entire region, as a pilot for economic reform, investments in industry arrived here earlier than, for example, in Shanghai or China's other coastal regions.

The Pearl River Delta is now home to a greater concentration of manufacturing plants than anywhere in the world, and is the origin of many consumer goods that can be found on store shelves worldwide. The delta region's gross domestic product reached 4,372 billion yuan by 2011 (550 billion US dollars), with an annual growth rate of 11% since the 2008 global economic crisis (Gstj, 2012). The explosion of manufacturing in this region has been

▲ Figure 2.1

Guangzhou landscape.

The drawing was made by Liang Youshi in the 18th year of Emperor Guangxu's reign during the Qing Dynasty (1892), 130 cm x 70 cm. It was made in the Chinese landscape painting tradition. The names of Guangzhou's main gates and important landmarks such as Guanyin Mountain and Zhenhai Tower were marked on the drawing. Note to the left of the walled city the fortified Shameen Island, an early treaty port for foreign trading companies in China. The caption says: "ships from many countries are sailing on the Pearl River day and night". (Guangdong Provincial Zhongshan Library.)

accompanied by rapid urbanization and a transformation of land, much of which has occurred more rapidly than the pace of the official planning process.

The economic reforms have created continuous urbanization reaching from Guangzhou in the north to Dongguan and Huizhou to the east and Shenzhen to the south. Topography and a significant protected wetland prevent urban attachment to Hong Kong. A proposed bridge from Hong Kong to Macao would connect urbanization to the western shore of the estuary. There urbanization continues to Zhuhai, Zhongshan and Jiangmen to the southwest and via Shunde and Panyu to Foshan and Zhaoqing and Lubao in the north-west. It would be misleading to focus only on these ten to twelve cities; already in the mid-1990s, ten years into the new era of an open economic region, research showed that urbanization in the Pearl River Delta was less a spatial extension of established cities, although that took place in a significant manner. The main volume of urbanization took place in the countryside as an extension of villages and small towns (Lin, 1997). The result is a type of urbanization that does not follow the typical urban–rural paradigm. Spatially, an urbanized metropolitan landscape formed, a polycentric conurbation shaped like an urbanized ring similar to Randstad Holland, not around a green heart, but around a large delta formed by three major rivers and eight estuaries. A population of 56.5 million lives in the Pearl River Delta conurbation.[2] The real number is much higher when the migrant working population is added: these residents have no choice but to maintain rural registration at the place where they originated. According to a Sun Yat-Sen University study (Xiang Dong, 2011) an estimated 36.7 million inhabitants fall into that category and need to be added. A Hong Kong based study estimated the total population of the region at 104 million inhabitants (China Labour Bulletin, 2013). When we consider that the region had only 16 million inhabitants in 1980, even young residents of the Pearl River Delta can claim to have experienced a magnitude of change of stunning proportions in their relatively short life time. The Pearl River Delta is one of the fastest growing conurbations in China, if not the world.

▶ Figure 2.2a
Urbanization of the Pearl River Delta in 1979, 1999, 2009. The three maps illustrate the magnitude of change to urbanization over 30 years. During the period prior to 1979, the pace of urbanization followed a history in which all physical change appeared slow. Urbanization's pace around the Pearl River Delta accelerated to a frantic tempo as a result of China's leader Deng Xiaoping's pragmatism to select Shenzhen and later the entire region as a pilot to allow foreign investment on socialist territories that would improve the regional and national economies. (Source: 1979 map by Wei Lang and Haoran Wang, 1999 and 2009 maps by Sarah Moos and Amna Alruheili.)

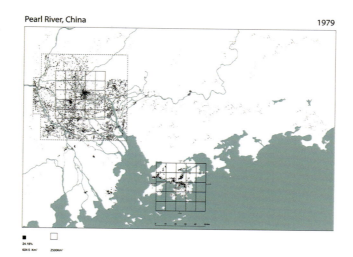

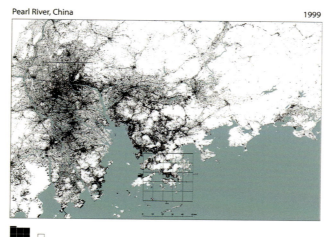

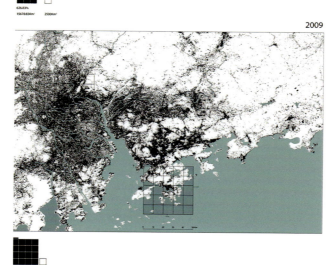

PART II The Pearl River Delta

The Pearl River Delta and estuaries is China's third largest delta after the Yangtze and Yellow River deltas. Three rivers, the Xi, Bei, and Dong, discharge into the South China Sea. The total discharge of the three rivers varies greatly, from 1,054 cubic meters per second to 66,500 during the monsoon season (Weng, 2007). The main contribution to discharge comes from the Xi Jiang (West River), where maximum discharge can measure up to 48,800 cubic meters per second (Anon., n.d.). This main branch of the Pearl River system, originates over 2,000 km to the west in Yunnan Province, a mountainous region to the east of the Himalayas. With its many tributaries, the Xi Jiang drains over 353,120 km² of southwestern China (Marks, 1998, p. 30). With an average discharge of 7,580 m³ per second, it is by far the largest affluent to the delta (South China University of Technology, 2007). Its main flow meets the northern branch of the Pearl River, Bei Jiang (North River), in the western portion of the delta and connects there during floods, then turns sharply to the south and exits west of Macao into the South China Sea.

The Pearl River Delta was formed by sediments deposited at the mouths of the western, northern and eastern branches. Much of the land in the Delta was deposited within the past millennium. Since the Ming Dynasty (1368–1644) this extensive open estuary has been filled by alluvial sediments, traversed by the many tributaries and distributaries of the three rivers. The city of Guangzhou was founded on what was then the main branch of the Bei Jiang. As the main flow of the Bei Jiang shifted southward in the 7th century towards another distributary, the city of Foshan developed along its banks. Foshan was one of the Four Famous Towns in Late Imperial China, and is now Guangdong's third largest city.

The natural history of the changing river system has been well recorded. The commercial importance of navigation made it necessary to chart the waterways. The approaches to Guangzhou and Foshan were well documented on maps made by Chinese and European navigators from the 17th century.

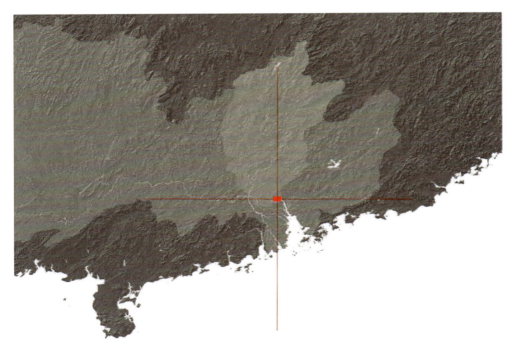

◀ Figure 2.2b

Pearl River drainage basins. The map shows the eastern portion of the West River and the entire North and East River drainage basins. The red cross lines are set on Guangzhou. (Map by Patrick Webb.)

▶ Figure 2.3

A water landscape.
　Map of Guangzhou with surrounding cities made between 1733 and 1738, 42 cm x 40 cm. The map was plotted onto a square grid to maintain a correct graphic scale. The city of Guangzhou is shown in the center of the map with its walls, gates and the Yuexiu Mountain. Other cities were plotted as castle-like symbols; army camps are shown in house-shaped fashion, and fortresses as gates. (First Historical Archive of China, Guangzhou Yuexiu District Archive.)

　Throughout recorded history, the Pearl River Delta was shaped by human intervention, mainly land reclamation, levee building and the construction of a levee pond landscape for intensive agricultural use. The extensive annual rainfall of 1,600–2,600 mm due to monsoon and typhoon events has needed drainage and channeling ever since the estuary was claimed for cultivation during the Sui Dynasty (581–618 AD) and Tang Dynasty (618–907 AD). For centuries, this channeling of the rivers through levees brought down large quantities of sediments; the 86.36 million tons of annual silt extended the delta seawards, a process that to this day continues to move the shoreline south into the South China Sea by 40 meters/year, in some coast stretches by 100 meters (Weng, 2007). Channeling waterway flow and river sedimentation between levees has raised river water levels above the level of adjacent fields (Weng, 2007).

　From the Song Dynasty (960–1279), large portions of the delta to the southwest of Foshan and Guangzhou, were characterized as a mulberry dike-fishpond landscape. Land below adjacent river water levels became subject to inundation after torrential rains, and thus difficult to drain. Farmers dredged the mud and deposited it on the levees. Inside ponds, farmers began raising carp and fertilizing the embankments with dredged fishpond

◀ Figure 2.4

Map of the watercourse systems of Guangzhou. The map was made in the last year of Emperor Guangxu, 1692, Qing Dynasty, colored drawing on silk, 80 cm x 73.6 cm. The map shows the eight estuaries, referred to as "gates", where the distributaries of the three main Pearl River branches discharge in the South China Sea from east to west: Humen, Jiaomen, Hongqili, Hengmen, Modaomen, Jitimen, Hutiaomen and Yamen. Numbers mark water depth, black points mark shallow water. (Guangdong Provincial Zhongshan Library.)

mud. The resulting highly productive agricultural system brought much wealth to the region from 1757 to 1839, when the demand for silk waned (Marks, 1998, pp. 118-120).[3] In areas of rice growing, the levee and pond practice increased agricultural production to two or even three crops per year: two rice, plus one vegetable or sugar cane crop. Agricultural practices increased the danger of severe flooding. Records exist for a 100-year period in the late Qing dynasty (1736–1839), when 44 major floods were recorded: one major flood every 2.4 years (Weng, 2007). Robert B. Marks gives a fascinating portrait of the region in his book *Tigers, Rice, Silk and Silt* set during the late imperial period. Taking a long-range view, the book documents how the environment with its naturally caused and anthropogenic changes affected people, their choices, and hence their history. "One hundred year floods" have most recently occurred in June of 1994, 1998, 2005 and 2010 (Zhang, et al., 2008).[4] With rapid urbanization of former agricultural land, comprehensive land-management practices have become imperative.

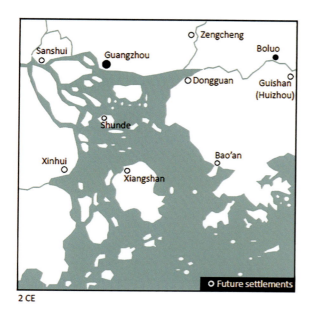
2 CE

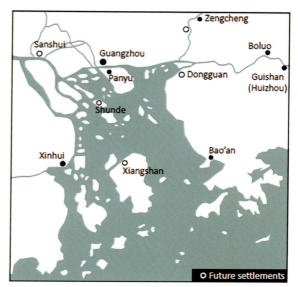
742 CE

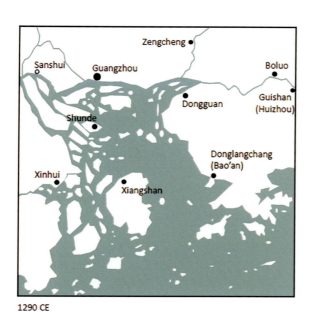
1290 CE

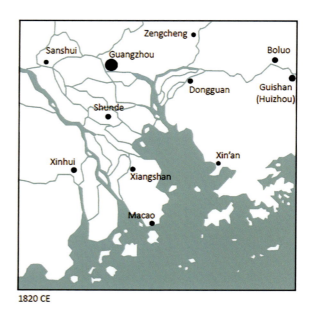
1820 CE

▲ Figure 2.5

The making of the Pearl River Delta. The term "making" refers to the anthropogenic actions that shaped the Pearl River Delta. Maps redrawn from R. B. Marks 1998, p. 68. (Source: Historical Maps of China, Shanghai, 1975–82.)

Urban Form

Historically, the form of cities in the Pearl River Delta can be explained by understanding their *Feng Shui* history, a history that locates cities in relation to mountains and water. This rationale for city design is highly pragmatic; water supports life, but in low-lying areas sudden floods have been notorious for taking human lives. Located on the slope of hills or mountains, cities provide refuge. Villagers who cultivate low-lying areas can, with some warning, flee towards towns on higher ground when floods inundate their fields. Guangzhou, Foshan, Shunde and

Jiangmen, to list the oldest cities, secured their existence by backing up against higher terrain. They are located on alluvial fans with hills or mountains to the north and water to the south. Ingenious in the layout of these cities is the construction of canals that connect to the flow of rivers somewhat upstream and direct water through canals into the center of the city. If engineered correctly, drainage of the river is controlled by multiple channels, water is delivered to the center and waste is channeled back into the river further downstream. Qingzhou Wu (2007) elaborates on the sophisticated water management practices in Chinese city design. Throughout history, the presence of water in the form of moats, canals and harbors aided the city's most important functions, including defence, firefighting, and hygiene, irrigation of garden plots, fish farming and transport. While many of these functions are of past importance, in the low-lying countryside the network of canals remains important as a system to store water during floods and to control discharge.

The forces to modernize the form of cities in globally recognized patterns has erased much history, and with it, its canals. With the astonishing pace of urbanization since the 1980s, water management could easily take a minor role in city design, were it not for the increasing occurrence of floods in cities of the Pearl River Delta. In the early decades, well into the 1990s, an integrated urban planning system did not exist. During that period, all investments

▼ Figure 2.6 Dike and pond landscape. A satellite view of Xiqiao town of Nankai, Foshan. The large curvature represents an elevated rail line above the dike and pond landscape that opened in 2005. (Source: Urban Planning Bureau, City of Foshan.)

were welcome in the delta. The result was a hodgepodge of forms: factories, former villages and isolated clusters of high-rise towers separated by fields and ponds still under cultivation. It is not uncommon to see brand new urban villas standing right in the middle of rice fields, with large factories in the distance. Starting with the first decade of the new century, strong land use controls were enacted. Since 2000 there has been a legal code for land use. To change land use or, for example, residential density is a difficult undertaking: "You need to go through a long process with different committees. Therefore, the development is generally better than before; we have more control over it. The city government is now very careful in clarifying and understanding the impact of different kinds of investments and projects," commented Jiang Feng (Feng, 2015). He goes on to say: "An interesting phenomenon although remains: planners usually assume that a parcel of land will be used for a single function, but people here prefer to create a mixed-use situation after a short time."

In the chapters that follow, we argue that a slowing in the pace of urbanization can be a blessing for cities, villages and small towns in the region. Such a slowing started to set in with the beginning of the second decade of the 21st century. A slower pace of development allowed for a better merging of historic settlement form with the forms of the new, what in China is called "chengxiang yitihua", the urban–rural integration. In the first few decades after

▼ Figure 2.7
Map of Guangzhou made between 1685 and 1722. The map was made in the traditional three-dimensional landscape painting style. It also shows the South China Sea Temple to the east of Guangzhou mentioned in chapter two; 47.5 cm x 64 cm. (Guangzhou Yuexiu District Archive.)

PART II The Pearl River Delta

1980, the trend was for industrialization to conceal the rural environmental and social structure, and now, due to a shifting model of production and society, environmental concerns push for a reinvention of the inherited spatial organization.

In support of this argument, we observe that with the turn of the millennium, industry in the Pearl River Delta is transforming to greater knowledge-based modes of production. This led to re-evaluating the merits of a seemingly endless supply of untrained migrant workers in favor of maintaining a qualified and well trained workforce.[5] Local government is aware that the economic vitality of their region increasingly depends on improved living conditions and quality of life for all residents.

In response to the greater frequency of flood events and the certainty of sea level rise, the three chapters address water management in various settings. The repair of the canal systems and stream restoration to manage water discharge and water storage capabilities in the low-lying delta are necessary, but the chapters also report on design experiments that address the larger context of repairing the dispersed settlement form of this delta region.

In 2007, when we started to work on Pearl River villages and towns with teams of young international design professionals, the presence of historic settlements, from our perspective, introduced a welcome social and spatial heterogeneity. As outsiders we greatly valued the diverse form despite the obvious overcrowding and the frequently deteriorated appearances. These villages and town centres were alive with people, where the new developments were sterile and lifeless. For sure, it was easy to imagine that villagers would prefer more space and better sanitation, but achieving those amenities did not require the radical removal of all existing urban form. Furthermore, the new forms of isolated clusters of high-rise towers were

◀ Figure 2.8

Map of Guangzhou drainage system. The map was presumably made in the ninth year of Emperor Tongzhi's reign during the Qing Dynasty (1870), 56 cm x 55 cm. "Six Veins Canal System" refers to six large drainage canals in the ancient city. They were built in accordance with the urban topography of the city. There is a saying, "ancient canals are like veins, canals connect with moats, moats connect with the ocean", Guangdong Annals, Ming Dynasty (1368–1644). The ancient canals were used by sampans, flat-bottomed wooden boats, to transport cargo and passengers into the city. Guangzhou's "six veins" canal system was established during the Song Dynasty (960–1276). The canal system was maintained and repaired throughout the Ming and Qing Dynasties. In the lighter shade of blue, the map shows minor drainage canals. (Guangdong Provincial Zhongshan Library.)

▲ Figure 2.9a

The former village Shi Pai as seen from the 26th floor of one of the many high-rise buildings that now surround the village. Right, close-up.

 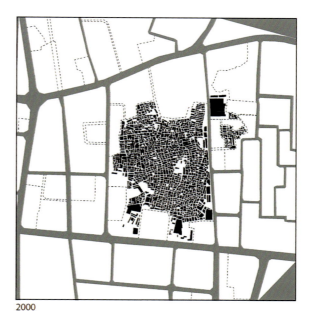

1980

2000

▲ Figure 2.9b

Shi Pai, a former agricultural village once surrounded by fields and ponds (left), but now entirely encapsulated by Guangzhou's new central business district (right). Lower income residents and members of the rural population who have migrated to Guangdong province find accommodation in urban villages like Shi Pai. There is nothing much village-like in Shi Pai's current settlement form. Buildings of three to six floors in height are tightly spaced along narrow lanes. The buildings are of a relatively recent age, generally built informally without government supervision. Only the ground plane reveals the village character with the original parcelization intact, but each parcel is covered by structures to the maximum extent possible. The map drawing on the left shows the village surrounded by agricultural land; the map on the right shows the village encapsulated by Guangzhou's new commercial district.

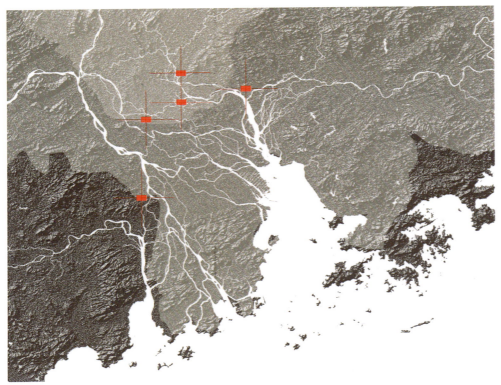

◀ Figure 2.10

Pearl River Delta with the locations of projects discussed in the chapters of the book (map by Patrick Webb, 2014).

financially unobtainable for many. For us, we saw little choice, but to incrementally improve living conditions through merging the old with the new.

Notes

1. Qing Dynasty (1644–1912)
2. 56.5 million in 2011, according to the Guangdong Statistical Yearbook (Gstj, 2012). It is an approximation of the permanent population (i.e. people who live for more than 6 months in the same place and hold a residence registration or a regular work permit).
3. The demise of silk production in China is tied to the opium war, 1839–1842, when China retaliated against the import of opium by British traders. The British in turn retaliated and blocked silk exports out of China. Silk was produced in Europe from the 7th century, first in Constantinople, later in Sicily, Venice and Spain, still later also in the Lyon region of France (Marks, 1998).
4. A 100-year flood is one with a 1 in 100 chance of occurring every year.
5. Evidence for this claim can be found in the official policy of the Guangdong Provincial Government that has started to centralize power at the urban district level away from the level of urban prefectures to directly guide economic transformation (Guangzhou Urban Redevelopment Office, 2013).

References

Anon., 2013. *Civil Society Portal*. [Online] Available at: www.eu-china.net/../2011_Wang [Accessed 28 May 2013].

Anon., n.d. *Gov HK*. [Online] Available at: www.epd.gov.hk/epd/english/environmentinhk/water/regional_collab/PRD_model.html

Braudel, F., 1992. *The Stuctures of Everyday Life*. Berkeley: UC Press.

China Labour Bulletin, 2013. *China Labour Bulletin*. [Online] Available at: www.clb.org.HK/ [Accessed 29 May 2013].

Feng, J., 2015. Preservation of the public. In: ETHZurich, ed. *Global Schindler Award 2015 Shenzhen Essays*. Zurich: Schindler, pp. 40–45.

Gstj (Guangdong Sheng TongjiJu), 2012. *Guangdong Tongji Nianjian. [Guangdong Statistical Yearbook, in Chinese]*. Beijing: China Statistic Press.

Guangzhou Urban Redevelopment Office, 2013. [Online] Available at: www.gzuro.gov.cn/ [in Chinese] [Accessed 20 November 2013].

Lin, G. C., 1997. *Red Capitalism in South China, Growth and Development of the Pearl River Delta*. Vancouver: UBC Press.

Marks, R. B., 1998. *Tigers, Rice, Silk and Silt: Environment and Economy in Late Imperial South China*. Cambridge: Cambridge University Press.

South China University of Technology, 2007. *Urban Water System Plan of Foshan 2006–07*. [Online] Available at: www.hydroinfo.gov.cn [Accessed December 2008].

Weng, Q., 2007. A Historical Perspective of River Basin Management in the Pearl River Delta. *Journal of Environmental Management*, 85(4), pp. 1048–1062.

Wu, Q., 2007. Urban canal systems in Ancient China, *Journal of the South China University of Technology*. Oct.35(10).

Xiang Dong, W., 2011. *Comparison between Migrant Workers in Pearl River Delta and Yangtze River Delta*, Guangzhou: Sun Yat-Sen University.

Zhang, H., Ma, W. & Wang, X., 2008. Rapid urbanization and implications for flood risk management in the Pearl River Delta hinterland: The Foshan study. *Sensors*, 28 March, 8(4), pp. 2223–2229.

Chapter 1

The Pearl River Delta as a Cultural Landscape – New Life for a Traditional Water Village[1]

The historian Spiro Kostof reminds us that the administrative coming together of proximate villages to form a town has been repeatedly attested to in world history since ancient times (Kostof, 1991, p. 59). He uses the term *synoecism* to describe how villages are absorbed into a new town in a process in which the villagers exchange their pastoral ways and the laws of their tribe or clan for the presumably free and durable institutions of the city. The transaction is of a political nature with strong physical and social consequences; and, as Kostof points out, history shows that such unions have mostly been involuntary, thus strongly resisted. The physical consequences of the merger produce a form that Kostof describes as "organic" next to planned or orthogonal development patterns. Through history, well known examples include Athens, Siena, and numerous cities in Iran, such as Kazvin. Calcutta and even Greenwich Village in Manhattan were also forced into synoecism. In these locations and many more, the juxtaposition of forms remains traceable, thus the dynamics of the long-ago social integration can still be recalled or imagined as part of cultural progress. For a historian (Al, 2014) or anthropologist interested in the morphology of cities, the Pearl River Delta is a rich study area where the small scale organic form of a villages is encapsulated by the orthogonal street grids of urban expansion.

▼ Figure 2.1.1

Left: proposed extension of Foshan's new central business district. Redrawn from a map by Sasaki Associates, 2003, Boston. Right: same map with four villages superimposed.

▲ Figure 2.1.2

Dadun village in 2000. A village in transition: factories replace ponds and fields.

Dadun, a Typical Water Village

Dadun exemplifies many characteristics typical of water villages in the Pearl River Delta. The history of the village reaches back to the late 13th century during the Song dynasty, and possibly the Yuan dynasty that followed it in 1279. It was during this era that the low-lying alluvial lands of the delta were settled in a characteristic pattern of compact villages that were connected by canals and surrounded by rice paddies, later turned into fishponds.

Frequently, an ancient banyan tree marks the entrance to the village. The tree-lined canals and dense spacing of buildings create a compelling, intimate urban experience and a cool micro-climate during hot summer months (Wu, 1995).

Although the many branches of the Pearl River near Dadun are lined with levees, major floods (2.5 m deep) inundated the village in 1915, in 1924 (knee-deep, or about 0.35 m), and again in 1962 (2.3 m deep) (Liang, 1988). In the 1962 flood, the levees failed, causing extensive inundation. Many residents took refuge from the flood on the second and third

▶ Figure 2.1.3

Water village in the Pearl River Delta; a large banyan tree marks the entrance to the village.

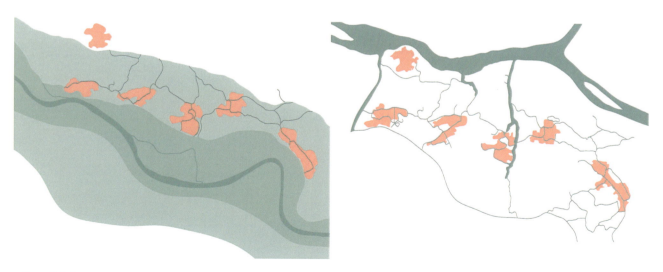

▲ Figure 2.1.4

Left: Fluvial morphology between the historic Yandu River, left, and the Dong Ping River, right. The historic Yandu River meandered greatly and flooded the low-lying land (shaded in light blue) until levees were built during the Song dynasty. Consequently, the Yandu River was reduced in width. Dadun is one of six villages that were built on slightly higher ground north of the historic Yandu River. Dadun had the advantage of being located on a north to south and west to east running drainage channel that boats could use. Thus the location prompted special bi-weekly markets. Right: the six villages in recent history with the channelized Dong Ping River to the north.

floors of buildings, an experience that has motivated the construction of multistory buildings in delta villages since.[2]

Traditionally, up until the 1980s, villagers like those in Dadun derived their livelihood from a combination of aquaculture, silkworm cultivation, and the growing of fruit trees, vegetables and flowers in garden plots. Villagers cultivated mulberry trees on the berms between ponds, and fertilized the trees with nutrient-rich mud, excavated from the fishponds at times when the ponds were periodically drained. Farmers harvested the leaves of the mulberry trees and fed them to silkworms, whose larvae they sold to silk processing facilities in the region (Marks, 1998, pp. 118-120). Organic matter, notably the dung of silkworms, served as food for fish.[3] Villagers also collected their "night soil" to put on garden plots as fertilizer (Bruenig, et al., 1986). After the construction of several large fertilizer plants in 1972, chemical fertilizers became widely available, and the traditional practice of collecting night soil for use as fertilizer was gradually discontinued. Since the human faecal matter was no longer used as a resource, it became a waste product, and toilets were installed that discharged either directly to canals or to pipes that drained into the canals.

When the south bank of the Dong Ping River was designated for the new city center for Foshan (Figure 2.1.1) a plan developed by Sasaki Associates in 2003 (Sanchez-Ruiz, 2003) was selected as a result of a competition, and adopted by the city. While the plan's text called for landscape elements to be "built according to the existing natural context, such as canals, lakes, islands, hills and wetland," the plan did not acknowledge the complex pre-existing system of canals and the traditional water villages. The plan evidently assumed the water villages would be erased and replaced with an entirely new urban structure. An eight-lane road was proposed to pass through what is now the center of Dadun village.

Observing and Listening

The villagers resisted annexation, asserting their ownership rights to village land and dissatisfaction with the compensation offered by the government. As a result, the new road stopped abruptly at the edge of the village.

The Sasaki Plan was only partially implemented. In 2007 a new bridge crossed the Dong Ping River along the center line of the new axis. Completed elements include the city's new stadium, a large media headquarters building, and a central park, whose water features include a meandering, decorative canal. Since the water quality in the canals in Dadun was compromised due to the discharge of untreated sewage, the authorities installed a water gate along the northern boundary of the village, disconnecting the polluted waters of the village canals from contaminating the decorative canal in the new park. This disconnection has exacerbated the contamination problem within the village by eliminating flushing from the north. The village canals still have one connection to the larger canal system (and ultimately the Dong Ping River) to the east, which induces a tidal range of about 1 meter in the upstream end of the village canal network.

The abstractions of the proposed plan contrasted sharply with the experience of the existing conditions. At the time of our work in Dadun in the winter of 2007/8, the great pressures on South China's cultural landscapes have helped to create an awareness of the lack of conceptual foundations capable of guiding past and current planning practices (Whitehand & Gu, 2006). Past development practices, such as encapsulating villages with new housing and industry, are being met with much resistance; the villagers of Dadun proved no exception. At the national level, land development practices were reconsidered in light of their social and environmental consequences (Asia News, 2006).

▶ Figure 2.1.5

An alternative future for Dadun; a new town in a greenbelt of villages and ponds flanked by urbanization (drawing by Peter Frankel, Sam Woodhans Roberts, Lin Yuming, Lin Feng, Quan Xuewen, Chen Wei, Gun Xin).

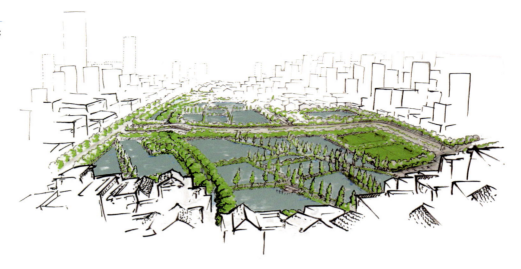

As an alternative to demolition, an integration of villages like Dadun into a newly developing urban fabric would create a green belt of ponds, canals and villages within the new center. The villages would play an economically viable and socially important role as districts within the new city. At the time of our work, there were no models for such successful integration of water villages in the Delta. However, if such an approach could be articulated and disseminated, it may be possible to avoid some future social conflicts, and preserve the unique cultural and environmental attributes of such villages while the surrounding landscape transforms. A "harmonious integration", mandated by the national government, would also need to acknowledge the changing demographics of the population that now occupies the villages, especially the large influx of a young migrant workforce from rural parts of China who have taken up residence in the villages in order to work in nearby industries.

The reasons why villages have been incorporated into the expanding cities and why villages were not simply erased by government fiat are related to historically defined rights. During the "Long March", Mao Zedong severed China's long feudal tradition, which had ruled the existence of an estimated 300 million agricultural workers (Ping Li, 2008). As a result of land reforms, the Chinese farming population was given autonomy of operation, including land ownership (Ping Li, 2008). At the same time, the land reform, known as "tu gai", solidified support among the rural population, who had been active participants in the Chinese revolution of 1949 – referred to in China as the 1946–1950 "War of Liberation" (Ping Li, 2008). In the mid 1950s, following Soviet Russian models, a farmer's individual rights to property were converted to collective rights, which have been maintained to the present day (Ping Li, 2008). The village as a farming collective holds authority over land use rights and controls development independent of neighboring city or prefecture government. As the neighboring city expands onto farmland, the collective is compensated for their loss of land. Inside the village, villagers maintain ownership of their homes and frequently rent space to migrant workers, the so-called "floating population". Thus, the former farmer becomes a landlord and the village becomes an enclave for migrants.

The incentive to increase density in the former rural village has led to new four or five-story cinderblock construction replacing the original one-story farm buildings. The already narrow lanes become narrower as building heights ascend and upper floors cantilever until they nearly touch each other across the lane. The lanes are damp and dark even during the day.

▲ Figure 2.1.6

Dadun villagers (left) and migrant workers (right) on a Sunday afternoon in October 2007.

◀ Figure 2.1.7

Stone-faced canal in the center of Dadun.

The migrant population quickly outnumbered the local villagers by a sizable factor. In 2007, Dadun's migrant worker population had reached 6,000 and the villagers remained at 3,500 residents. The villagers gained rental income to be invested upgrading their homes. Other villagers preferred to move into nearby modern high-rise apartments. At the prefecture level, authorities frequently perceived village conditions as undesirable; urban villages were considered slums, overpopulated, full of precarious construction, and plagued by severe infrastructure deficiencies and sometimes social disorder. Rarely acknowledged were the benefits for the migrant population. For the growing number of migrant workers, much work was readily available, but affordable places to live were rare. The relatively cheap housing in the urban villages remained vital to the economy of the region (Ma. & Wu, 2005).

The setting of a village in a river landscape held great attraction for the participants in our collaborative work with students and faculty from the South China University of Technology. Dadun's spatial structure of lanes, canals and public spaces was of high quality. Two centuries ago, in a concerted effort, the walls of the canals had been faced with natural stone. Stone masons had carved identical stone rings into natural stone blocks and placed them at regular intervals to serve as ties for sampans. Wherever a lane meets a canal at right angles, steps lead down to the water. Ancestral halls of the two predominant families, the He and the Liang, open out to medium sized squares. The village is divided into eight parts, or "Shes"; minor deities guard each island surrounded by canals for each of the eight families of the village. Remnants of two watchtowers remind visitors that the village was once a wealthy market town that needed protection from river pirates. Apparently, the two leading families had been in a state of feud from 1922 to 1925. Remnants of a wall that separated the village into two parts could still be seen near an ancient Zhushuai temple. There, in the center of the village, members of all families maintained mutual access to the Thao shrine, a neutral territory near a bosque of old trees enclosed by a formal stone-faced pond.

▶ Figure 2.1.8

Liang ancestral hall, rebuilt in 1870. Below: survey of the Liang family ancestral hall by Zhimin Zhang. The residential typology described above is also evident in the Liang family ancestral hall, but with the far more generous dimensions of 35 by 25 meters.

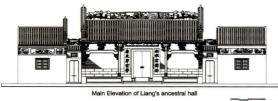

Main Elevation of Liang's ancestral hall

Section of Liang's ancestral hall

CHAPTER 1 The Pearl River Delta as a Cultural Landscape

Yumenliang's Ancestor Hall
Wennu Temple
Tianhou Temple
Fuxue He's Ancestor Hall
Former Silk Factory
Liang's Family Ancestor Hall
Huaiyou's Family Ancestor Hall
Former Primary School
Quan He's

Observations of Dadun quickly led to an understanding of how the village had functioned in the river landscape of the Pearl River Delta. The elements of the landscape that we observed had formed the basis of Dadun's social and cultural existence, an existence that had abruptly disappeared in the last two decades. Admittedly we looked at the disappearing river landscape with much appreciation, but with full realization that the changes to the landscape were irreversible. At the same time, we realized that our observations could lead to a better understanding of how the former landscape had evolved and how a future landscape could be constructed that is attentive to the balance of natural and social forces, such as the interplay between the water system, vegetation, climate and settlement patterns and the dynamics of changing demographics.

In January 2008, the chairman of the village committee, Liang Jinghua, told us that the committee of Dadun villagers was faced with two choices. On the one hand, they could negotiate with land developers who would offer higher compensation for the land than the Foshan city government. If the villagers agreed to an offer, they would gain funds and could invest in property outside their village. Under the then existing rules, the local government would return 15% of the land areas to them and the villagers would have the right to develop it. A real estate developer, together with the City of Foshan, would implement the city center plan, which would call for the demolition of the village, the building of a park connected to the new sports stadium and completion of the road grid. The details of this planning scenario were never worked out, but could have included the preservation of historic structures within the village, the canals and some of the ponds. One could imagine a museum-like park landscape that evokes memories of the past, including displays of fish farming and mulberry-silkworm cultivation. Unresolved in this scenario would have been the future of the 6,000 migrant workers who rented space in the village.

A second scenario, the one pursued by the local village committee, was not to sell the development rights, but to maintain collective ownership and control over the village's planning and building permit process. We set to work in support of the second choice.

▲ Figure 2.1.9

Social structure of Dadun. The village consists of eight parts, generally islands between canals; each part is protected by a minor deity referred to as "She". Stone tablets indicate the boundaries between the extended families that have settled in Dadun, first the Cai followed by the Liang, Yu, He, Feng, Wu and Li. The Liang and He families are the most numerous; their families built large ancestral halls. They are indicated on the map together with the Zhushuai temple.

Specifically, the villagers' control over land use and building renewal activities made possible a gradual renewal that will lead to the village's transformation. To finance the renewal, the villagers invest the lease and rental income into new revenue generating ventures that support commercial, recreational and cultural activities for the anticipated city center population of 30,000 new residents. The intent was to guide the transformation of Dadun towards a more "harmonious" synoecism, a coming together of new and old that gave the villagers more say about their future.

Designing for Dadun's Future

In our minds, most urgent at that time were improvements to the historic canal system. Household sewers had to be separated from the canal system, and new sewer lines had to be placed along the margins of the canals. The canal system had to reconnect more robustly to the river; this would increase the natural flow as well as permit tidal action in both directions of the system. This would improve water quality in the canals. The water system of ponds and canals, together with the trees that line them, would again play an important role in attenuating potential floods. The improved canals would have an important ecological function, beneficial to plant and animal life, thus importantly contributing to air quality and a comfortable micro-climate.

Canals, Water Quality, and Micro-climate

It had become clear from our observations that villagers made frequent use of the multiple steps leading down into the canals. In the past, villagers traditionally drew water, washed clothes, and swam in the canals, all activities reflecting good water quality (some long-time villagers in Dadun insisted that they could drink the canal water in the past). Drinking water was drawn from shallow wells, which are hydrologically connected with the canals. However, once night soil was no longer applied to crops, and raw sewage began to be discharged into canals, the waters became too contaminated for these practices.

As part of our field work, the hydrologist on our team, Matthias Kondolf, with his students, collected water samples and sent them to a laboratory at Sun Yat-Sen University to test for faecal coliform. Students took samples from the nearby Dong Ping River, from a fishpond, from a domestic well and from several other locations within the Dadun canal systems. Lab results showed extremely high concentrations of faecal coliform in the canals and the well. It is worth noting that the water samples from the middle of Dadun and the well would not be suitable for agricultural or general landscape use according to the water quality standards for surface water in China (Ministry of Environmental Protection, The People's Republic of China, 2002). The water sample from the canal between Dadun and the neighboring village, Xiaochong, met the standard for industrial uses and recreation with no direct contact. We measured concentrations an order of magnitude lower in the mainstream river and fishpond samples. These samples met the standard for direct human contact in China, such as swimming, but do not meet the standard in the United States.[4] Clearly, water quality was compromised in Dadun, and the domestic well and canals were heavily contaminated and not fit for human contact.

The loads of sewage and constituents from runoff make the canals vulnerable to eutrophication, the over-enrichment by nutrients, which, when combined with sunlight, can result in algal blooms that rob the water of dissolved oxygen. Wherever possible the impervious ground near the canals should be redesigned to include small to medium sized wetlands.

(Figure 2.1.11). Human waste would no longer discharge directly into the canals but be collected in sewer pipes that would be laid along the margins of the canals. In addition, former fishponds no longer in use can be stocked with submersed or floating water plants local to the delta. Such ponds can be used to store water and improve water quality.

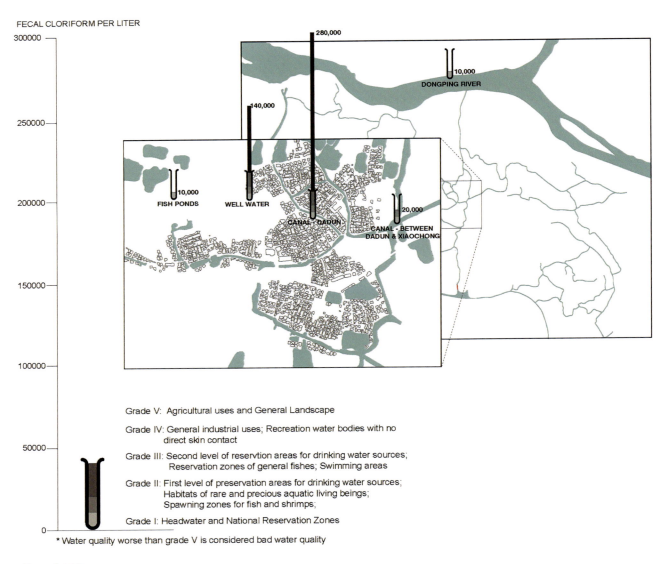

▲ Figure 2.1.10

Testing water quality. Map showing sampling locations and test results (map by Kirsten Podolak and Matthias Kondolf).

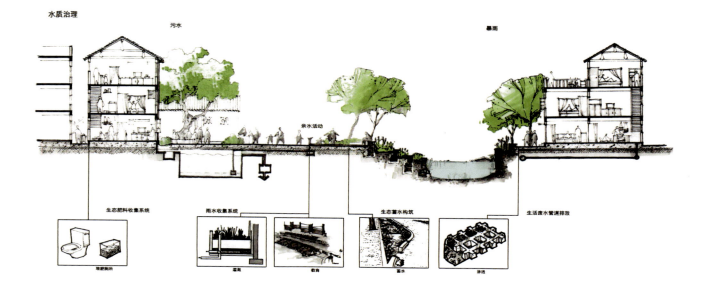

▲ Figure 2.1.11

Water management included treatment of runoff and storage and the installation of sewer lines along the margins of the canal system (drawings by Nadine Soubotin, Kirsten Podolak, Jin Lei, Li Yue, Hu Lan, Li Boxie, Luo Yushan and Matthias Kondolf).

Village Comb Structure

As part of the workshop, we made our own maps from satellite information. When we carried the maps around the village they attracted much attention. Villagers had rarely seen a map image of their village, especially not one that showed buildings and lanes in photographic detail. For us, the maps became a way to analyse the village's fine-toothed comb structure of buildings in rows along narrow lanes; the walks along the canals form the ridge of the comb, and the teeth of the comb are formed by the narrowly spaced lanes. The distance between lanes allowed for a single property with front and back entrances opening onto parallel lanes. The buildings fronting the canals along the ridge of the comb were generally executed in a more elaborate design and frequently housed small ancestral halls belonging to one of the eight family clans. Some comb structures accommodated two separate properties between lanes. These properties were generally smaller and would have only a front entrance, but no back door. This fine grain pattern could have emerged through divisions among family members. The tree-shaded canals and close spacing of buildings with alleys 1.5 meters wide, just wide enough for two people with poles to pass, created a cooler micro-climate. By virtue of the shading from trees and buildings, the cooler air above the canal provided natural ventilation along alleys. Most canals in Dadun are oriented roughly NW–SE, along the axis of the south-easterly breezes that prevail during the hot summer.

The spacing between parallel lanes rarely exceeded 10 meters, with 7.8 meters being a more common dimension. The property frontage length alongside the lanes also generally measured 10 meters. Thus, the properties were square or nearly square and measured between 80 and 100 square meters. Judging from the roof structures, ceiling beams span from 4.5 meters to a maximum of 5 meters, which is typical of single span wooden roof construction between masonry walls in other parts of the world. Thus, property dimensions produced a main structure with gable walls of 5 meters in width and a length of 7 to 10 meters measured along the roof ridge. The single orientation of the main structure is directed towards a small court in the center of the property. Two very small rooms flank the court, serving as entrances to the court from the lanes; they were generally also used for storage. The

◀ Figure 2.1.12

Dadun's comb structure. Throughout history, villagers guided by family ties had built their houses in rows, one behind the other, starting with the family's ancestral hall, along the canal. Generally the oldest members of the clan would occupy the structure nearest to the ancestral hall, followed by younger family members' households. Long rows perpendicular to canals resulted, a form similar to a comb, where the rows form the fingers and the canals form the rim. The lanes between the rows were generally spaced 7.5 to 10 meters apart. (Drawings by Krishna Balakrishnan, Carrie Wallace, Guan Feifan, Zhang Yunyuan, Li Junjun, Hua Sha, Li Zheng, Chen Yipin, Gan Yile Chen Jingxiang.)

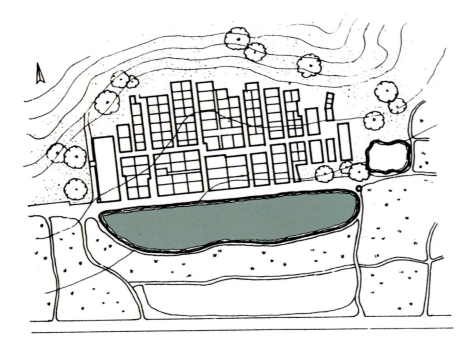

◀ Figure 2.1.13

Typical Pearl River Delta village farm house typology. (The figure was redrawn from *Chinese Vernacular Architecture*, Yuanding Lu, editor, 2004: p. 525, Guangzhou: South China University of Technology Press.)

settlement pattern described here constitutes a regional adaptation of an ancient Chinese building typology; it is still visible in Dadun, but only traces can be found on the aerial views.[5] As a result of extensions and remodeling, the courtyards and small flanking buildings have almost disappeared. Although the ridged roof with gables facing the lanes is still most common, new flat roofed structures and some pavilion shaped roofs have started to appear. This type of roof suggests a freestanding structure with an orientation to four directions and it is always associated with multistory structures.

Public Life

A major attraction of Dadun village is its public realm. The large square in front of the Liang ancestral hall also served as the school yard in front of the former school house. It measures 30 meters between the entrance to the ancestral hall and the canal. The length of 74 meters appears too generous nowadays, but must have been adequate when the square was used by children. In the 1980s, a new primary school was built three blocks away, at the western edge of the village. The square in front of the Her family ancestral hall is more modestly dimensioned. It measures 18 meters from the canal to the front steps of the ancestral hall and is 35 meters long. The two main ceremonial squares are not used much on a daily basis. Elderly residents and children sit or play on the paved walks alongside canals; these walks widen in places and sometimes have a width of 10 meters, but generally measure only 3 to 5 meters. Especially popular is a place alongside a canal in front of the Tao shine. A cluster of male residents gather here to sit in the shade under the bosque of trees we mentioned earlier. Clearly, people gather in the places that are comfortable and subject to shade and light breezes from the canals.

If cities are generally places for strangers, as the sociologist Louis Wirth wrote in his *Urbanism as a Way of Life* (Wirth, 1938), villages are places for extended families. This is also true in China, more so prior to economic reforms. Unless families made their living in trade, as civil servants, in the military or in scholarly pursuits, the majority of Chinese society is still so very few generations removed from its agricultural roots. When the sociologist Wirth wrote his famous essay in 1938, he was reflecting on his youth in a remote village in the Hunsrück Mountains of Germany. Wirth later became a leading figure of the Chicago School of Sociology. It is interesting to note that the Chinese historian Jiang Feng refers to Louis Wirth by saying:

> In the past, our tradition was not to build a place for strangers, but for people who were familiar with and linked with each other. We need more places that are not only for strangers. Today, we create public space only for strangers, like a park, where anybody can enter, and that's good, but not good enough. Today, we offer a blank space as open space; it's a space without meaning. So when people get there, maybe they feel comfortable because there is no pressure, but they will also feel lonely, because there's no community to share things with, no clear idea of what to do in the space. So we tried to create meaning – but meaning does not just come from architecture. Without social meaning, you cannot create spatial meaning, so I don't think architects can do a lot. But urban designers and urban planners have more to contribute.
>
> Feng, 2015

▲ Figure 2.1.14

Like their parents and grandparents before them, contemporary teenagers enjoy a cool breeze on the riverbank. Note the woman to the very left. She might be keeping an eye on matters.

The Implications of Policy Tested Through Design

Upgrading existing buildings and building new modern homes on the village outskirts required little guidance. More difficult for the villagers to address were the issues related to water quality and water circulation, and the repairs necessary to the system of canals and ponds. Therefore, our team prioritized tasks, designed solutions and illustrated them as principles that could direct the integration of the village into the new Foshan city center. The first group of principles addressed the water system.

Improve water quality in canals up to a level that permits human contact, including swimming. As trunk sewer lines will serve the surrounding new urban development, it will be possible to collect sewage within the village by laying sewer pipes under the paved walkways, along the margins of the canals, and connecting them to the sewer main. At the same time, grey water from homes, together with runoff after rains, can be locally treated under the pavement of the canal margins and stored there to be fed into the canal system as needed.

Preserve waterways and wind flows. This policy will restore the important function of canals as a cool air resource. This requires maintenance of the perpendicular orientation of lanes to water in order to avoid blocking ambient wind flow patterns.

Distinguish the village from the surrounding urban center. This can be accomplished through retention of a ring of fishponds around the village, or similar strategies that create a sense of entrance to the village. To address the gradual transformation of the village's

PART II The Pearl River Delta

▶ Figure 2.1.17

Distinguish the village from the surrounding central business district by maintaining traces of the pond-dike landscape (drawings by Kirsten Johnson, Stacy McLean, Wang Ge, Li Wenxuan, Sui Xin, Li Xuesi and Chen Siyun).

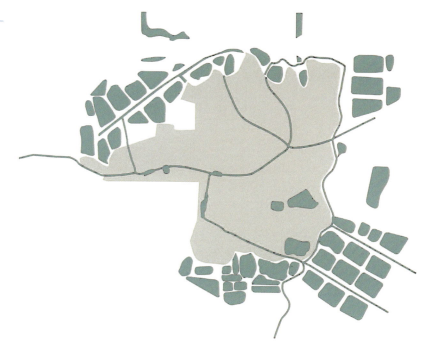

▶ Figure 2.1.18

Allow new construction that is consistent with Dadun's scale and parcelization.

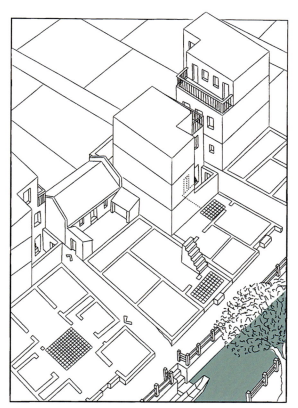

CHAPTER 1 The Pearl River Delta as a Cultural Landscape

The increase in building heights should be limited to four floors. The spacing of neighboring structures should be set to 4 meters across lanes that are narrow. This rule would apply for all structures exceeding two floors. Land coverage by new building construction should be reduced and, as a result, the open space area on a given lot will increase from the current 10% to 25%. Some parcels will prove too small to accommodate new development under these rules. In that case, assembly of neighboring parcels should be encouraged, but land assembly should be limited to not more than two parcels. Parcels should never be assembled across lanes, since that would result in the closure of lanes. The building frontage facing canals should be maintained; new construction along canals should be built up to the frontage line established by neighboring buildings.

These detailed rules would apply to all new construction. In addition, the village's two significant family heritage halls and the Tao shrine with its three separate temples should be placed on a historic register. The team illustrated rehabilitation proposals for the abandoned historic school house, two partially ruined fortification towers, numerous small ancestor shrines, the abandoned silk factory building, and a former social hall. While not necessarily of great historic significance, these structures contribute significantly to the character of the village and they could be reused as commercial enterprises, restaurants or shops to serve the influx of population in the new developments surrounding Dadun.

The aim of our work was not to simply preserve a rural way of life that has largely disappeared from the outskirts of cities in the Pearl River Delta, but to bring new life into Dadun that could serve as a viable cultural, residential and commercial place within the new business district of Foshan. The proposal was based upon the premise that Dadun with its ponds and canals transformed in the manner described here would be in stark contrast to the urban high-rise development that will soon surround it and therefore, because of its contrast, remain attractive to the current residents as well as to newcomers, in a mutually beneficial symbiosis.

Reflections

We presented our proposal to members of the Foshan city government and to the village council in January 2008. It was favorably received by the villagers. The reaction by the government officials was more guarded. For them, our proposal was of a politically delicate nature, because it was based upon land use controls that originated in the early communist era and rest with the village central committee. For the Foshan government the question remained: will the villagers maintain their rights to the land and thus their rights to self-determination? The rising land values on former village land might provide a powerful incentive to sell. In addition, professional advice on how to structure the incremental renewal envisioned here was without precedent. A private developer or government entity might be reluctant to satisfy such a specialized sector of the housing market in such an incremental fashion. We have observed very few projects of this kind in the Guangzhou area. One project, on Jiefangzhong Road, designed by the architect He Jingtang together with architects Jiang Feng and Lui Hui, incorporates traditional row housing and combines it with new commercial space and new affordable housing.

We were alone at the time in pointing out that the demand for a skilled workforce was growing in the industrialized areas of the Pearl River Delta. More so than in the past, industry will try to hold on to qualified workers, and that can only happen if the workers are compensated with a higher quality of life, including decent and affordable living conditions.

In January 2008, when we left, we were uncertain about Dadun's future. In March 2009, on a return visit, we learned that the City of Foshan had entered into an agreement with the

Dadun Village Committee. The villagers agreed to pay for the installation of a local sewer system that the City of Foshan agreed to connect to a new sewer treatment plant. In return, the City of Foshan has cancelled the water-lock; the barrier to the free flow of river water to the village's canal system has been removed. In retrospect, our measurements of water quality in the ponds, canals and wells had been our strongest contribution to a healthier future for its residents. We suspected that it was the collection of water samples by us, an international group, and the subsequent analysis by an independent laboratory at Sun Yat-Sen University,[6] which raised the issue of Dadun's future to a higher level of government.

On 17 August 2009, the Shunde district government was elevated to prefecture level on a par with the City of Foshan. A year later, we learned that the provincial government had reverted all land on the southern bank of the Dong Ping River, including Dadun and the neighboring villages, back to Shunde, where the land had been administered prior to Foshan making plans for its new center. This reorganization at the province level indicated a shift in policy to strengthen the centralized authority of the Guangdong province and reduce the power of prefecture level cities like Foshan. For the land around Dadun, it means a transformation from labor intensive manufacturing towards more knowledge-based industries. The land there, south of the Dong Ping River, was selected to house a collaborative Sino-German industrial service zone.[7]

When we agreed to work on Dadun, an alternative development proposal might have been expected from us. Developing a central park in Foshan's new center might be simpler from the official planner's perspective. Government officials in many Chinese cities were impressed by the success of Xintiandi in Shanghai. However, on closer examination, here the control over land use does not rest with local residents, but with a real estate developer. Xintiandi is a successful development in Shanghai that incorporated historic structures into a commercial entertainment district. Literally translated as "new heaven and earth," Xintiandi is located in the center of Shanghai, a car-free two-city block area, where only 15 years ago, a crowded neighborhood stood, with up to 30 families per courtyard house. The inhabitants were moved out. China's first "lifestyle center"[8] now serves as the "value generator" for the adjacent high-rise office and residential development complex that is part of the same development. Incidentally, at the

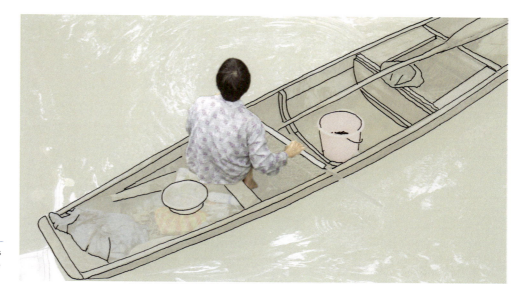

▶ Figure 2.1.19

Improved conditions in Dadun's canal system, 2015. Aquatic life returned to Dadun's canals.

CHAPTER 1 The Pearl River Delta as a Cultural Landscape

time of our work in Dadun, the City of Foshan was talking to the developer of Xintiandi about a similar development in the historic center of Foshan, adjacent to the famous Zumiao temple, the ancient water temple that has survived wars and revolutions. Our proposal was not to follow the Xintiandi example. We might be ahead of our time and some readers will criticize our proposal as too academic, but the pace of change in the Pearl River Delta is still rapid. Social and environmental problems are mounting; a more comprehensive approach that involves local concerns in the dynamics of urbanization is urgently needed.

Notes

1 First published as an article on the preservation of Dadun, China (Bosselmann, Peter; Kondolf, G. Mathias; Feng, Jiang; Bao, Geping; Zhang, Zhimin; LU, Mingxin, 2010).
2 Chairman Liang Jinghua of Dadun Village, personal communication with the author and Matthias Kondolf, January 2008.
3 Chairman Liang Jinghua of Dadun Village, personal communication with the author in January 2008.
4 The US standard for swimming correlates to eight added gastrointestinal illnesses per 1,000 swimmers.
5 The Chinese courtyard typology is well known. In 1934, the Danish architect and planner Steen Eiler Rasmussen might have been the first to describe it for European readers (Rasmussen, 1935, 1950).
6 The author paid 300 RMB in cash for the analysis.
7 *The Economist*, Jan. 11, 2014, "Urban Renewal, New Frontiers, Foshan".
8 Goldberger, P. 2005, "Shanghai Surprise: The radical quaintness of the Xintiandi district," *The New Yorker*, 25 December 2005.

References

AI, S. ed., 2014. *Villages in the City: A Guide to South China's Urban Informality*. Honolulu: University of Hawaii Press.

Asia News, 2006. [Online] Available at: www.asianews.it/view.php?l=en&art=7332 [Accessed 27 September 2006].

Bosselmann, Peter, Kondolf, G. Mathias, Feng, Jiang, Bao, Geping, Zhang, Zhimin, LU, Mingxin, 2010. The future of a Chinese water village. Alternative design practices aimed to provide new life for traditional water villages in the Pearl River Delta. *Journal of Urban Design*, 25 March, 15(2), pp. 243–267.

Bruenig, E. F. et al., 1986. *Ecologic-Socioeconomic System Analysis and Simulation: A guide for application of system analysis to the conservation, utilization and development of tropical and subtropical land resources in China*, s.l.: Compiled from the proceedings of the China Resources Conservation, Utilization and Development Seminar.

Feng, J., 2015. Preservation of the public. In: ETHZurich, ed. *Global Schindler Award 2015 Shenzhen Essays*. Zurich: Schindler, pp. 40–45.

Kostof, S., 1991. *The City Shaped: Urban Patterns and Meanings through History*. London: Thames & Hudson Ltd.

Liang, H. X., 1988. *History of Dadun Village (unpublished handwritten manuscript)*, Foshan, China: Committee of the Village of Dadun.

Ma., L. & Wu, F., 2005. *Restructuring the Chinese City: Changing society, economy and space*. New York: Routledge.

Marks, R. B., 1998. *Tigers, Rice, Silk and Silt: Environment and Economy in Late Imperial South China*. Cambridge: Cambridge University Press.

Ministry of Environmental Protection, The People's Republic of China, 2002. *Environmental quality standard for surface water (GB 3838–2002)*. [Online] Available at: http://english.mep.gov.cn/standards_reports/standards/water_environment/quality_standard/200710/t20071024_111792.htm [Accessed December 2008].

Ping Li, D. J., 2008. *Rural land reforms in China. Land reform, settlement and cooperation, 3.* [Online] Available at: www.fao.org/docrep/006/y5026e/5026e06.httn#bm06 [Google Scholar] [Accessed 24 June 2008].

Rasmussen, S., 1950. *Towns and Buildings.* Cambridge, MA: MIT Press.

Rasmussen, S. E., 1935. *Biledbog fra en Kinarejse.* Copenhagen: Bianco Lunus.

Sanchez-Ruiz, M., 2003. *Foshan Urban Design Plan, Sasaki Associates, Inc..* [Online] Available at: www.sasaki.com/what/portfolio.cgi?fid=306&region=6&page=2 [Accessed December 2008].

Whitehand, J. W. & Gu, K., 2006. Research on Chinese Urban Form: Retrospect and Prospect. *Progress in Human Geography,* 30(3), pp. 337–355.

Wirth, L., 1938. Urbanism as way of life. *American Journal of Sociology,* 44, pp. 1–24.

Wu, Q., 1995. *Protection of China's Ancient Cities from Flood Damage.* Beijing: China Architecture & Building Press.

Chapter 2

Whampoa Harbor

It takes time to structure in one's mind an urbanized region as large as the Pearl River Delta. Unless mountains and water set limits to urbanization, urban form appears continuous but in patches. Views from the expressway show a jarring juxtaposition of old and new. To gain a deeper understanding, it helps to learn about the structure of the many waterways that dissect the land between the Baiyan Mountains to the north and the eight Pearl River estuaries with the South China Sea to the south.

In this chapter we concentrate on Guangzhou, the largest city in the region and capital of Guangdong Province. To graphically represent urban form of such a large urbanized area is always a challenge. A map view that shows the entire city provides little information about the scale of its elements; only the very large elements of the urban structure stand out. To better understand the range of form, we adopted Alexander von Humboldt's transect method that we introduced in part I of the book. As a sampling method with reduced dimensionality, transects not only represent the smaller elements of urban form but show the interconnectedness of the various elements. To produce such an abstraction we selected eight frames each measuring 4 by 4 kilometers and placed their center points 12 kilometers apart on east–west and north–south transect lines.

As a result, Guangzhou is shown in four squares in the east–west direction and five squares in the north–south direction. For more detailed analysis, each 4 by 4 kilometer frame contains one square kilometer that is gridded into 10 by 10 squares of 100 meters by 100 meters. This was done to measure the distribution and scale of elements that make up the metropolitan landscape.

The selected frames depict a patchwork. Except for the frame in the center, which shows Guangzhou's historic core, each square shows a juxtaposition of fields, villages, industry and new residential developments. The distribution of the elements is clearer when an abstraction is applied that selects elements within the gridded squares, for example, water surfaces, blocks and streets and the patterns of agriculture.

The distribution of roads is telling: a pattern of widely spaced roads indicates large industrial areas that until recently covered agricultural fields. We can tell by looking at the scale of residual agriculture, and by the much more narrowly spaced road structures that characterize villages. The agricultural landscape is rapidly transforming. Additional high capacity roads are the first new traces that are laid onto the land. The roads, in the form of large-scale orthogonal grids, are graded in straight lines, removing and dominating all previous forms that block their path. The new roads emphasize mobility; access to adjacent properties becomes sporadic. As a result, the form of new development becomes insular and is structured on superblocks with little connectivity to adjacent blocks. The intersections are designed for the high capacity needs at peak hour traffic times. Traffic reaches and exceeds such capacities, because all movement in a given area is confined to a very limited number of crossings.

GUANGZHOU, GUANGDONG PROVINCE, CHINA

▲ Figure 2.2.1

Guangzhou metropolitan transects. The figure shows four squares in the east–west direction and five squares in the north–south direction. The center points of each square are selected every 12 kilometers along transect lines following the cardinal directions. Each frame contains one square kilometer inside a 4 by 4 square kilometer area. The inscribed square kilometer is gridded into 10 by 10 squares of 100 meters by 100 meters, and this was done to measure the distribution and scale of elements that make up the metropolitan landscape. (Source Google Earth, 2009.)

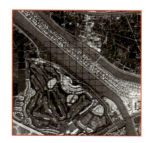

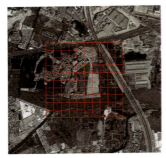

▲ Figure 2.2.2

Scale and grain of Guangzhou. The four west to east squares are shown in separate layers of streets, blocks, fields and water. (Drawn by Jassu Sigh and Brinda Sengupta.)

    The scale of the road grid is very coarse at the Canton Fairground area shown on the third frame of the west to east transect. Here, an 800-meter long structure provides space for the biannual international trade fair. The new fairground opened in 2008 and replaced the old fairground closer to the center that had housed the fair in the past.

    Twelve kilometers to the east, the last frame on the west to east transect, an inlet can be seen that forms the historic edge of Guangzhou at the former shoreline of the Pearl River's Humen estuary. Historically, sea voyages into the South China Sea departed from here after prayers were given at the Taoist temple near Miaotou Village. The temple is dedicated to Nanhai, the Divine South China Sea God.[1] Today, a gigantic, 600-meter long coal-fired power plant blocks the axis from the historic temple towards the South China Sea.

    On the western edge of Guangzhou, the first frame of the west to east transect shows the village Bishuiwan near the border towards neighbouring Foshan. This frame gives a sense of the prevailing settlement pattern of the metropolitan landscape prior to the reforms that established the Pearl River Delta as part of an economic development zone.

    In this first pass, the selection of frames along a transect line seems arbitrary. However, I had selected frames of places that I had visited. They were representative of Guangzhou as I had experienced it up to that time. Seeing them together gave me an understanding of my mental grasp of the city as a whole. The selected frames only claim to be representative of my personal understanding at that time. As with all representations, information is selected to allow for meaningful interpretations. For me it was essential to establish a firmer mental hold over the larger spatial structure prior to working on a finite location, like the villages south of Foshan. Eventually a much finer grid of frames would need to be placed upon the urban landscape and that would happen in years to come. However, even the limited set of frames gave me the information I was looking for: how to design in response to a very large physical, social and cultural context and in response to traces left in the cultural landscape by natural processes.

    In the winter of 2010, for our second project in the Pearl River Delta, a site was selected at a location 6 kilometers between the Canton Fairground and the South China Sea God

▶ Figure 2.2.3

A survey of the Humen. The map was made in 1786 by officers of the British East India Company, 61 cm x 51 cm. The Humen – the British cartographer called it Tigris – refers to one of the eight "gates" or estuaries of the Pearl River system. The map shows detailed cues or navigational instruction for travel from Macao/Hong Kong upstream to the Whampoa Harbor in Guangzhou. The historic Whampoa Harbor is located at the top of the map. (Hong Kong University of Science and Technology.)

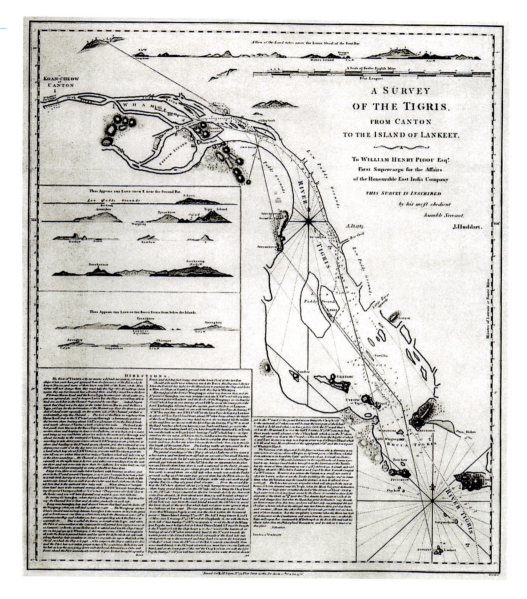

Temple, halfway between the third and fourth frame on the west to east transect. Here, at the former Whampoa Harbor (World Port Source, n.d.) a 60-hectare site became available that had been used until recently to receive bulk shipments of steel and exotic lumber. These activities were in the process of relocation to Guangzhou's new port facilities that are located closer to the open sea.

As always in this low-lying region, sites near the distributaries of the Pearl River system need to be understood with respect to their fluvial history. Figure 2.2.4 illustrates the system of waterways to the north of the former Whampoa Harbor, itself a former arm of the main river. The canals of the Pearl River Delta once served a system connecting myriads of small waterways to villages and agricultural activities. Their role as a transportation system has now been abandoned, and the canals have been partly filled with debris, but they still function as an open

CHAPTER 2 Whampoa Harbor   111

sewer for the remaining villages. In the future, the canals will take on an additional important role as drainage channels after the heavy monsoon rains that last from April to August and drop up to 30 cm of rain per month or an average annual rainfall of 1.7 meters (Wikipedia, n.d.). The canals provide storage space for water, and thus delay the outflow to avoid flooding. More room for water will be especially important in the future, when more hard surfaces replace the formerly permeable surfaces of fields, and when more water accumulates quickly that needs to drain towards the Pearl River. As in other delta locations around the world at the confluence of large drainage basins that debouch into a common estuary, flood events occur more frequently due to rising groundwater tables and due to more abrupt mountain snow melt and higher than normal ocean tides that are forced inland by – in this case southerly – storm gales.[2]

Figure 2.2.5 illustrates a tentative design for the 36-hectare former Whampoa Harbor site at Yuzhu. The professional staff of the Whampoa district of Guangzhou had only

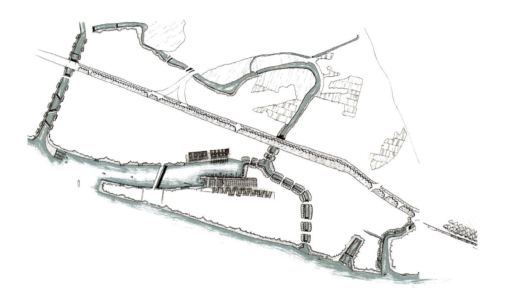

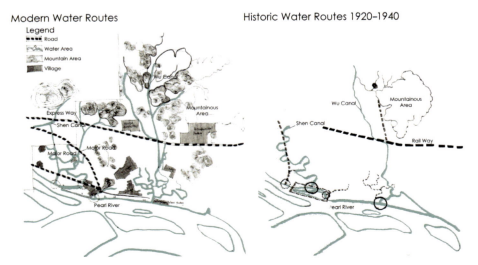

◀ Figure 2.2.4

Water system at Whampoa.

112　　　　　　　　　　　　　　　　　　　　　　　　　　　　　PART II The Pearl River Delta

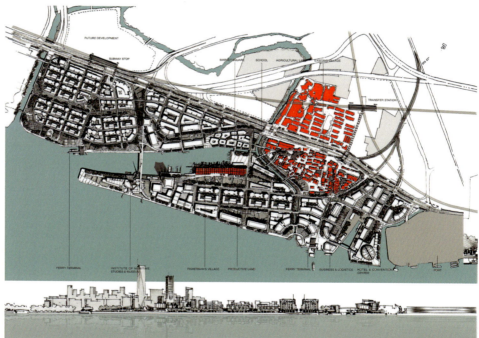

▶ Figure 2.2.5

The new Whampoa Harbor. Design for Guangzhou's Whampoa Harbor at Yuzhu (drawings for this project were made by Rebecca Finn, Dario Schoulund, Brinda Sengupta, Jassu Sigh, Supaneat Chananapfun, Jennifer Hughes, Patrick Race, Jessica Look, Robin Reed, Beth Harrington, Huang Qiaolun, Chen Qian, Liyue, Lin Yuming, Zhang Zhenhua, Xie Daibin, Zhang Lei, Cao Xibo, Zhang Yingyi, Liu Ping).

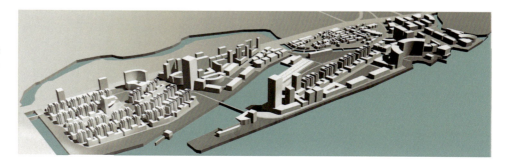

CHAPTER 2 Whampoa Harbor

programmed a mercantile lumber exchange facility for the site. Such an exchange regulates the trading of exotic woods imported into China from Indonesia, Brazil and Africa. Staff was surprised to see how intensively the site could be used and how new activities on the site could integrate with the existing village and the science and technology island across the Pearl River. There is room to house many interrelated and overlapping activities in the vicinity of the shoreline and to design a river esplanade with hotels connected to the Canton Fairground and Guangzhou's new and historic center by ferry and subway. The ideas illustrated were viewed favourably and they triggered discussions among the staff and politicians about integration, including the preservation of a historic village near Yuzhu. As in the Dadun example in the previous chapter, the positive integration of villages into new developments amounts to a clash of lifestyles. Only recently have scholars demonstrated how the typologies found in Chinese villages and small towns have evolved and how they could further evolve in order to satisfy the need for modernization (Gu, et al., 2008).

Spatial integration does not necessarily mean social integration, but if villages are preserved, the difficult process of relocating village residents is, if not entirely avoided, certainly slowed. The relatively small parcel and block structure allows residents to remodel, expand and add on to buildings at their own initiative. Thus, residents belonging to less affluent social groups can remain in established villages. To our western eyes, a community of "water people" who lived in the Yuzhu harbor basin on boats and other floatable devices was a group that also needed to be integrated into the design. In fact, the district government had provided permanent housing for the community in the form of tightly spaced two-story structures. As so frequently in China, within a short walk a visitor can cross from the present to the past and observe people in an environment that appears unconnected to the economic advances of the last 30 years. The student members on our team, who grew up in the new China of economic opportunities, were sceptical about a possible integration of the water people. Our Chinese students adopted the slightly romantic, but plausible, view that in a waterlogged landscape like the Pearl River Delta, aboriginal people had adapted to a water-based lifestyle prior to the beginning of the Han Chinese civilization (Anon., n.d.).

In Chinese, the land to the south of the Nanling mountain range is referred to as Lingnan. The Meiling Pass across the mountains connects to the Pearl River's North River valley. If Han Chinese now predominate in Lingnan, they are not the only ethnic group. From R.B. Marks we learn that four ethnic groups lived in Lingnan (Marks, 1998), groups now referred to as ethnic minorities. The lowland Tai and Zhuang people cultivated wet rice long before the Hun Chinese conquest in 1094. The Tai migrated south to what became Thailand, the Zhuang remained and might be the remnant ethnic group at the Yatsu harbor basin. However, in the hard reality of urbanization the water people will in all likelihood be pushed further out into one of the eight Pearl River estuaries.

Reforming New Stream

Two years later, in the winter of 2012/13 we returned to work again in the Guangzhou Harbor district of Whampoa. At the time, the Whampoa district was one of the then ten administrative districts of Guangzhou. We focused on the former agricultural village Xinxi, or New Stream, located to the north of the historic harbor on the Bei Jiang branch of the Pearl River. After having worked on the incremental transformation of Dadun, we used the Xinxi case study to test the design implications of an affordable housing policy that, if it were established, would address the need to house migrant workers in proximity to their workplaces. Xinxi in our case is again a village where the villagers were inclined to hold on to their collective rights to ownership, at least for the time being.

As in other villages that we have worked in, Xinxi villagers are in the minority. Here approximately 800 residents are outnumbered threefold by migrant workers who pay rent to the villagers for their living spaces. The villagers maintain a limited amount of farmland that is used to grow produce. Much of what is grown supplies a large-scale outdoor restaurant that can seat several hundred guests at a time. Apart from the farm and restaurant, the villagers own a hotel that was built on land they kept after most of their agricultural land was sold. The villagers also built a set of warehouse structures with space for small trucking operations. While the farm, hotel and restaurant are viable operations, the warehousing has become less important as port activities have moved away from the historic Whampoa Harbor. Xinxi is located next to a new subway station that links the nearby Whampoa district government centre to the rest of Guangzhou in an east–west direction. The station will be further improved by a not yet existing line that will make a north–south connection to the emerging science city and Guangzhou's recently built South Station.

Of course, Xinxi is a microcosm operating within a larger regional, even global, dynamic. We considered a number of macro-trends that will have implications on Xinxi in its location. The economy of the Whampoa district will gradually transform with the reduction of port activities and the growing concentration of science and technology research centres on an island directly to the south of Xinxi. Household income will grow slowly, but demand for decent housing will increase more rapidly. Both trends will keep the area as a residential resource to supply housing for employees with low income and few choices in Guangzhou's steadily more expensive housing market.

At the same time, the national government through Guangdong Province has strengthened local regulation on environmental protection to address water quality, waste disposal,

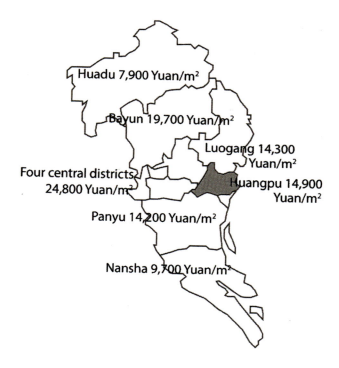

▶ Figure 2.2.6

Housing cost in Guangzhou's ten administrative districts (diagram drawn by Francesca Frassoldati).

air quality, vehicular circulation and public transport issues. These measures will require significant public expenditures, making local initiatives to increase housing supply for those in need even more necessary.

At the level of the individual households, young people in China, like elsewhere, live together before marriage and share living space with others, chiefly to reduce expenses. The demand for locally managed housing solutions will increase, and their success will largely depend on lower costs for financing, management and land acquisitions. Cost savings cannot be expected as much from construction costs but from moderate unit size. Therefore in any affordable housing model, collective land disposition would need to be regulated and made consistent with district plans that identify housing needs by income. Such plans would also favor an integration of land use with public transportation to reduce dependency on vehicular movement. The plans would encourage redevelopment of existing underused areas, like Xinxi's cluster of warehousing.

In the transformation of agricultural land to industrial use, the villagers received compensation. In Xinxi's case, land acquisition for urban use happened in 1994 with a compensation of 150,000 to 200,000 yuan per hectare, depending on the then prevailing crops or use. Government officials estimated a ten-fold increase in the current land value. In all likelihood, the funds gained from the compensation were invested in the construction of the hotel and warehousing facilities. Apparently, the village collective took a long-range view: once agricultural land was transferred, the village collective as "landless farmers" had no choice but to seek non-agricultural revenue streams.

Individually, villagers benefitted from rental income. They either rented out existing living space directly, or individuals created additional space through horizontal, or more frequently vertical, extensions. The latter is best described as an informal process, only subject to supervision by the village council.

Inside villages like Xinxi, the derogatively labelled "floating population", as mentioned, outnumbered the villagers. However, the Guangdong's working population with rural registry "floats" less than assumed.[3] A second generation of migrant workers has been born locally with fewer ties to the rural origins of their parents. To western understanding, the distinctions between urban and rural registration, *Hukou* in Chinese, resembles remnants of a feudal order that prohibits free movement of citizens. The registration system, however, was legislated in 1953 during the post-revolutionary period led by Chairman Mao. Thus far, villages like Xinxi have provided a place of transition in which migrants are gradually introduced into urban life without formally becoming citizens of a city (He, et al., 2010). Frequently, groups of migrants settle in the same village with peers from the same home town or region, building sub-enclaves where language, food and traditions can be easily shared.

I now invite the reader to suspend all disbelief in a future for Xinxi that includes the welfare of *all* its residents, including members of the migrant workforce. We simply did not know what the villagers would decide, nor did the villagers seem to know at the time of our work in January 2013. Instead, I would like to introduce a hypothetical case and make assumptions about conditions that would have to be met if housing were to be provided for a population in need, a population that is left out of the formal housing market, yet a population that makes significant contributions to the economy of the region.[4]

The land currently used by warehousing operations in Xinxi measures 3.8 hectares and has a value of 4,000 yuan per square meter. Our colleague Francesca Frassoldati established the value by comparing the land in Xinxi to nearby areas, not for reasons related to sale but considering the land as collateral and to calculate financing and mortgage costs. Our team had produced two alternative designs for the warehousing portion of Xinxi. The first envisioned a compact development of 623 units at 75 square meters per unit and land coverage

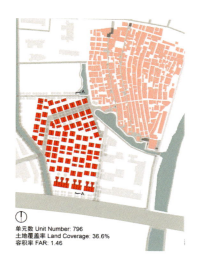

▲ Figure 2.2.7

Xinxi, New Stream Village in Guangzhou's Whampoa district.
  The map on the left shows the existing condition of the historic village with its typical "comb" structure built on a south-facing slope. The map on the right shows our proposal to replace the warehouse structures with affordable housing.

of 29%. The construction cost would amount to 93.45 million yuan and 16.19 million yuan for site improvements, streets, walkways, trees and permeable surfaces. The calculation of the financing cost resulted in 4.43 million yuan spread over a period of 15 years at an interest rate of 6.5%. Thus a loan of over 114.1 million yuan would be needed, which is lower than the value of the collateral, the land value of 152 million yuan.

To push the envelope, we developed a second scenario, where we increased the land utilization for buildings from 29% to 37%, which generated a unit count of 879 units and a cost of 131.85 million yuan for construction, plus 13.4 million yuan for site improvements. The financing cost would amount to 6.88 million yuan distributed over 15 years. This resulted in a loan amount of 152.1 million yuan, a figure in balance with the collateral.

In the lower density model, each unit had to generate a minimum yearly payback[5] of 19,473 yuan, which resulted in a 1,623 yuan rent per month per unit. The question now was: is such a rent affordable for residents who currently rent space in the existing village of Xinxi? We designed the 75 square meter units with three rooms plus kitchen and bathroom. If three wage-earning renters would qualify to cover the monthly rent, the three would pay 541 yuan each.

That might be tight for a wage earner who makes 1,200 to 2,400 yuan per month. The slightly higher density model with its 879 units on the same piece of land resulted in a monthly rent of 511 yuan per month for each of three hypothetical occupants. The increase in density provided only a marginal lowering of rental fees, but was more affordable. Clearly, if indeed the monthly income of a worker is limited to 1,200 yuan, a 40 yuan saving is not insignificant. If two established workers with an income of 2,400 yuan per month each shared a unit, there would be extra space to bring up a child.

While we were reflecting on the housing needs of literally millions of workers in the Pearl River Delta region, the merits of our modelling became apparent. What also became apparent was covered in an article in the *Economist*. The journal reported on so-called

CHAPTER 2 Whampoa Harbor

"handshake buildings" in Shenzhen that were built illegally on collectively owned rural land:

> China has managed a more orderly system of urbanisation than many developing nations. But it has done so on the cheap. Hundreds of millions of migrants flock to build China's cities and manufacture the country's exports. But the cities have done little to reward or welcome them. Rural migrants living in the handshake buildings are still second-class citizens, most of whom have no access to urban health care or to the city's high schools. Their homes could be demolished at any time.
>
> *Economist*, 2013

The need for a shift in policy became apparent. Housing prices in cities are increasingly out of reach for migrants. The central government has encouraged the construction of low-cost housing in cities with limited success, since only local *hukou* holders are eligible.[6]

Tao Ran of Renmin University in Beijing[7] says the solution lies in the handshake buildings of Shenzhen. Government should legalize such buildings around the country – allowing rural dwellers near cities to develop them and rent out flats to migrants – and then levy taxes and fees to pay for expanding services. Yes, that would help, but our proposal went further. It called for locally managed housing solutions. As commercial real estate developers are not providing affordable housing and as state regulated social housing does not serve the migrant population, a new model is needed.

Designing such a new model caused much discussion among faculty and student participants. We asked if it would be conceivable for a group of young professionals to organize a not-for-profit organization that would make their services available to manage the financing

▼ Figure 2.2.8

A new addition to Xinxi. Comb structure of Xinxi in the background and the new addition in front. New Stream Village with 620 units of affordable housing built on village land. Note on the section drawing, the height of buildings alternate to provide sun access to all south-facing facades.

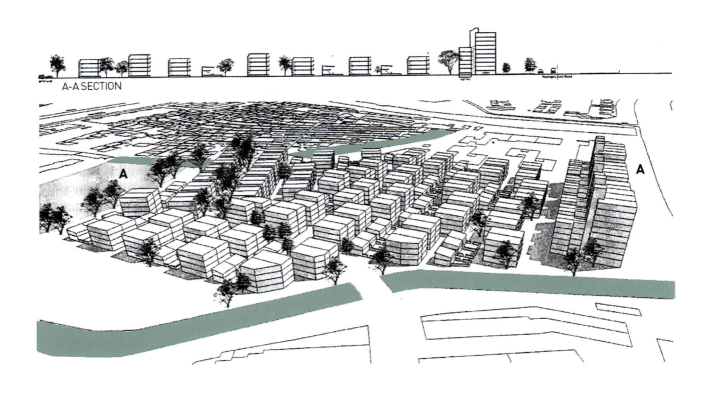

for new housing construction on village land. Not only in our case here in the Whampoa district of Guangzhou, but elsewhere, the concept of a not-for-profit organization that is dedicated to providing affordable housing appealed to students in urban planning. Such an organization would bring together the village council, local industry and district government in a model where the villagers provide the land, industry would underwrite loans and local government would have oversight to ensure that construction was in compliance with safety regulations. Government would also extend services to the new housing, such as sewerage, water and power.

We quickly discovered in our discussions that such a model hinges largely on the availability of financing. The villagers own their land collectively, but are prevented from using their land as collateral to secure loans. Informal financing systems exist in China, but are apparently based on traditional family networks and do not follow the microfinance structures known in India and Africa (Turvey, 2010).

To overcome such lending obstacles, in our hypothetical case the lending agreement would have to be signed by both the village committee and the urban district, and if necessary be guaranteed by local industry. Affordable housing for low and middle income families in a modest but decent environment would be consistent with local safety regulations and planning codes, and thus constitute the conditions for formal lenders to accept collective land as collateral for a precise scope. We argued that a not-for-profit organization established by a university institute at the school of urban planning and contracted by the collective could maintain the interest of the collective and the public goal of decent housing.

Designing New Stream's Future

While the urban planners on the team focused on the production of affordable housing, the designers worked on design principles that would have general applicability when designing for former villagers and migrant workers alike. The challenge here is to design spaces that foster community. Chinese building regulations, due to their tower separation rules, produce much undesignated open space: the higher the towers or residential slabs, the greater the undesignated open space between such structures. The challenge here is to increase land coverage by building structures of different heights, reducing the height of towers, but keeping the overall density high.

Historic Xinxi's main street runs east–west from the river to farmland. Movement along the main street is more concentrated than along other lanes. We designed a bridge across New Stream and continued the main street through Xinxi's new extension. The street is lined by four and five-story buildings, making the street 15 meters wide. Walking along this street is defined by the canopy of closely spaced trees. Near the bridge and under the trees we expected residents to gather in the evening hours. There would be benches and room for children to run around.

According to Feng Shui principles, Xinxi village was settled on a south-facing slope of a hill. The main passage through the village has remnants of an ancestral hall. Eight narrow lanes lead up the slope in the characteristic comb-like fashion. Currently, raw sewage drains into the tidal channel. Runoff from roofs and lanes drains into the ponds. As a consequence, both water bodies are contaminated. The place near the former confluence had traditionally been used for gatherings, like watching dragon boat racing. The steps leading down to the channel now sit empty. Our proposal provided a series of ecological systems, combined with places for social gathering that would connect New Stream to its water. Constructed wetlands for grey water treatment formed the backbone of the system. This network transitions to a

◀ Figure 2.2.9

Connect old and new. The sketch shown here illustrates the new tree-lined street that connects via a bridge to the old village.

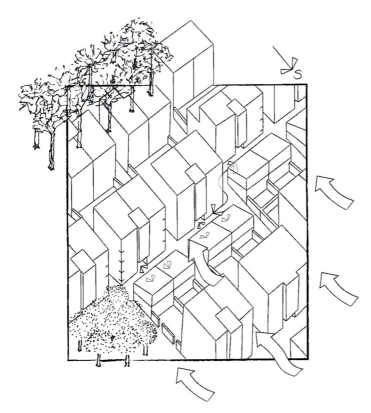

◀ Figure 2.2.10

Public life for streets and lanes. It was important to us that entrances to homes and flats would be accessible from streets and lanes and not from undesignated open space. Streets and lanes are defined by the cross-section of the buildings that flank them. In order to achieve such geometry, buildings of two stories in height are placed to the south of four to six-story buildings. A separation by 6 meters defines the width of lanes. As a result, residents on their walk towards entrances encounter others in a well-defined space. The dimensions of the lanes are comfortably narrow and in the shade during midday hours, but wide enough to satisfy building separation rules and the need to allow access for emergency vehicles. In addition to satisfying functional concerns, space would be sufficient to give entrances to buildings special character and distinction. We designed the 6-meter wide lanes to have a length of 50 meters. Such a lane would typically serve a community of 40 to 50 households. Even with one child per household, a sizable little group of children can play in that short lane. A person walking along the lane would change direction at the end, step into a north–south running lane, but only for less than 10 meters, and continue to turn again into the next segment of a 50-meter long lane.

PART II The Pearl River Delta

tidally influenced marsh near the confluence. Staged in elevation, the system is gravity fed. Irrigation runoff from the farm is used in newly constructed fishponds. Here, fish are able to reduce agricultural pollutants before water is released into the tidal channel.

The designs were ambitious to the point that some of our government counterparts could not hide their scepticism. Others responded with supporting smiles: how much fun it is to study what ideally should happen. Yet others shared our conviction that in cases like Xinxi, incremental modifications, or regulated transformations of spaces over time, can prove

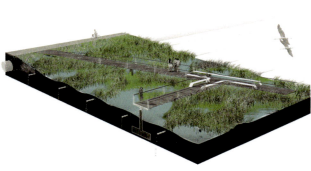

▲ Figure 2.2.11

Bringing the stream back into New Stream. As the earlier chapter on Dadun shows, the incremental renewal of villages necessarily addresses the repair of water systems. Historically, Xinxi was located at the confluence of two streams. The eastern stream was channelized and is tidally influenced. The western stream was diverted to a new channel. In its former course, a sequence of ponds remained. From spot elevations we created a contour map that clearly showed a gentle hill between the two streams and the possibility of connecting the water courses again at the place of confluence. (Drawings for this project were made by Alana Sanders, Hyun Young Kim, Miriam Aranoff, Benedict Han, Bin Cai, Kushal Modi, Ethan Paul Lavine, Erick Jensen, Benjamin Townsend Caldwell, Ruemel Sanchez Pangalo, Tian Liang, Xi Hu, Rui Wang, Jianzhao Zheng, Jing Xu, Kuan He, Xinyu Liang. Wenji Ma, Fei Du, Xinjian Li, Xiaofei Xie, Xiaolan Zhou, Haoxiang Yang, Shibo Yin, Junmin Xiongg, Min Luo, Binsi Li, Shansi He.)

more effective than eradication of the village. The realization that triggered our professional interests was to recognize how people of very limited means lived together, and how they made significant contributions through their collective and organized work.

It can be argued that students were encouraged to articulate visions of a future that will probably never become reality; at least not in the same idealized forms as were conceived by their authors. Be that as it may, clarity about design intent matters greatly in the educational setting, and not only there. The understanding required to work with an existing fabric can transmit the misleading message that architecture as in quality of building design is not important. Such an interpretation would indeed be misleading, because in this type of urban design work tentative architectural designs are chiefly made as decision making devices that help different parties to visualize conscious professional efforts within a larger social, political and economic context.

Notes

1 The temple dates back to 594 AD, Sui Dynasty. It marks the beginning of the Maritime Silk Road towards India, the Arabian Sea, Egypt and the Mediterranean Sea.
2 Reports on the most recent floods in the Pearl River confluence can be found in *China Daily*, May 24, 2010.
3 For a critical discussion of migrant worker conditions in Guangzhou see H. F. Siu (2007).
4 An article on Xinxi was first published in 2014 (Bosselmann, P., Frassoldati, F., Xu, H., Su, P., 2014).
5 (Total loan)*(0.065*(1+0.065)^15/(((1+0.065)^15)-1))
6 Urban population in China: 36.22% in 2000 (459.1 million people), 49.68% in 2010 (665.6 million people in the last national census). Urban population in Guangzhou: 83.79% in 2000 (8.3 million people), 83.78% in 2010 (10.6 million people).
7 Tao Ran has extensively elaborated on the role of urban villages in providing housing for migrant workers (Ran & Su, 2013).

References

Anon., n.d. [Online] Available at: www.wordiq.com/definition/Zhuang

Bosselmann, P., Frassoldati, F., Xu, H., Su, P., 2014. Incremental transformation of a traditional village in China's Pearl River Delta. *Territorio*, Issue 71, pp. 121–129.

Economist, 2013. Some Are More Equal Than Others. *The Economist*, 1 June.

Gu, K., Tian, Y., Whitehand, J. & Whitehand, S. M., 2008. Residential building type as an evolutionary process in the Guangzhou area of China. *Urban Morphology*, 12(2), pp. 97–115.

He, S., Liu, Y. T., Wu, F. L. & Webster, C., 2010. Social groups and housing differentiation in China's urban villages: An institutional interpretation. *Housing Studies*, 25(5), pp. 671–691.

Marks, R. B., 1998. *Tigers, Rice, Silk and Silt: Environment and Economy in Late Imperial South China.* Cambridge: Cambridge University Press.

Ran, T. & Su, F., 2013. *China's road-map for reform.* [Online] Available at: www.uchicago. cn/2011/05/renmin-university-professor-tao-ran-teaches-uchicago-course-in-beijing/ [Accessed March 2014].

Siu, H. F., 2007. Grounding displacement – uncivil urban spaces in post reform China. *American Ethnologist*, May, 34(2), pp. 329–350.

Turvey, C. G., 2010. Borrowing amongst friends: The economics of informal dredit in Rural China. *China Agricultural Economic Review*, July, 2(2), pp. 133–147.

Wikipedia, n.d. *Guangzhou/weather.* [Online] [Accessed 15 August 2010].

World Port Source, n.d. *World Port Source.* [Online] Available at: www.worldwideportsource.com/ports/CHN_Port_of_Guangzhou_403php [Accessed 15 August 2010].

Chapter 3

Jiangmen, a Historic City Remembers its Center and the Urban Expansion on Pazhou Island in Guangzhou

In the fourth decade since the Pearl River Delta's rapid transformation, greater value is given to places that have retained their historic identity. This trend is positive, because the preservation of buildings and districts limits the relocation of people with lower income who frequently occupy the historic parts of cities. Threatened by demolition in the recent past, rents in villages remained affordable for migrant workers and the less mobile members of society. The trend also preserves a way of life where the integration of living and working have always prevailed. Finally, once committed to repairing the urban fabric, the preservation of towns and buildings reduces the need for urban extensions and the serious deterioration of natural conditions, especially the quality of air and water.

Since the turn of the millennium, these issues have begun to receive attention in the Pearl River Delta, but implementation frequently falls by the wayside due to the unrelenting pace of change that city governments need to manage. We were greatly encouraged when we learned from the planners of Jiangmen, a city of five million, that the government had given up plans to demolish the historic center, but had embraced strategies to improve the quality of life for all its current residents. The historic center of Jiangmen is called Changai. It covers a large 93-hectare urban district with 14,500 residents. Here a substantial urban fabric can be transformed gradually to demonstrate alternatives to the predominant modes of urbanization in China.

Granted, holding up the preservation of Jiangmen's historic center as an example for the future to address social, economic and environmental progress can be a leap. The crowding of workers with rural registry into historic town centers and villages resulted in deteriorated conditions: a lack of sanitary sewer and much unauthorized vertical building extensions. The historic center of Jiangmen is no exception.

Natural History has Shaped a Cultural Landscape

Jiangmen is located at the edge of the alluvial flood plain between the Xi (west) and Tangjiang Rivers. During the past two centuries, ocean-going vessels could sail up the Yamen or Hutiaomen estuary. At the foot of the Jiangmen hills, on a river branch that connects the two estuaries, a protected harbor emerged that could be sufficiently guarded against the yearly summer monsoon floods. Here, cargo was trans-loaded to and from river barges. The natural history of the location has shaped the location of the city and its cultural landscape.

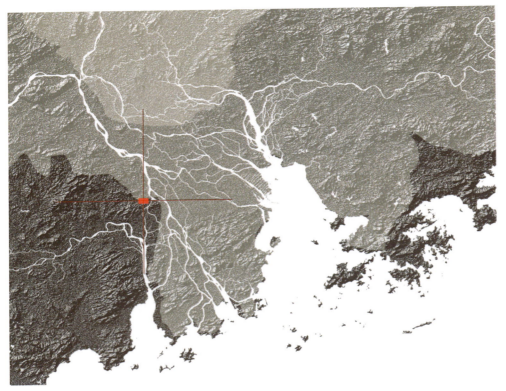

 Figure 2.3.1

Jiangmen's location between the West River and the Peng Jiang River (map by Patrick Webb).

Although barge activities have largely disappeared from riverbanks in the historic center, the city maintains the third largest river port in the Pearl River Delta nearby. In 1902, European colonial powers forced the river port to open to foreign trade. As a result, urban blocks were built on land reclaimed from the river. Their design shows much uniformity of arcaded streets running parallel to the river. Two to three-story shop houses were constructed in tight rows on narrow, deep lots. All structures were built around a time in China's history when American and European powers introduced new influences. The architecture is of a colonial character. However, Jiangmen's historic district did not entirely originate during the colonial period; many streets and lanes are much older and follow a pattern that relates to the city's hilly topography.

One of the reasons why the preservation of Jiangmen's historic compact form enjoyed serious consideration was related to land ownership patterns. Not only is the small scale land parcelization difficult to assemble into more easily developable larger parcels but many properties are owned by individuals who no longer reside in China, but in other South East Asian countries, in Australia, or in the Americas. We were surprised to learn about the importance of foreign ownership. Why would decisions about redevelopment be influenced by the fact that property is owned by someone who has left China? Well, the matter is very important. Overseas Chinese were instrumental in China's recent history: Sun Yat Sen and his brother greatly benefitted from financial support by overseas Chinese to purchase weaponry to overthrow the Qing dynasty and to start the republic in 1912. Overseas Chinese financed the struggle against Japanese occupation. Then in 1949, when China was very poor, financial support from abroad prevented starvation. The overseas Chinese maintained a tight network through their extended family, so when in 1979 foreigners were encouraged to invest in China's industrialization, it was the overseas Chinese who channeled the investments. As a result, for the time being, a property owned by an overseas Chinese person is protected from confiscation or demolition by government. Vacant, but foreign owned, buildings were rented out by remaining family members to migrant workers, including lower income residents, and many elderly people also remained in the center of Jiangmen.

When we learned on our first visit that the preservation and the upgrading of streets, blocks and buildings in Jingmen's historic district should be done with the goal of improving quality of life for all its current residents, we understood that this mandate suggested the importance of incremental renewal consistent with the small-scale urban fabric and economic conditions of its residents, a population that cannot readily be relocated. While the preservation of the commercial arcade architecture enjoyed much local support, even strong encouragement from the national government, there is a host of issues to be addressed in making the buildings and streets useful and livable for the future.

▼ Figure 2.3.2

Jiangmen's historic center. Map shows the pattern of ownership. (Map redrawn from material at the Foshan Planning Bureau.)

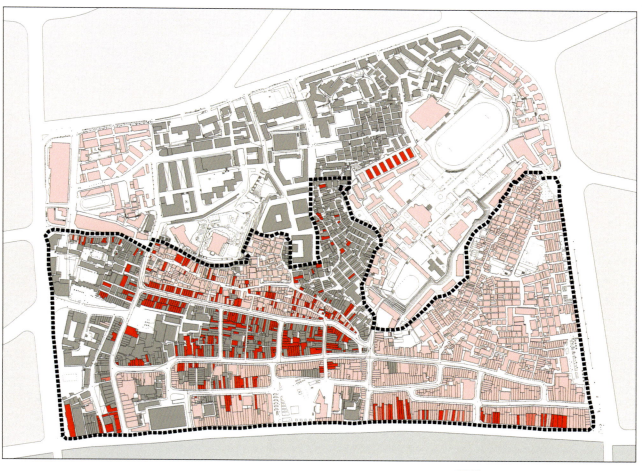

OWNERSHIP MAP
产权性质分布图

CHAPTER 3 Jiangmen, a Historic City

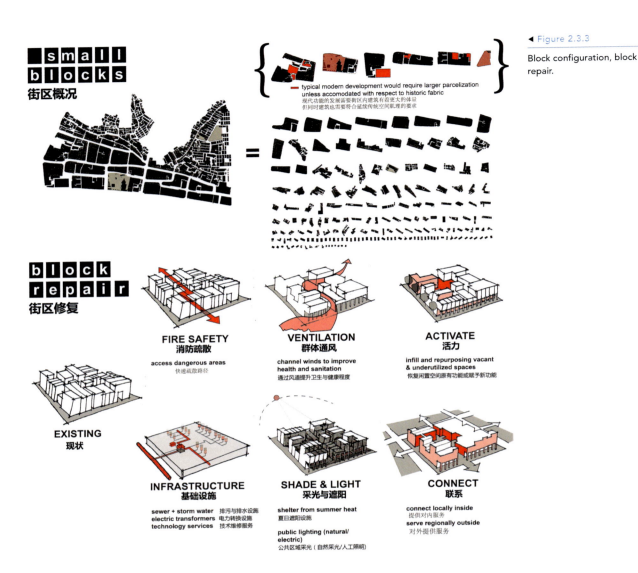

� Figure 2.3.3

Block configuration, block repair.

The commitment to preservation brought obligations for the Jiangmen government. For example, Figure 2.3.3 illustrates design strategies for a variety of city blocks and building typologies. The long, narrow shop-house typology presented major challenges when re-designed for improved fire safety and sanitary conditions. These buildings are referred to as *bamboo* structures, because rooms are lined up between parallel walls like the cells of a bamboo stick. Very narrow along the street frontage, the buildings reach 30 to 50 meters into the block. Shop houses can be a fire trap, with only one exit towards the front. Close to the midpoint in each block, room has to be made for a sizeable break between back-to-back facing structures. When connected to the breaks between neighbouring structures, these spaces serve as lateral escape routes in case of fire; a break at midpoint also provides access to sewer connections and acts as an air space to improve natural ventilation.

When designing infill projects for vacant sites, we enjoyed the challenge of inventing new expressions of historic building forms. The work demonstrated how to preserve the

▶ Figure 2.3.4 (opposite)

Contemporary expressions of the historic shop-house typology (drawings for this project were made by Brian Chambers, Hugo Corro, Richard Crockett, Karlene Gullone, Leo Hammond, Kelly Janes, Se-Woong Kim, Qinbo Liu, Mohammed Momin, Sarah Moos and Deepak Sohane).

126 PART II The Pearl River Delta

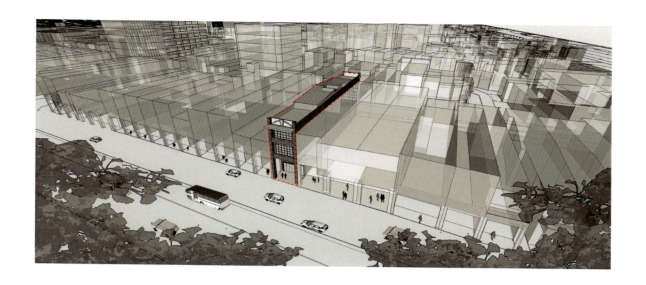

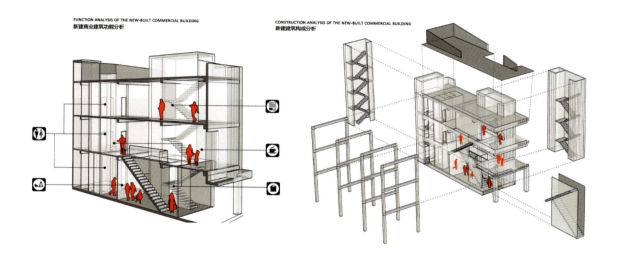

FUNCTION ANALYSIS OF THE NEW-BUILT COMMERCIAL BUILDING
新建商业建筑功能分析

CONSTRUCTION ANALYSIS OF THE NEW-BUILT COMMERCIAL BUILDING
新建建筑构成分析

CHAPTER 3 Jiangmen, a Historic City

traditional compact urban form typical of delta cities. If implemented, the typological work would not only exemplify the restoration of historic districts, but might also be applicable as sustainable urban form in new developments outside historic city centers.[1]

Along the river promenade, people of all ages gather. The same is true for the pedestrian shopping street. Streets in the hot and humid monsoon climate are comfortable when narrow and well ventilated. The heat exchange between sunny and shaded surfaces produces ambient ventilation. Walking under the thick canopy of banyan trees along the river is surprisingly comfortable, even on hot days; the same is true for the arcaded streets.

The reality in modern-day China of course is that residents who can afford car ownership have moved away from historic settlements to modern developments. In the traditional settlements, pedestrians, bicycles and mopeds dominate the streets, and this is certainly not due to a preference for a car-free lifestyle. Observations about income, car ownership and mobility raise important questions about social justice. The reader might wonder who in the

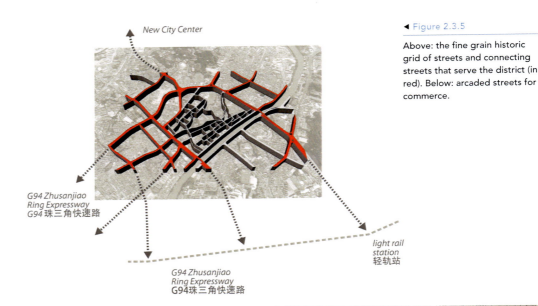

◀ Figure 2.3.5

Above: the fine grain historic grid of streets and connecting streets that serve the district (in red). Below: arcaded streets for commerce.

128　　　　　　　　　　　　　　　　　　　　　　　　　　　　　　　　PART II The Pearl River Delta

end will benefit from incremental renewal of historic districts like Jiangmen. For current residents to benefit from improvements, the improvements must remain affordable for workers who earn surprisingly low wages in an economy where the costs for housing and transportation have risen disproportionately to wages. Updating historic structures to meet current safety standards would require code enforcement grants from the national and prefecture governments. Low-interest loans would also be necessary to support individual owners and institutions with the upgrade of their properties. On balance though, the value created in this manner would outrank the new dispersed housing on the city's periphery.

What is touched upon is an old story, relived again and again in different parts of the world. At first the new towers and housing blocks on the outskirts provide welcome relief from the crowded, unsanitary conditions of the historic city. Access to light and modern furnishings hold great appeal. But then social deprivations set in. Starting with city extensions or slum clearance projects that were built in the mid-20th century, 30 to 40 years later they were demolished or in need of significant repair. Even in settings of high rise towers, there is surprisingly little life on the ground. Much of the ground-level space was only necessary because of tower separation laws. For human activities, the space remains deserted; buildings are not oriented to places where people need to be. The disintegration of the new housing from streets, or from other highly organized public spaces, became seemingly inevitable. Much of recent urbanization in China followed that paradigm. One can only imagine the amount of repair that will be needed 30 years from now, when the merits of new high-rise clusters in Pearl River Delta Cities will be questioned. One could even speculate that a new generation of people who have grown up with ubiquitous digital communication could become place bound in such historic structures of arcaded streets and blocks, because a city designed for physical mobility is no longer part of their way of life.

What Walter Gropius Could Not Have Known

Much urbanization in China follows design principles associated with the Modern Movement. Slabs and towers are placed using a misinterpretation of Walter Gropius' 1929 building separation diagram (Rowe & Koetter, 1979, p. 57); the result is undesignated open space. City life near the ground level of buildings is deadened by the lack of supporting human activities.

The prospect of climate change has made city designers come full circle, to no longer advocate for broad streets and structures detached from their context, but for a compact urban form. As Richard Rogers explains:

> the compact city – with development grouped around public transport, walking, and cycling – is the only environmentally sustainable form of a city. However, for population densities to increase and for walking and cycling to be widespread, a city must increase the quality and quantity of well-planned beautiful public spaces that are human in scale, sustainable, healthy, safe, and lively.[2]

▶ Figures 2.3.6a and 2.3.6b

Four-minute walk into the historic center of Jiangmen. The 30 frames describe a walk of about 4 minutes in length. To experience the sense of motion, the reader should hold the pages of the book closer to the eyes than customary and "read" the images from bottom to top by scanning the columns of images upwards from the bottom to the top of the page. The upwards movement of the eyes produces progression forwards. As in allegorical paintings, what lies in the future is above, what is past lies below.

PART II The Pearl River Delta

CHAPTER 3 Jiangmen, a Historic City

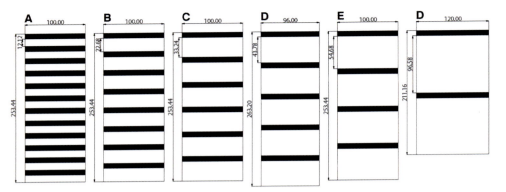
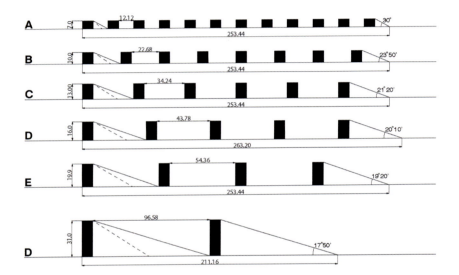

◄ Figure 2.3.7

Walter Gropius: diagram showing the development of a rectangular site with parallel rows of apartment blocks. Sun access angles determine the separation of structures. (Source: Bauhaus Archive, Berlin.)

Pazhou Island, an Urban Extension of Guangzhou's New Central Business District

Development on Pazhou Island in Guangzhou is typical of urban extensions in China. Located across the Zhujiang, a branch of the Pearl River, the island now belongs to Guangzhou's central business district. The new district came into existence prior to the Asia Games of 2010. Consistent with Chinese Feng Shui tradition, a new axis was laid out from the mountains in the north to the river branches in the south. The axis defines five major functional zones in neat hierarchical order. In this day and age, one would assume that there is no need to separate high-end commerce from administrative offices, or waterfront housing from a science and technology innovative zone, or from an ecological and recreational zone. An integration of these five functions would be more desirable, because the weaving together of uses and functions creates a higher level of urbanity, reduces movement between zones and results in a more compact urban form. Most importantly such integration would have saved space. But that was not to be. The new axis was centred to the south on the 600-meter high Canton Tower. From the tower, when completed in 2010, fireworks rained down onto the opening and closing ceremony at a large stage built on Haixinsha Island. Also ready in time for the games and near the foot of the tower, Guangzhou new Opera House[3] opened in 2010.

Prior to the conditions that came about when the new axis was laid out, the islands between the distributaries of the Bei River were referred to as "south of the river" and had a folkloristic appeal. Pazhou Island was the site of the Pearl River Brewing Company, a very popular Chinese beer with 48,000 bottles consumed per hour! Further to the east on Pazhou Island, the Pazhou Convention and Exhibition Center opened. Inside huge hangar like structures, Guangzhou hosts the bi-annual Canton Import and Export Fair. Between the fairground and to the south of the former brewery, traces of a former village exist on Pazhou Island. The village was mostly demolished and residents were relocated into rows of 30 floor slab type towers, but a school remained and some villagers still live in their historic structures. There is also an agricultural farm on the island that is run by the Vegetable Science Institute and is part of the Guangdong Agricultural University. The institute is a remnant of the island's historic agricultural use. Low-lying and subject to periodic floods, the entire island was used by villagers for traditional agriculture.

City government converted the remaining farmland on Pazhou Island and designated the land as a cultural and new media center. The concept is simple: Guangdong Province needs new types of industry; every forward-looking politician would agree. The region's excellent universities produce young engineers trained to work on software development for new media, integrated technology and marketing tools for a growing consumer-oriented society. Nobody knows exactly what form such activities will take, but planners felt that a generous street grid of 160 meters by 160 meters should be able to accommodate various types of buildings.

▼ Figure 2.3.8

Aerial view of Guangzhou new axis. The Canton tower is visible just to the south of the river. In its current form, the axis projects across a small island to the northern bank of the river and towards the upper right hand corner of the view. (Source: Google Earth, October 2015.)

CHAPTER 3 Jiangmen, a Historic City

▶ Figure 2.3.9

The morphology of an island. From top:
   First: the historic maps reveal that four east–west running canals once drained the island after floods and irrigated the fields when needed. Also, the northern riverbank of Pazhou Island is shown in a condition prior to river regulation.
   Second: in 1970 the site is still used predominantly for agriculture.
   Third: in 2000 the riverbank along the Pearl River is reclaimed with a new levee and a new bridge is built for the privately financed South China Expressway. Xingang Road, a new east–west street is built and historic Pazhou village is relocated.
   Fourth: in 2010 a second highway bridge across the Pearl River was completed prior to the Asia Games.
   Fifth: in 2015 at the former brewery site, the large hops kilns and bottling plants are dismantled. A regular grid of 160 by 160 meters is laid onto the agricultural land to develop a cultural and new media center. The three canals are abandoned. One new canal is built. Two additional subway lines are planned to serve the new development.

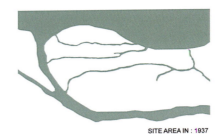
SITE AREA IN : 1937

SITE AREA IN : 1970

SITE AREA IN : 2000

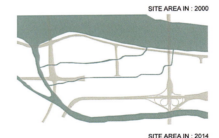
SITE AREA IN : 2014

SITE AREA IN PROPOSED MASTERPLAN : 2015

In California's Silicon Valley, activities similar to those mentioned here are housed in different configurations that range in form: cramped converted loft spaces with only a business card taped to a glass sliding door or campus-like settings where even internationally renowned firms reuse nondescript buildings.[4] Rarely have companies built ostentatious lakeside towers with fountains like ORACLE. The latter is rare; the former more common. New technology is a volatile industry, expanding, contracting and constantly changing. Predictable are the ever larger servers that everyone depends on. On Pazhou Island it might have been better to leave the bottling and fermentation plants in place after the racks of stainless steel containers and conveyors were removed. New technology can operate inside conventional office towers, but that is not where it thrives. The masterplan for Pazhou Island did not consider keeping the structures of the former brewery. In 2015, a new conventional office tower for a telecommunications firm was under construction on one of the 160 meter by 160 meter large blocks. Neatly centered in the middle, the building left much undesignated open land around the block's perimeter.

Adaptation to a new form of urban expansion calls for a rethinking of decisions that so fundamentally influence city form and the way of life of workers who will occupy these towers. For example, the integration of working and living should be encouraged. A government official after our presentation said, "there is no law that prohibits us from considering housing on these new blocks. . . and we should, it would cut down the commute trips office workers make". The wide streets with intersections every 160 meters would significantly discourage pedestrians. The telecommunication headquarters will not allow pedestrians to walk through their new city block, nor will others in the future. A gated perimeter is preferred. Streets are dedicated to vehicular movements, cumbersome to cross on foot, thus a barrier for other modes of movement. Smaller block sizes serving multiple functions like housing integrated with work spaces, more streets, and streets designed for pedestrians and cyclist are the answer.

Adaption to a new form of urbanity starts at a more fundamental level. Literally, it starts with the water table of the Pearl River. Demolition debris has been placed on top of Pahzou's low-lying agricultural land, but with the significant increase in impermeable surfaces in the future, the land will still flood after heavy rains, and it will be inundated during rising tides, or periods of increased river discharge. The worst case scenario is that all three processes occur simultaneously.

In future, low-lying land with an elevation barely one meter above the water level of adjacent rivers should be designed like a sponge. Significant areas for water storage will be needed as buildings and roads seal the surface of the island and make it impermeable to water. The work starts with computations of the area needed for water storage. Most variables are known, others follow reasonable assumptions about precipitation, tidal movement and river discharge. The two remaining lakes need to be retained and will serve as managed ponds to store water after heavy rain events. The low-lying land of the agricultural institute should also be retained at its current low elevation to serve as a seasonal wetland. The agricultural institute might move in the near future, but here the land could still be used for water storage, or for recreation when dry. What is left of the canal system is also needed for storage and to drain the land after floods. Figure 2.3.12 shows the calculations that we did to compute the amount of land needed for water retention and for the design of a drainage system.

New roads built on the island will need to accommodate a significant number of pipes of sizeable diameter below their surfaces. Next to roads, strips of land will be designed to absorb water and connect to the underground pipes in cases of an overflow of rainwater.

▼ Figure 2.3.10

In our proposal, a finer grain of urban blocks on the developable land of Pazhou Island encourages the integration of housing, work and recreation.

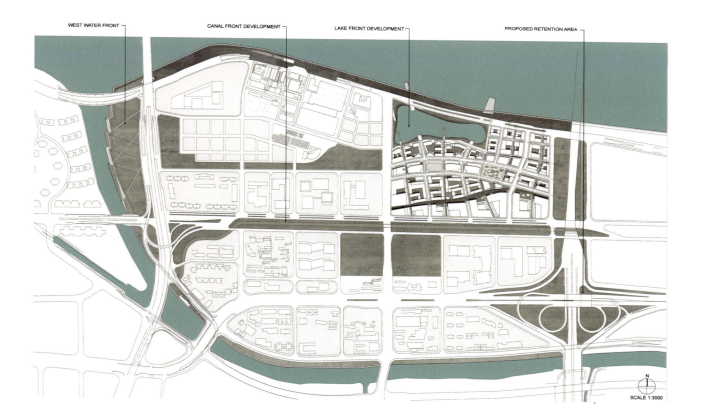

CHAPTER 3 Jiangmen, a Historic City

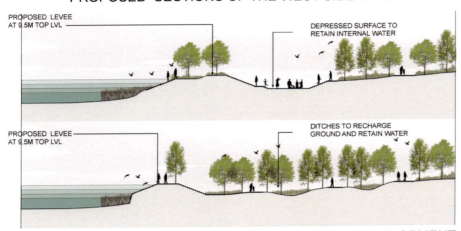

◀ Figure 2.3.11

Top: the section shows the low-lying land on Pahzou Island at its historic elevation with a projected flood level superimposed.

Top middle: the land along river and canals of the island will be protected by a new levee with an elevation of 9.5 meters above m.s.l.

Below middle: low-lying surfaces are designed to retain runoff water.

Below: managed pond to retain surface water.

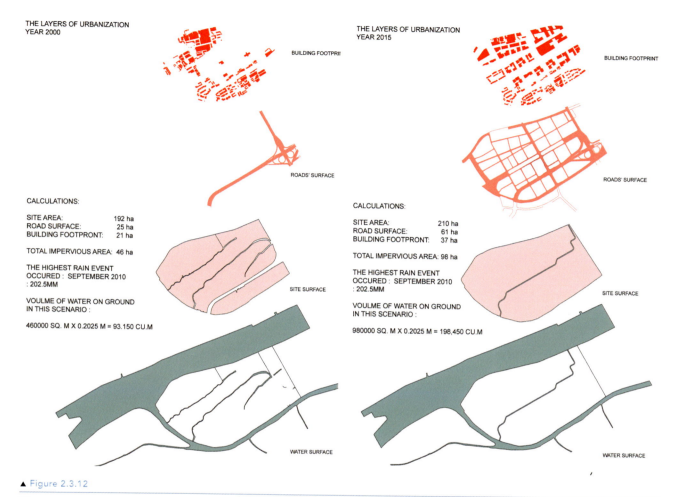

▲ Figure 2.3.12

Water storage computation comparing predevelopment conditions with development proposed under the 2015 Masterplan. The bottom of the riverbed is at 3 meters above m.s.l., the water table of the Pearl River at Pazhou Island measures 6.3 meters. The ground elevation on the island measures 7.5 meters above m.s.l. The surface area of the site slated for development is approximately 200 hectares and the impervious surface in its predevelopment condition totals 46 hectares, an area that will increase to 98 hectares once developed. Given a rain event similar to that of 10 September 2010, when 202.5 mm fell, the volume of water on the undeveloped site measured 93.150 cubic meters. With new development, the amount of water on the site would increase to 180.000 cubic meters.

Living with Water – Strategies for the Future

When Chinese settlers first arrived in what we call the Pearl River Delta, the area was not a delta but on open sea. When the city of Guangzhou had its beginning, it was located at the shore of this large inland sea. The landform started to change very slowly at first but more noticeably by the end of the Song Dynasty, 960–1279 and during late imperial China. What is now a delta could then be best described as a large bowl-shaped inland sea filled with shallow water and chains of small islands. Agricultural practices and early water control projects along the West River changed the channeling of river sediments. The deposits first formed sand banks and then an interconnected shoreline between, eventually, eight estuaries. But these topographies only formed during the Qing Dynasty, 1644–1911.

The modeling done at Key Laboratories for Coastal Studies in Shanghai, at the Hong Kong Observatory and at the Atmospheric, Marine Coastal Environmental Program at Hong Kong University of Science and Technology predict inundation of the delta to the condition that prevailed in history. Like elsewhere in the world, scientists there use for their predictions the Fourth Assessment Report of the Inter Government Panel on Climate Change from 2007.[5] The panel predicted sea level will rise during the remainder of this century by 0.41 meters, due to the thermal expansion of water molecules. The physics of this phenomenon are well explained; they relate to a rise in water temperature in the global oceans. Added to that, the panel projects a melting of glaciers, or the so-called "mountain ice", by another 0.17 meters. Finally, and here is where uncertainty sets in, the melting of the Greenland ice shield – land ice, as it is called – would add another 0.17 meters. The uncertainty of these predictions is now the focus of much discussion. The panel concluded in 2007 that the total sea level rise would amount to 0.59 meters. Among scientists today, there is agreement that such predictions were conservative and that the melting of ice at both polar ice shields would be faster, thus sea level rise higher and sooner than estimated.

It is probably the very slow process of sea level rise that has led to so much complacency among policy and decision makers in all three settings covered by this book. In Hong Kong, the gauge at the observatory in Victoria Harbor shows only a 2.6 mm annual rise in seawater, or a 14 cm rise since the station was established in 1954 (Lee & Woo, 2010). That is seawater when conditions are still. More concerning and noticeable in the recent past have been the shortened times between extreme storm events. These are storm surges generated by tropical or extra-tropical typhoons, and their increased frequency and intensity is related to global warming. Six tropical typhoons per year have occurred on average. Such typhoons raise sea level by 0.5 meters to 1.0 meters. In extreme cases, when typhoons coincide with atmospheric high tides (twice a month), seawater has risen by 3 meters or more. Such a catastrophic event occurred in 2009, when typhoon Koppu reached Hong Kong. One year earlier, typhoon Hagupit reached the shore near Hong Kong on Sep 24, 2008 and produced 3.96 meters above m.s.l. datum. Both events caused extensive coastal flooding. Such events are considered 100-year floods, meaning the likelihood of their occurrence is one flood in 100 years. A flood reaching a height of 340 cm above m.s.l. datum now occurs every 20 years. Typhoons Koppu of 2009 and Hagupit of 2008 were preceded by typhoon Ellen in 1983 and the legendary Wanda on 1 September 1962.

There is another variable to consider in making sea level rise predictions. As in other river deltas, the Pearl River Delta is subject to long-term geological subsidence. Using interferometric synthesis aperture radar (ISAR) a team of scientists measured coastal subsidence near Shenzhen, 500 meters from the coast and estimated an annual subsidence of 2.5 to 6.0 mm per year (Wang, 2012). Miniscule, even trivial, as these numbers might seem, they add up. Thus the current prediction that sea level will rise to 30 cm by 2030, taking ground subsidence and coastal sediment deposits into consideration (Huang, et al., 2004). Coastal sediment deposits total 86.36 million tons of silt annually (Weng, 2007) and continue to produce a southwards migration of coastlines into the South China Sea. If shaped into horizontal barriers, they can protect the shoreline in the estuaries by ameliorating the forces of storm surges.

A long-range view is necessary to address the response to climate change. Responses will need to be designed for the entire delta region, but importantly responses will be shaped by local conditions. A uniform urbanization pattern will no longer be viable. All new construction, whether it be the repair of towns and villages or new urban extensions, needs to focus on water management as a primary concern. Inundation of the Pearl River Delta is currently predicted to cover 42% of its 17,200 km² by 2030 (other estimates are higher). Most affected will be the low-lying plains that measure 0.7 to 0.9 meters below mean sea level and those

▶ Figure 2.3.13 (opposite)

Making room for water under streets and along the river front. The map view recommends a more finely scaled block pattern that encourages a better integration of workplaces and residential functions, thus a lower dependence on commuting and a greater encouragement to walk. (Drawings for this project were made by Justin Kearnan, David Cooke, Huiyi Zhang, Chuwei Yang, Ying Ding, Haochen Yang, Xingling Cai, Ken Hirose, Cacena Cambell, Yi Hu, Junxi Wu, Zeyue Yao, Yining Ying, Bilin Chen and Lolein Bergers, Stephanie Brucart and Katrina OrtizJiang Hewen, Li Chenxue, Shen Xinxin, Xu Xiang, Zhang Ao; Adam Molinski, Eden Ferry, Kaleen Juarez and Kevin Lenhart.)

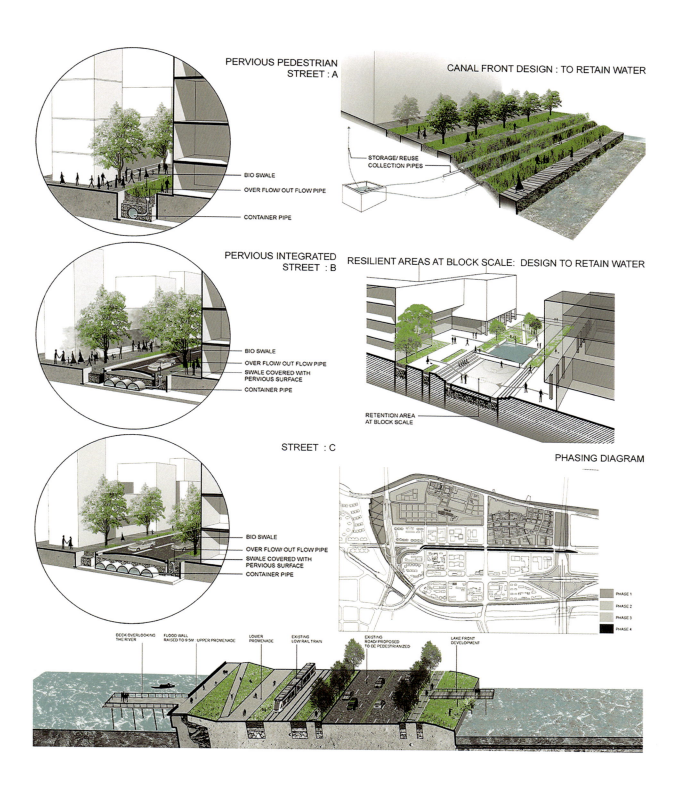

CHAPTER 3 Jiangmen, a Historic City

▲ Figure 2.3.14

Aerial view of Pazhou Island (source: Google Earth, Pazhou Island in December, 2015).

higher plains up to 1.0 m above sea level. As we have seen in the preceding chapters, substantial low-income communities have lived in these low-lying areas. Here the urbanization strategies will address how to house a large population in a manner that is affordable, safe and livable.

Much will be done to prevent a 42% inundation of the Pearl River Delta's 17.200 km² with now over 100 million inhabitants. Adaptations will be imperative and they will continue to affect the form of cities. Reasons for adaptations not only come from the need to address sea level rise and the more frequent return periods between coastal floods along the delta's extensive shorelines, but also from flood danger in the upstream reaches of the deltas. With the very low longitudinal gradient along rivers and channels of 0.0023% in the West River (Weng, 2007), rising tides reach far inland, and with them saltwater will intrude into agricultural land. Rising tides and floods will also block discharge channels at times of intensive rainfall. Living with water in Pearl River Delta communities will require more water storage areas and interconnected systems of canals that store water until discharge is possible through gravity. Therefore, in all projects discussed here we have addressed water management strategies together with improved urbanization practices.

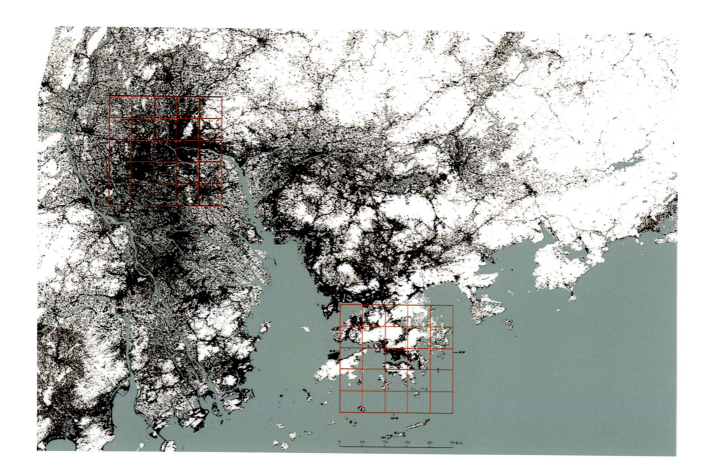

▲ Figure 2.3.15

Urbanization in the Pearl River Delta in 2015. The two squares superimposed on Guangzhou and Hong Kong measure 50 kilometers by 50 kilometers.

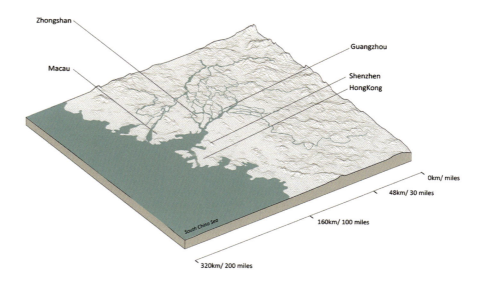

▶ Figure 2.3.16

Pearl River Delta topography with vertical elevations exaggerated twentyfold (map by Kushal Lachhawani).

CHAPTER 3 Jiangmen, a Historic City

Existing Sea Level + Flood

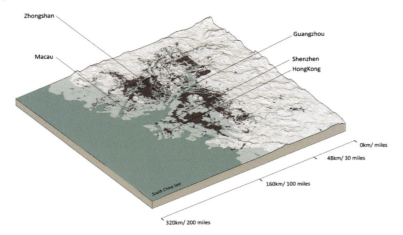

1m/ 39" Sea Level + Flood

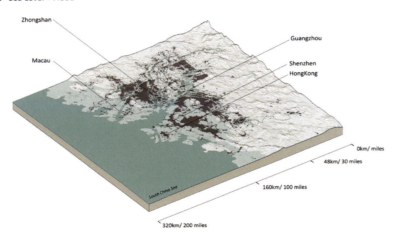

6m/ 236" Sea Level + Flood

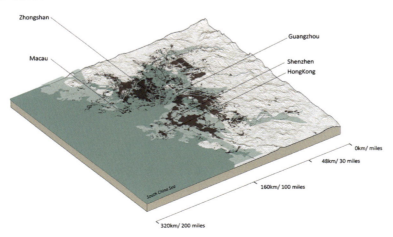

◀ Figure 2.3.17

Pearl River Delta topography with vertical elevations exaggerated twentyfold, a) existing condition, b) 1-meter sea level rise, c) 6-meter storm surge. (Maps by Kushal Lachawani based on Wong, Lau, & Gray, 2007.)

Notes

1 The architecture typology described here was echoed by Renee Chow (2015).
2 Richard Rogers in the introduction to Jan Gehl's book (Gehl, 2010).
3 Designed by Zaha Hadid.
4 The Google and Facebook campuses come to mind.
5 Intergovernmental panel on climate change (Solomon, et al, 2007).

References

Chow, R., 2015. *Changing Chinese Cities: The Potential of Field Urbanism*. Honolulu: U. of Hawaii Press.

Gehl, J., 2010. *Cities for People*. Washington DC: Island Press.

Huang, Z., Zong, Y. & Zhang, W., 2004. Coastal inundation due to sea level rise in the Pearl River Delta. *Natural Hazards*, 33(2), pp. 247–264.

Lee, W. T. W. & Woo, W., 2010. *Sea-level Rise and Storm Surge–Impacts of Climate Change on Hong Kong*. Hong Kong, Hong Kong Observatory, pp. 1–8.

Rowe, C. & Koetter, F., 1979. *Collage City*. Cambridge, MA: MIT Press.

Solomon, S. et al., eds, 2007. *Contribution of Working Group I to the Fourth Assessment Report of the Intergovernmental Panel on Climate Change*. Cambridge, UK & New York, USA: Cambridge University Press.

Wang, H., 2012. NSAR reveals coastal subsidence in the Pearl River Delta, China. *Geophysical Journal International, Oxford Journals*, 91(3), pp. 1119–1128.

Weng, Q., 2007. A historical perspective of river basin management in the Pearl River Delta. *Journal of Environmental Management*, 85(4), pp. 1048–1062.

Wong, A., Lau, A. & Gray, J., 2007. *Impact of Sea Level Rise on Storm Surge in Hong Kong and Pearl River Delta*. [Online] Available at: www.hkccf.org/download/iccc2007/31May/S6B/Agnes WONG/... [Accessed 27 February 2017].

Part III | The Dutch Delta

Fernand Braudel starts his environmental history of the Mediterranean (Braudel, 1996) with the heading "mountains come first". To likewise start a narrative on the Rhine-Maas-Scheldt Delta with a reference to mountains will strike most readers as counterintuitive. The highest elevation in the Netherlands is 322 meters in the extreme southern corner of the country. Nevertheless, starting with mountains makes geological and historic sense, because it changes the perspective from which we view the Low Countries. Several mountain ranges in particular hold importance for the Dutch Delta. At the "Roof of Europe" in Switzerland's Grion Alps, tributaries of the Rhine, Danube and Po Rivers have their origins at the 2,645-meter high Piz Lunghin next to the Septimer Pass. There are, of course, many tributaries to the Rhine River, but here at the Septimer Pass, a crossing of the Alps is possible by traversing only one mountain ridge. In antiquity, this pass was known to connect the Mediterranean south of Europe to the north via the Upper Rhine Valley. The Romans made more extensive use of that passage than the other well-known crossings used today, and so did Venetian traders. Once across the Alps' Albula Range, traveling along the Upper Rhine Valley was the obvious route, a route that led to the Low Countries.

Another good reason to begin a narrative on the Rhine-Maas-Scheldt Delta with mountains is that it dates the age of the delta's rivers. The Maas, or Meuse as it is called in France and Belgium, is among the oldest rivers in the world (Nienhuis, 2008) with an age of 380 million years; the Rhine ranks sixth, at 240 million years. Geologists are relatively certain about these facts. The Maas is older than the mountains it dissects, meaning the force of the water continued to cut its path through the Ardennes as this mountain range folded upwards. This crustal upheaval took place during the Hercynian age for the Maas. In the case of the Rhine, mountains rose during the Triassic age, but here the geologists are not as certain. The Rhine also transverses the mid-Rhine range, only somewhat younger than the Ardennes, thus the river could be older than currently assumed. Why are observations about the age of mountains and the rivers that dissect them important in a book on the form of cities? To think about natural processes, in the form of river dynamics, is a reminder (Mann, 1973) that water has held a permanent place in earth's history, thus in the origins of civilizations, the movement of people and the need to build cities near rivers, but also underlines the precariousness of doing so.

I use the term "Low Countries" to include the northern and western part of the Netherlands, where land is located barely above, and in many places significantly below, sea level. This definition of the Low Countries also includes parts of Belgium and East-Friesland in Germany.

The term "Holland" follows a political definition, indicating the Dutch provinces of North and South Holland, two of the twelve provinces that make up today's Netherlands. When Holland is mentioned in history, reference is made to the domain of the Counts of Holland. The Netherlands is a relatively recent label for a country that came into existence as an independent kingdom after the Napoleonic wars in 1815; initially it included Belgium

▲ Figure 3.1

Rhine–Maas–Scheldt catchment areas. The map also includes the Ems River catchment area to the east. (Map by M.T. Pouderoijen, TU Delft.)

▲ Figure 3.2

The Netherlands from satellite (source: http://geodus.com).

PART III The Dutch Delta

and Luxemburg, and after 1830 in its present boundaries. Prior to French occupation, from 1795 to 1813, a union of seven provinces formed at Utrecht after the defeat of the Spanish Habsburgs in 1579; the new country was internationally recognized as a republic at the treaty of Münster in 1646 and referred to in the English-speaking world as the Dutch Republic, or the Seven United Provinces (Prak, 2010).

The term "Randstad" was coined by planners in 1968. The term describes the polycentric form of the urbanized region, where cities like Amsterdam, Harlem, Leiden, The Hague, Delft, Rotterdam, Dordrecht, Utrecht and a number of smaller communities form an urban rim around a green heart. Finally, the definition of the term "delta" follows geological reasoning. For the purposes of this book, I use the term "Dutch Delta" to include the mouths of the Rhine, Maas and Scheldt rivers and drainage basins from the IJssel in the north-east to the Western Scheldt in the south-west.

References

Braudel, F., 1996. *The Mediterranean and the Mediterranean World in the Time of Phillip II*. Berkeley: University of California Press.

Mann, R., 1973. *Rivers in the City*. New York: Praeger.

Nienhuis, P., 2008. *Environmental History of the Rhine–Meuse Delta: An Ecological Story on Evolving Human–environmental Relations Coping with Climate Change and Sea-level Rise*. Dordrecht: Springer Netherlands.

Prak, S., 2010. The Dutch Republic as a bourgeois society. *BMGN Low Countries Historical Review*, 125(2/3), pp. 107–139.

Chapter 1

The Making of the Dutch Delta

At a time 130,000 years ago, at the end of the Saalian Glaciation, when large surface areas of the earth were covered by ice, the south to north draining Northern European rivers discharged water below the ice shield and started to shape the land and the deltas of the Low Countries.

The Great Rivers

Between Arnhem and Nijmegen, the Rhine branches into several distributaries. The northern one is the IJssel, which runs into the IJsselmeer. In counterclockwise direction, the Lower Rhine separates near Utrecht into the Crooked Rhine, then the Old Rhine, and enters the North Sea near Leiden. At Utrecht, the Rhine is also met by the Vecht, which connects to the IJmeer near Amsterdam. To the east of Nijmegen, most of the Rhine's discharge runs due west through the Waal. From there, the Waal runs parallel to the Maas until their confluence, and creates common outlets through the Neder Rijn, the Lek, the Old Maas and the Merwede. To add to the multitudes of Rhine River distributaries, there is also a Hollandsche IJssel, different and distinct from the IJssel mentioned first. The river Scheldt originates in France and joins into the Dutch Delta from the south. In addition, a great number of canals make connections between rivers. The water system of river, canals and distributaries is full of complexity and has been subject to much change over the centuries.

The combined discharge of the Rhine and Maas is seasonally conditioned. Over the last 50 years, the average discharge of the Rhine at the Dutch border with Germany has been 2,200m³/sec. The Rhine is both a rain-fed river and a snow-melt-water river, with two different drainage peaks per year, in January and February, and then in June and July. The Rhine's lowest discharge takes place in October, with an average of 1,600 m³/sec (Van de Ven, 1993). The highest known discharge at the Dutch–German border was measured in January 1926 at 13,000m³/sec. The river was then 6 meters higher than normal.[1] The discharge of the Maas is considerably lower, with an average of 250m³/sec. But the Maas is notorious for its sudden rises due to the fact that the Maas traverses the solid granite of the Ardennes with little water loss absorbed into the ground. Only very recently have countries upstream from the Netherlands received the political mandate to monitor water quality and discharge along the Rhine, Maas and Scheldt (European Union Directive 2000/60/EC, 2000).

For centuries, rivers with their changing paths dispersed across the large expanse of the Low Countries. Tributaries silted up and rivers found new stream beds that channeled around glacial moraines and through barrier dunes at the seashore. The ice age had left the surface of the land highly compacted with boulder clay. Encouraged by the warming climate and the high amount of surface water, intensive vegetation covered the land between the coastal dunes and the glacial moraines. Along streams, mineral deposits encouraged the growth of trees, which eventually resulted in a woodland landscape that would change its form and composition depending upon the constantly changing configuration of rivers, creeks and fens. The decaying plant material produced layer upon layer of peat, and depending upon the composition of the decaying plant material, raised bog peat areas built up on top of earlier peat from reed and sedges, both on top of the compacted boulder clay.

As a result of this process, around 100 AD, the western part of the Low Countries behind the barrier dunes was dominated by large areas of peat moor, which rose several meters above sea level and above the level of the rivers. The change at that time and in the centuries that followed was a rise in sea level induced by climate change. From 300 to 800

▼ Figure 3.1.1

Map of rivers, estuaries and places named in the text. In dark blue, all elevations below 10 meters. (Map by Steffen Nijhuis.)

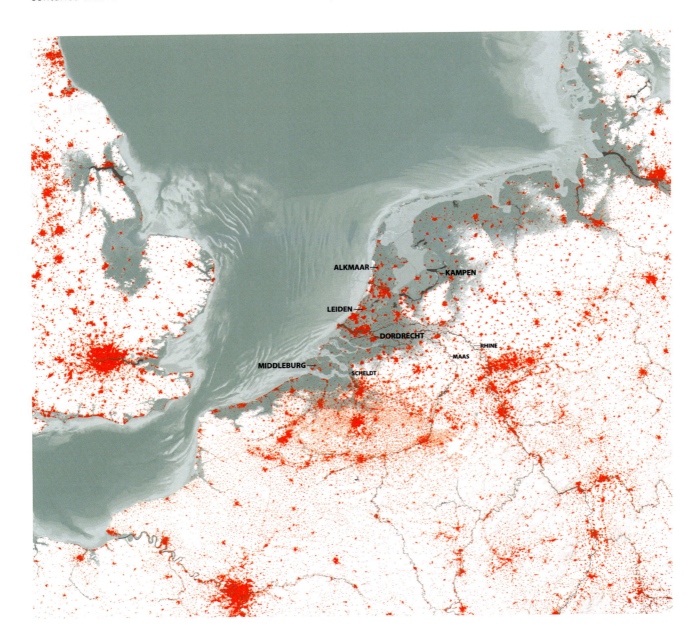

150   PART III The Dutch Delta

AD, continued sea level rise breached the barrier dunes at the mouth of the Maas and Rhine, tore inlets into the peat deposits, drained deposits out to sea, and covered their remnants with marine clay. The contours of the present coastline and delta became evident (Nienhuis, 2008, p. 30). The draw from the new coastal incision of that time changed the drainage pattern of the Rhine away from its northerly course to the west through the Waal and formed the Maas-Rhine-Scheldt Delta.

The time when rivers directed their own freely braiding and meandering channels largely disappeared from the 12th century onwards. A dike here, a lock there, dams, pumping stations, and weirs everywhere turned the Netherlands into a vast control panel. Control indeed is necessary; it is designed to manage rivers, lakes, estuaries and canals, thus greatly influencing the fate of human settlements. Without it, towns and villages would have drowned below the waves as they did in Zealand (Meyer, et al., 2010),[2] and in North Holland, where towns and fishing villages disappeared or were cut off from their access to the open sea.

Currently a control station near Arnhem controls the water distribution of the Rhine in a highly sophisticated manner. For as long as possible in any given year, the water discharge from the Rhine sends 285m^3/sec into the IJssel, the Rhine's former northern course (although there is some debate about whether the IJssel ever was a distributary of the Rhine), and 25m^3/sec into the Old Rhine. The remainder goes into the North Sea through the Waal, Merwede and the New Waterway between Rotterdam and Hook van Holland. The control station at Arnhem directs sufficient water into the IJsselmeer for storage, prevents the intrusion of saltwater, and maintains water levels for navigation along canals and rivers. Especially important here is the oceangoing navigation on the North Sea Canal between Amsterdam and the North Sea.

Shoreline along the North Sea

After the last ice age, the main rivers deposited large amounts of sediment, which accumulated along the shoreline. This material created a shoreline along the North Sea with a closed configuration of barrier dunes. Four tidal inlets formed through the dune barrier creating estuaries into which the rivers drained. The most northern estuary, *Flevum*, formed in correspondence with the glacial valley of the IJ. This ancient riverbed, in Dutch referred to as the *OerIJ*, is believed to have functioned as one of the northern drainage channels of the Rhine during the ice age. Its mouth was located to the south of today's Alkmaar, but silted in during Roman times. A second, called *Rhenus*, further south at Katwijk near today's Leiden, provided the mouth of today's Old Rhine, a third, the *Helenium*, seaward of the combined Maas-Waal-Lek-Merwede discharge, and finally a fourth, the *Scaldis*, at the mouth of the Scheldt (Nienhuis, 2008, p. 30). In my curiosity to explore the shape of towns in response to water, I have selected a town near each of the four river drainage basins: Alkmaar in the North, Leiden near the central coast, Dordrecht in South Holland and Middelburg in Zealand.

I had to add a fifth town, Kampen, at the mouth of the IJssel, and that has to do with the history of the IJsselmeer, the former Zuiderzee, and before that known as the Almere or Flevo Lacus. The four names refer to a body of water that greatly changed its shape through recorded history and alternated between saline and freshwater, tidal and still water in its 2,000-year history.

The former Zuiderzee (South Sea) as an estuary originated in the 13th century after North Sea storms broke through the northern barrier dunes to flood the large low-lying land that stretched inland and connected the Almere (Great Lake) to the open sea.

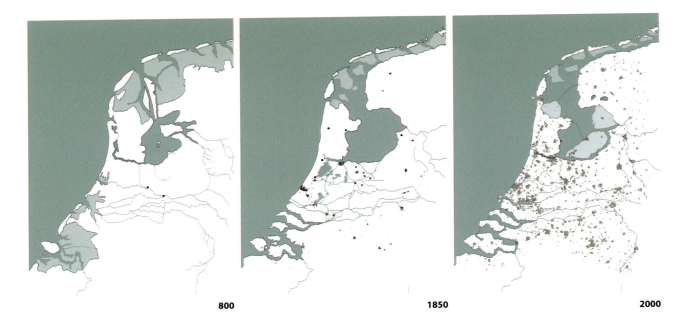

800   1850   2000

▲ Figure 3.1.2

Dutch coastline and river system. Left, around the year AD 800: Flevo Lacus – Almere. Middle, around 1850: Zuiderzee. Right, 2000: Ijsselmeer.

The Roman general Claudius Drusus, in 12 BC, on a naval campaign to explore Friesland, had traveled downstream from today's Cologne to a ford of the Rhine River near Trajectum. One would like to assume that the ford was at Trajectum, but the Roman *Castrum Trajectum*, today's Utrecht, was not started until AD 46, though *Batavorum Noviomagnus*, near today's Nijmegen, had its start in 12 BC during the time of Drusus' repeated campaigns into Germania Inferior. It became a town in 5 BC. We know that the silting of the northern branch of the Rhine, the Crooked Rhine, and Old Rhine had already set in during Roman times and it is believed that Drusus ordered the digging of a canal between 12 BC and 9 BC. The Roman historian Tacitus (Harbers, 1981) gives evidence of such a project. Unconfirmed by archeology, the canal would have been the first large-scale diversion of water away from the Waal to the IJssel, the Lower Rhine, and Old Rhine. The reasons for the canal were of a military nature. Drusus needed a transport route to bring in troops and supplies for his campaign against the Frisians (Lambert, 1985, p. 45). His mission was to confirm the *Limes* as a boundary of the Roman Empire by conducting forays against Germanic tribes across the Rhine. After Drusus, who was a stepson of the Emperor Augustus and father of the later Emperor Claudius, Rome fortified the northern *limes* from Colognia Ariquippa, Cologne, with military camps (*castra*), on the left bank of the Rhine up to the sea near today's Leiden at Katwijk.[3]

From Batavorum/Nijmegen, either through the IJssel or through the Vecht, Drusus reached a body of water that in Roman times was named Flevo Lacus and which connected to the open sea via the Vlie, a strait between today's islands of Vlieland and Terschelling. From there he sailed eastward along the Frisian coast and reached the mouth of the River Elbe in 9 BC (Lambert, 1985, p. 46).

Thirteenth century floods broke through the dune barrier, flushed out the peat deposits around the Almere and brought the sea inland to create a large saline estuary. These acts of nature gave a set of small fishing villages around the Zuidersee, most prominently among them Amsterdam, but earlier Kampen, access to ocean trade, first to trade with the Baltic countries and England, later with the rest of the world. The former Zuiderzee ranks among

PART III The Dutch Delta

estuaries for its short history. Human influences have changed many estuaries, but the largest of such interventions in Holland was the 1932 saline closure dike that separated the Zuiderzee from the North Sea and changed the water body into what is now known as the IJsselmeer, Marken Meer, and IJmeer, three connected inland lakes.

Delta Cities

The historian Rudolf Haepke (1908) in his work on Bruges fittingly refers to the Low Countries as an "Archipelago of Towns". That is what towns must have looked like, and frequently still look like, when seen in their horizontal landscape near water, one clearly in view, others in the distance, sometimes entirely surrounded by water.

We already mentioned a number of towns that came into existence during the Roman occupation, but dissolved with the fall of the Roman Empire in the late third century. Apparently a cold period began around 500 AD and lasted for two centuries (Nienhuis, 2008, p. 38). Sea level rise and more frequent transgressions of the sea through the dune barrier rendered the extensive peat moors behind the barrier dunes uninhabited. However, between 800 and 1250 AD the population of the Delta increased from 100,000 to 800,000 inhabitants (Van Dam, 2001). This period is marked by increased pressure to cultivate land and the forming of towns. The period is also characteristic of a systematic draining of the extensive peat landscape in the Low Countries. We mentioned that the raised peat bog had risen 1 to 3 meters above sea level and above the level of the dissecting rivers. That land would now be systematically drained. Peat was extracted and used as fuel for heating and, at a larger scale, for beer brewing, brick making and to gain salt. The newly exposed peat layers below the extraction

▶ Figure 3.1.3

Historic view of Alkmaar from the still undiked Schermeer by Hendrik Corneliz Vroom, 1638, oil on canvas, 103 x 209.5 cm (source: Stedelijk Museum Alkmaar).

oxidized due to their new surface exposure and due to cultivation; the surface compacted and land started to subside. The land, now under cultivation, required more and deeper trenches for drainage, which resulted in additional subsidence until the level of land became as low as the level of the rivers. Inadvertently, occasional flooding resulted. Sea level rise due to greater climate variability, high tides and storm events brought water inland. Left with no choice but to block the water from entering the land, the people of the Low Countries learned the art and science of water defense. They started to build levees and sluices. This is when the famous Dutch water boards came into existence. The planning, building and upkeep of dikes and sluices required sound organization. Johan van Veen, chief engineer of the water board in the 1940s, in his classic book, *Dredge, Drain and Reclaim, the Art of a Nation* (Van Veen, 1948, p. 23), gives a lucid account of the highly empirical and localized approach towards water management in Holland and Zealand. Van Veen's observations are taken a step further by the historian Geert Mak, who sees the roots of Dutch political culture in the localized and democratic manners in which water issues were dealt with. Since the dynamics of water affects virtually all aspects of life in towns and villages, water boards became powerful institutions, ruled not in a top down fashion, but in a decentralized manner through locally elected dike masters, so called *dijkgraven*, and participating boards (Mak, 2001, p. 11). In contrast to this widely held belief, the origins of the water boards are best described as that of a military organization with clear lines of command that need to be obeyed. Democratic elections of representatives became customary only in recent decades.

The years from 1150 to 1200 were a period of fundamental change in agriculture, trade, ship building and the growth of towns. This was also when typologies of town design emerged, characterized by a town on slightly elevated ground, on sandy soil and with gravel transported there by rivers. Such elevated grounds carried different names: *terp*, *burcht* or *fluchtberg*. These terms describe an elevated place, constructed or created by natural forces or both; a place to escape onto during floods but also to gather on for reason of defense. On such elevated dry ground, settlements started like clumps, often around a chapel. As the town expanded onto surrounding peat bog, strategies were needed in guiding the spatial structure that would only allow the construction of buildings and roads in a highly organized manner. Scattered built form could not be tolerated, because all structures on wet soil needed protection. The town on a mount mutated or expanded into a town on a dike or levee. Dikes became necessary when systematic peat extraction lowered the surrounding land. Water started to fill the excavated sites to form lakes. At this time in the history of Dutch urban form a second type of town resulted based on the *dam*. The *dam*, as in Amsterdam, Rotterdam, Edam, Monikendam, and other towns, is fundamentally the damming of a river with a sluice gate that prevents seawater from entering cultivated land during high tide and allows surface water to exit during low tide. One decision led to another, and the dam also took on military importance; it became the place for trans-loading from river barges to seaworthy vessels; it became the public square where business was conducted, frequently the

▼ Figure 3.1.4

Dam typology in the design of (left to right) Amsterdam, Rotterdam, Edam and Monikendam, by Jacob van Deventer around 1560. (Source: Environmental Design and Architecture map room at the Technical University, Delft.)

▶ Figure 3.1.5a

Aerial perspective of Amsterdam, 1538, by Cornelis Anthonisz (courtesy Amsterdam Historical Museum).

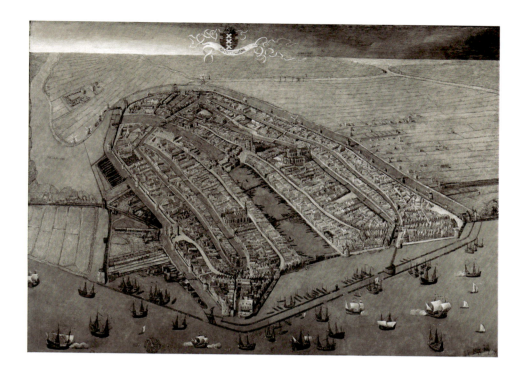

▶ Figure 3.1.5b

Dikes, dam and sluicegates of 16th century Amsterdam.

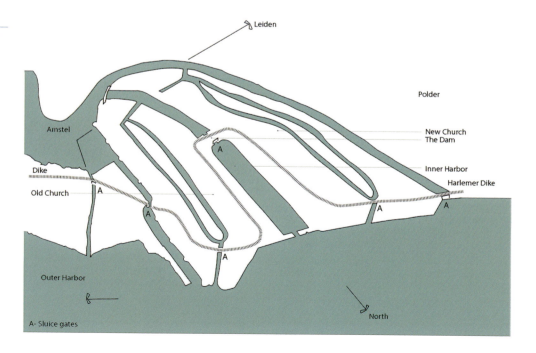

CHAPTER 1 The Making of the Dutch Delta

place for weighing goods and paying tolls and, in the case of Amsterdam, the place of the nearby mercantile exchange, where shipping gains and losses were traded.

Cartography

The art and science of water management required knowledge in surveying and mapmaking. Holland has produced some excellent mapmakers. One of them, Cornelis Anthonisz, produced an astonishing bird's-eye view of Amsterdam in 1538. The oil painting on a panel was intended as a gift for the Emperor Charles V, to be presented to him on his visit to Amsterdam. Unexplained is the fact that the Emperor never took the map with him when he left Amsterdam. Anthonisz's map can still be admired at the historic museum of the city. Also unexplained is the method that Anthonisz used to prepare an aerial perspective that appears so contemporary, detailed and accurate. In 1538, survey methods were of recent origin and came from Portugal or Italy (Bosselmann, 1998). I suspect Anthonisz must have prepared a geodesic survey, or partial survey, upon which he would have constructed his aerial perspective. Noteworthy is the detailed portrayal of the polder landscape around Amsterdam. The painting makes us reflect on the similarities between urban and rural land divisions that are only possible with detailed knowledge of surveying (Mak, 2001, p. 53). Also noteworthy and useful in the context of this book is Jacob van Deventer, who for 15 years until his death in 1575 mapped all Dutch cities of his time. The commission came from Phillip II of Spain for a set of maps drawn to the same graphic scale: 1:8,000. Clearly the maps were intended for military purposes, therefore kept secret. Deventer's life work was only rediscovered in 1859[4] in libraries in Madrid and Brussels.

Notes

1 Water levels in the Netherlands are measured against Normal Amsterdam Pail (NAP). In 1682, Johannes Hudde, the then Mayor of Amsterdam, established the NAP convention based upon a record of 48 water-level measurements daily. The number of daily measurements was later reduced to 24; at the German border the normal water level of the Rhine is +11m NAP (Van de Ven, 1993, p. 26).
2 Christian Sgroten, as cited by Joost Schrijnen and Jandrik Hoekstra in "The Southwest Delta: Towards a new Strategy" (Meyer, et al., 2010).
3 *Capitum Germanorum*, a fort now submerged under the waves off the coast.
4 I counted 97 maps (Fruin, 1923).

References

Bosselmann, P., 1998. *Representation of Places: Reality and Realism in City Design.* Berkeley: University of California Press.
European Union Directive 2000/60/EC, 2000. *Water Policy Framework.* [Online] Available at: European Union Directive 2000/60/EC, 23 Oct.2000. Water Policy Framework [Accessed 27 February 2017].
Fruin, R., 1923. *Nederlandsche steden in de 16e eeuw. Reproducties van de platten gronden door J. van Deventer.* 's-Gravenhave/The Hague: Martinus Nijhoff.
Haepke, R., 1908. *Bruegges Entwicklung zum Mittelalterlichen Weltmarkt.* Berlin: Curtius.
Harbers, P. &. M. J., 1981. Een poging tot reconstructie van het Rijnstelsel. *Koninklijk Nederlands Aardrijkskundig Genootschap,* 15, pp. 404–421.
Lambert, A., 1985. *The Making of the Dutch Landscape: An Historical Geography of the Netherlands.* London and New York: Academic Press.
Mak, G., 2001. *Amsterdam: A Brief Life of the City.* London: Vintage.

Meyer, H., Nijhuis, S. & Bobbink, I., eds, 2010. *Delta Urbanism: The Netherlands*. Chicago/Washington: APA Planners Press.

Nienhuis, P., 2008. *Environmental History of the Rhine–Meuse Delta: An ecological story on evolving human–environmental relations coping with climate change and sea-level rise*. Dordrecht: Springer Netherlands.

Van Dam, P. J., 2001. Sinking peat bogs, Environmental change in Holland, 1350–1550. *Environ History*, 6, pp. 32–45.

Van de Ven, G. P., ed., 1993. *Man-Made Lowlands: History of Water Management and Land Reclamation in the Netherlands*. Utrecht: Uitgeverij Matrijs.

Van Veen, J., 1948. *Dredge, Drain, Reclaim: the Art of a Nation*. The Hague: Uitgeverij Martinus Nijhoff.

Chapter 2

An Archipelago of Cities – Five Delta Towns

To write descriptions of the five towns in this chapter, I followed the morphological approach that started with initial visits and direct observations. All observation suffers from the well-known fact that we only understand the things we see if we know something about them. Consulting maps made by Jacob van Deventer and topographic maps from the early 20th century allowed me to verify or refute my observations. Even then, the interpretations developed from such observations risk being short-lived unless verified from sources with in-depth knowledge. Fortunately, information about the form of Dutch towns during their development from the 12th to the 15th century (Zweerink, 2011) has received recent attention in the literature (Borger, et al., 2011).

Selecting five towns from a large number of Dutch cities is, of course, an arbitrary task. Already in medieval times, the Low Countries supported a larger number of towns per land area than other regions in Europe north of the Alps (Braudel, 1992, p. 484). As mentioned, what guided me in the selection was a town's location in relation to river drainage basins. More important, for the purposes of this book, was the idea of a town as a set of constructed elements in the context of a larger environmental system. I have borrowed from Joseph Rykwert the concept of a town from his book *The Idea of a Town*: "A town is not really like a natural phenomenon. It is an artifact of a curious kind, compounded of willed and random elements, imperfectly controlled. If it is related to physiology at all, it is more like a dream than anything else" (Rykwert, 1976, p. 24).

I have already mentioned that many towns drowned, especially in Zealand. Dutch people therefore knew about the importance of a town design in the context of natural processes that act on a chosen location. At the time when decisions were made about a town's placement, the obvious criterion was to select a somewhat elevated location that would be robust enough to sustain high winds, ocean waves and river floods. But designs that aimed for such robustness in the light of potential extreme events did not always succeed; to rely on resilience is not enough. Rarely have town designs bounced back to the equilibrium of their previous condition after sudden extreme events. The inhabitants adapted their town designs, and adaptation generally required knowledge in engineering. What I hoped to take from history was an understanding of adaptability in the light of the many interrelated forces that continue to influence the design of cities in the Netherlands.

Climate change and sea level rise are nothing new to the Low Countries; both phenomena have occurred since the end of the ice age. The issue has always been the human response to such phenomena. With continued land subsidence in the Netherlands and an acceleration of climate change and sea level rise due to human induced causes, design responses will try to demonstrate robust approaches. Some solutions will have temporary success, such as building higher and higher dikes along rivers, or disguising major new sea dikes as dunes. More promising will be a design approach that acknowledges the need to

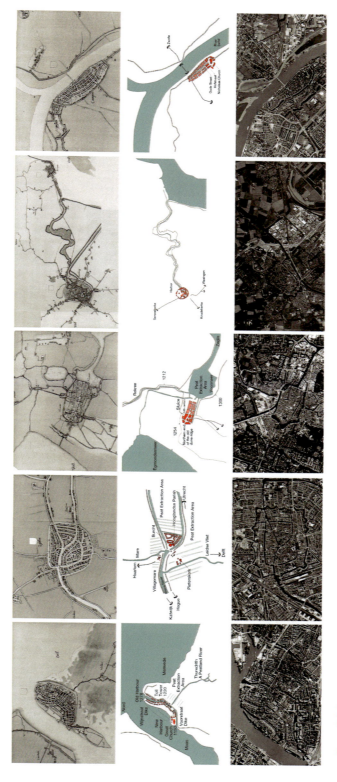

▲ Figure 3.2.1

Top row from left to right: Jacob van Deventer's maps of Dordrecht, Alkmaar, Middelburg, Leiden and Kampen; middle row: the "idea of a town"; below: the towns in 2010. Van Deventer's maps were scanned from originals found in the map room of the Environmental Design Library, Delft Technical University. Source of the 2010 row of maps, Google Earth. The maps in the middle row were drawn by the author and show the concept of a town in response to landform and climate. Here I borrowed from Joseph Rykwert who traced the design of a town to those original elements that were deliberately placed on the land.

give room to water; such designs work with water, not against it, to make room for rivers and to address sea defenses without trapping the flow of water. The three river systems, Rhine, Maas and Scheldt, drain a significant portion of the European continent. New strategies that adapt cities and landform are intensively debated in the Netherlands. We will return to this topic in the last chapter.

DORDRECHT, A Town between Two Great Rivers

Starting with the premise that towns in the western Netherlands were shaped by water, I traveled to Dordrecht to better understand what was implied by such a premise. It is fitting to start with Dordrecht: not only is the town reputedly one of the oldest cities in Holland, with city rights since AD 1220, centuries older than Amsterdam and Rotterdam, but Dordrecht, like no other, was the first city located near the concentrated discharge of the Rhine and the Maas. Like other coastal cities, Dordrecht lies at the head of the tidal influence from the North Sea. The connection to international sea and land routes has been the reason for its existence.

Standing on the bank of the broad Old Maas River at Dordrecht, a slightly inwards curving bend is obvious to the observer. Generally, in the lower course of a fast-flowing river, deposits occur in the slack waters of inside bends. It is here where natural levees form. They consist of gravel and sand deposits, but also plant material. Such a natural levee can easily build up to a crescent-shaped island with a smaller watercourse running along the land side in a parallel arch to the river. That watercourse could fill during high water and be dry at other times. The raised ground on top of such an island would support tree growth and smaller riverine vegetation. It would have been visible in this vast expanse of peat and water. The raised ground would also support structures, including sizeable structures with their foundations supported by gravel and river clay. In fact the soil conditions would provide the only buildable ground in the surrounding peat swamp. With a reasonable amount of certainty, I deducted that the origins of Dordrecht can be found on the gravel and clay that fluvial geologists refer to as a "point bar". Plausible as my theory about the origins of Dordrecht sounded to me, I would later learn that my "city on a point bar" theory had to be abandoned. What I did not know, but what is now clear from research, is that the river referred to as the Old Maas did not exist when Dordrecht was formed prior to the 12th century.

Before leaving the place on the riverbank, I looked around at the nearby buildings for clues as to their age. The massive tower of the Great Church stands out. The tower is out of proportion, even with the monumental Gothic church that is attached to it. Crossing the town on foot along a line perpendicular to the river reveals first a set of harbor basins, called New Harbor. They form a row parallel to the river and must be of a more recent date. As I crossed the New Harbor, I encountered a slight rise in the land centered on Wijnstraat (Wine Street) followed by a downslope towards the Wijnhaven (Wine Harbor), apparently the old harbor. From there I walked up to another more noticeable rise, centered on Voorstraat. Land parcelization along this street is very small. These first observations led to tentative conclusions about the shape of the original settlement in this location: probably a form that grew on top of a levee along Voorstraat. The harbor, in the form of a canal, would have provided shelter for modestly sized boats; only at Wijnhaven does the harbor widen. If correct, Dordrecht would have been a city on a levee with a harbor on the northern end and accessible from the Merwede.

Dordrecht is first mentioned in 846 in the Annals of Xanten as a place plundered by Vikings and set on fire (Halsall, 1997). A port near the confluence of the major Rhine River discharge, via the Merwede and the Maas, must have been of strategic importance. The archeological record shows that the Wine Harbor has natural origins as an inlet of the

160   PART III The Dutch Delta

▶ Figure 3.2.2

Top: Dordrecht in 1545, map by Jacob van Deventer, Environmental Design Library, TU Delft. Middle: "the idea of the town between two rivers". Below: Dordrecht in 2010 (source: Google Earth).

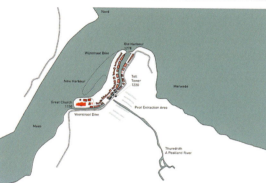

▼ Figure 3.2.3

(From top) Great Church at Dordrecht; view from the Voorstraat dike downwards across the harbor to the Great Church; view upwards towards the Voorstraat dike; view downwards from the Wijnstraat dike towards the New Harbor; view along the Wijnstraat dike.

CHAPTER 2 An Archipelago of Cities

161

Merwede and is connected to a small watercourse, a so-called peat river. Traces of early buildings were found 8 meters below the present surface of the Wijnstraat and Voorstraat (Benschop, et al., 2013, p. 8).

On a second visit, I came by waterbus from Rotterdam along the Noord to the Merwede. I went to the city's museum and obtained a recent book with historic maps (Benschop, et al., 2013). Studying the maps, I was no longer certain about my initial interpretation. What I had not taken into consideration were the changing configurations of the river system. Rhine River discharge via the Waal–Merwede broke new passages through the land where peat extraction had lowered the surface. In the decades from 1100 to 1180, aided by major floods in 1134 (Benschop, et al., 2013) and the years thereafter, the Merwede altered its course to make a more direct connection to the Maas, thus to the North Sea.

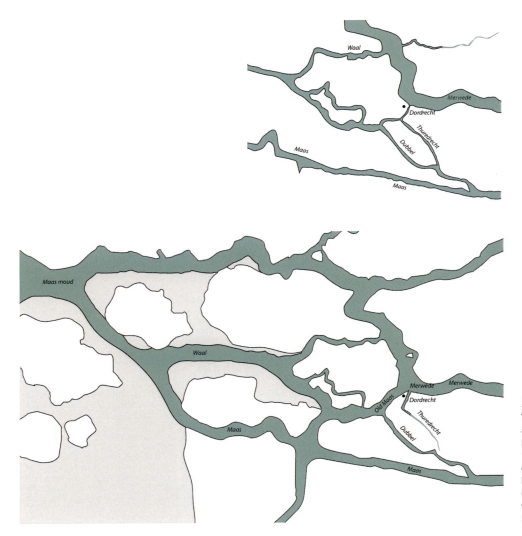

◀ Figure 3.2.4

The changing river landscape at Dordrecht between Merwede and Maas in the 12th century. Top: location of Dordrecht 1100; bottom: location of Dordrecht 1180. (Source: maps redrawn from the 2013 Historischer Atlas van Dordrecht, Vantilt.)

▶ Figure 3.2.5

Dordrecht between Lek, Merwede and Maas. River dikes in red. (source: Topographic map from 1920. Environmental Design Library, TU Delft).

CHAPTER 2 An Archipelago of Cities

Dordrecht's Urban Form

In mediaeval times, Dordrecht was called Thuredrecht; a small watercourse, the Thure, made a connection between the Rhine drainage channel, Merwede, and the Maas via the Dubble. My revised interpretation of the evidence is that there, at the mouth of the Thure with the Merwede, a harbor was established from where boats could be "dragged" to the Maas, thus the Dutch word "drecht". In this part of Holland, the Maas runs in a parallel course to the Merwede about 10 kilometers to the south. Consistent with that assumption, a levee became necessary after the Merwede broke through the peat formation and connected to the Maas. As the river was under tidal influence from the sea, the levee had to protect the cultivated land and the town from inundation. If these interpretations are true, it is more likely that Dordrecht started as a town on a rise of the land where the Great Church is located and where the foundations of a 12th century chapel were found. Explicit mention of a church in Dordrecht was made in 1203 (Benschop, et al., 2013, p. 8). An inscription at the base of the Great Church indicates that the massive church tower on the southern end of historic Dordrecht was started in 1339. At that time the tower was a useful marker on the Old Maas, the still relatively new approach to Dordrecht. The tower clearly signaled the way to Dordrecht for ships entering Holland's waterways from the sea via the Haringvliet or the Hollands Diep. A new harbor became necessary; it offered docking for ocean-going ships at the foot of the Great Church in basins parallel to the Old Maas. Using the Voorstraat levee, the town mutated to a city on a dike typology (Zweerink, 2011, p. 156). About midway on the Voorstraat levee, the Count of Holland established a toll tower in 1220, a stronghold to collect tolls from passing ships.

The orientation and reorientation of Dutch towns in response to water is a common theme during the development of cities in the Low Countries. Did those who made decisions about the form of cities understand the interconnectedness of water discharge, peat extraction, subsidence and marine floods? The historical record is not clear. There was certainly a pattern of floods that started in the 12th century and occurred repeatedly until the 15th century and beyond (Nienhuis, 2008). In the night of 18 to 19 November 1421, the famed Saint Elizabeth flood surrounded Dordrecht with water. The Grote Waard was inundated; an area of 400 square kilometers directly to the south-east of Dordrecht was lost under the waves. Peat extraction on a massive scale was responsible for land subsidence. Signs of looming danger had been evident: since the storm of 1134, floods caused by rising tides or river floods had occurred roughly every 25 years (Nienhuis, 2008, p. 77).

Nor was the Saint Elizabeth flood the last. Other devastating floods followed, such as the flood of November 1530. Deventer's map of Dordrecht, from around 1545, shows Dordrecht still attached to the Grote Waard, but rather timidly. The most memorable flood, on All Saints Day of 1570, was a combined marine flood and river flood that devastated large parts of the south-western delta (Nienhuis, 2008, pp. 244-252). Dordrecht again became an island in the Hollands Diep. The response had always been the same through the centuries, to build higher and stronger dikes, but obviously not high and strong enough. The pattern of marine and river floods continued in events that are still part of the collective memory of Dutch people today, such as the devastating flood of 1 February 1953.[1] The toll of human lives amounted to 1,835. The western portion of the former Grote Waard was abandoned and given over to sea and rivers, where it remained the largest tidal estuary in Europe until 1970, when the Delta Works completed the sealing-off of the coastline at the Haringvliet, the Grevelingen and the Eastern Scheldt. With the Delta Works in place, flooding from the North Sea is no longer possible, but high water along the Waal and Maas could still produce flooding at Dordrecht, where the Merwede, Noord and Oude Maas join together (Nienhuis &

164   PART III The Dutch Delta

Stalenberg, 2005). The current thinking is that the former polder near Dordrecht will need to be "depoldered" and used for water storage during periods of high water.

LEIDEN, a Town on a Mount, the Burcht

My visit to Leiden started with a cycle ride to the Burcht, a constructed hill from the 11th century. The hill was purposely built by the Count of Holland for defense near the confluence of the two Old Rhine River branches. The hill, with a circular wall on top, also functioned as a place of refuge to escape to during river floods. Today the Rhine River at Leiden is confined to two modestly sized canals. To imagine major water discharge inside these canals is a challenge. However, when Leiden was first mentioned AD in 860 the water discharge via the Old Rhine was more substantial.

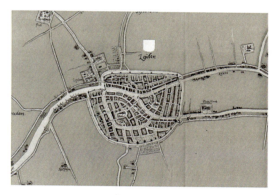

▶ Figure 3.2.6

Top: Leiden in approximately 1550, by Jacob van Deventer (source: Environmental Design Library TU Delft). Middle: "the idea of the town on a mount"; the fortified 11th century mount known as the Burcht at the confluence of the two Old Rhine River branches. The settlement extended towards the village Mare in the north, and a trading settlement on the Breestraat dike to the south, with both built on river dikes. Later, the Counts of Holland established a court with a chapel on land protected by dikes and perimeter canals. Below: Leiden in 2010 (source: Google Earth).

CHAPTER 2 An Archipelago of Cities

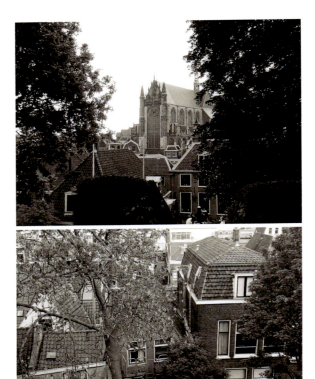

◀ Figure 3.2.7

Above: view from the Burcht towards Hooglandse Parish Church; below: view from the Burcht towards the west.

As in Dordrecht, the river forms a gentle inside bend. More noticeable than in Dordrecht is the rise between the river embankment and the nearest street that runs parallel to the river. The Breestraat is located on a river dike, a former natural levee where an early trading settlement had its beginning. Crossing the Breestraat, the land dips down noticeably when walking along Pieterskerk Choor Steeg (Street). Deventer's 1560 map reveals a canal in this location. It runs parallel to the Rhine, where today's Langebrug is located. From there, the land rises again towards Pieterskerkhof, where Leiden's oldest church once stood and where the town's 13th century Gothic cathedral is now located. Here, on high ground, the Counts of Holland erected a court to collect tolls. The observations about Leiden's form in response to the Rhine were confirmed when I found a study about the spatial transformation of towns in the Western Netherlands (Borger, et al., 2011). Three nuclei formed: an ancient village called Mare on the north bank that left very few traces; a trading settlement on the south bank on top of the Breetstraat Dike extending towards Pieters Kirke; and the development at the foot of the Burcht and around Leiden's second church, the Hooglandse Parish.

At Leiden, I also expected to find traces of the former *Renus* discharge basin. Here the Rhine must have followed a passage through the barrier dunes, prior to debouching into the North Sea. I wondered how a river – already at sea level – discharges through a dune barrier, or interacts with a dune landscape that is shaped by wind and tides. Following the Old Rhine from Leiden to the sea at Katwijk provides no clues of the former drainage basin that must have taken the form of a tidal estuary. The river meanders only slightly and ends

▶ Figure 3.2.8

Topographic map of Leiden from 1920 (source: Environmental Design Library, TU Delft).

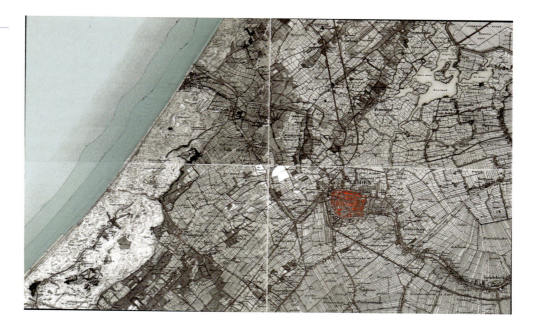

▶ Figure 3.2.9

Soil map of Holland. Shaded red indicates old dunes; bright red shows the new dune barrier (redrawn from the original at Alterra, Wageningen-UR, NL).

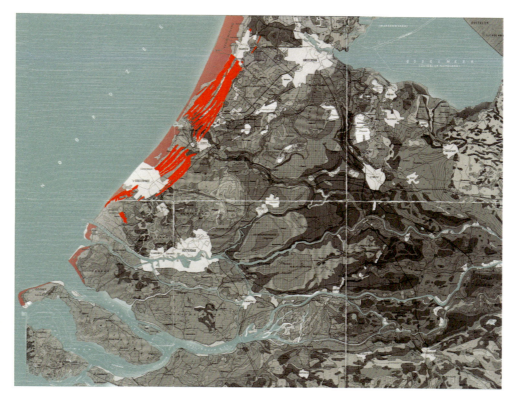

CHAPTER 2 An Archipelago of Cities

at a constructed sea defense that is designed to keep the sea out and to a lesser extent to discharge the water of the Old Rhine.

Evidence of the natural form at the Rhine River mouth is not visible at Katwijk, but can be found on soil maps. The maps reveal that the old dune barrier is interrupted. Three elongated dune fingers show up on both sides of the Rhine's mouth; they line up but are without correspondence. In between the finger, the map shows a fan of marine clay that is broad towards the sea and narrows along the present course of the river towards Leiden. A new dune barrier has formed in front of the old dunes, but there is evidence of a weak point in the coastal defense at Katwijk. In early 2014, a major sea dike was under construction. The signs said that in order to protect the Randstad from inundation during storm tides, a very large concrete structure would be completed prior to the winter of 2014. The structure would be disguised as a dune and provide a large parking garage below the surface inside the artificial dune. Clearly, the millennia old gap in the dune barrier caused by the Rhine poses a serious liability today for the coastal defense against sea level rise.

Other solutions for Katwijk were contemplated, solutions that would not create a fortress in the dunes and would leave the existing seaside villages as they are. Such a solution would have created a barrier island in front of the present coastline. We shall return to such alternative responses in the next chapter.

ALKMAAR, A Town on the Northern Tip of the Old Dune Barrier

Alkmaar was chosen for its location at the most northern end of the old barrier dunes that protect the Dutch coastline. In prehistoric times, the most northerly branch of the Rhine, the Oer-IJ, discharged into the North Sea near today's Castricum, just to the south of Alkmaar. On paleographic maps, the discharge basin is labeled *Flevum*.[2] The opening through the dune barrier closed when the river silted up in Roman times and closed completely. A set of new dunes formed over the gap around AD 50. A smaller tidal estuary, the Zijpe, existed in mediaeval times and from there Alkmaar could be reached from the sea via the Rekere, which at Alkmaar connected to a large system of lakes, including the Schermeer and the Beemster. These lakes formed after extensive peat extraction. Through these lakes, boats could reach the Zuiderzee until the 13th century, when land subsidence as a result of peat extraction forced the building of levees to protect the low-lying land from inundation. The dune barrier to the west of Alkmaar is stabilized by dense forests. However, in mediaeval times the area north of Alkmaar showed continuous transgression from the sea. This resulted in dike building along the Rekere in 1212 and the Westfriese Omringdijk in 1220 (Van de Ven, 1993, p. 56). Both dikes considerably reduced storm surges on the cultivated land. Three and a half centuries later, the dikes were willfully opened to flood the land outside the city, thus helping in the famous defense of Alkmaar against the Spanish during a siege under the Duke of Alba in 1573.[3]

On my first visit, I had arrived by train and found my way into the historic town from the north-west. The first noticeable sign of the old town is the moat and the large St. Clemens Church on a slight rise of the land. It is here at the northern tip of the old dune barrier that a village, and later the town, had its beginning. Different from the other towns I visited, Alkmaar stood out for its clear geometry of streets, canals and urban blocks. The regularity reminded me of a planned city. A long straight street runs from the church towards the east and ends at the historic harbor. Here the Rekere, a small waterway, enters from the north and intersects with two east–west canals. The harbor is partly covered by a wide vaulted stone bridge. Near there is the municipal

▶ Figure 3.2.10

Top: Alkmaar, approximately 1550, by Jacob van Deventer (source: Environmental Design Library, TU Delft). Middle: the "idea of the town on the northern tip of the old barrier dune ridge". Below: Alkmaar in 2010 (source: Google Earth).

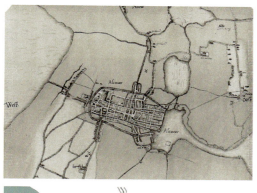

weigh station. The tower of the structure can be seen from far away by boats approaching from the north. In fact, the tower design is very handsome, decorated in a playful manner with a spire that looks like an open onion dome.

On my second visit, I reached Alkmaar from the south along the Nord Holland Canal. The canal was completed in 1824 to improve Amsterdam's connection to the North Sea at Den Helder. The canal connected Alkmaar to a major shipping channel and brought much prosperity to the city. At Alkmaar the canal forms a large basin. Facing the basin, a tower marks the new entrance into Alkmaar, also decorated with an open onion dome spire. The Accijnstoren sits on an axis with the approach to Alkmaar from the North Holland Canal and can also be seen by navigators from far away. The tower had the same function as the weigh house; both signaled the sense of arrival for barges coming into the market town.

Facts and interpretations gathered thus far could only provide a sketch of Alkmaar's morphology through time. No explanation emerged to refute or confirm the observation that the town looked planned. Then, upon closer examination of Jacob van Deventer's 1560 map, the regular east–west canals stood out. In addition to the two that still exist today inside the historic perimeter of Alkmaar, I counted six parallel canals drawn a roughly equal distance from each other. Of course, the canals must have been deliberately laid out. The equal distance between them suggests that they originated as ditches during peat extraction; first to drain the land and then to transport the extracted peat inside shallow boats. The process that generated urban form was clearly planned, but how? To lay down straight parallel lines

◀ Figure 3.2.11

The open onion dome design of Alkmaar civic buildings. Top: Town Hall. Middle: Accijnstoren in line with the Zeglis waterway, now North Holland Canal. Below: weigh station in line with the Rekere.

170 PART III The Dutch Delta

▲ Figure 3.2.12

The landscape around Alkmaar, topographic map from 1906 (source: Environmental Design Library, TU Delft).

on a large terrain at an equal distance from each other is not a trivial task. To my surprise, nothing is known about the art of surveying in Holland during the Middle Ages. We do not know how it was practiced or what instruments aided the process, only that surveyors were much in demand from 1200 onwards (Boerefijn, 2010).[4]

Orthogonal urban blocks formed along the former drainage ditches on wetland. Not all ditches were needed in the long run; those that were became canals and would be faced with stones along their embankments. Once I understood the origins of Alkmaar's regular canals and urban blocks, the same spatial pattern with its origin in peat extraction could also be detected on Deventer's maps of Leiden and Dordrecht. Outside these towns and others, the extraction of peat was practiced on a large scale. As decomposed plant material, peat is light and could be sliced off with long spade-like tools. The process called for digging away layer upon layer in regular rows until the excavation site filled with water. Once extracted, the material was stacked and dried, ready for shipping. The Counts of Holland granted extraction rights in a concessionary manner to the highest bidder, frequently to a syndicate of shareholders. What remained after the extraction process filled with water and became shallow lakes. These lakes became characteristic of the peat landscape. The first reclamation schemes of such lakes started in the Achter Meer and Egmonder Meer near Alkmaar in 1533. Enclosed by dikes and drained dry by a ring canal, the former lakes became polders, land that could be cultivated for grazing or as farmland. If land below the water table could not be drained through gravity, it was kept dry through wind-powered pumps, the characteristic windmills of Holland (Van de Ven, 1993, p. 201). The first large polder in North Holland, with

CHAPTER 2 An Archipelago of Cities

▲ Figure 3.2.13

Left: North Holland's peat extraction areas that turned into lakes. Right: starting in the 17th century, the large lakes were drained and polders were built.

7,100 hectares, was the Beemster, laid dry from 1609 to 1612 (Van de Ven, 1993, p. 131); the Schermeer followed in 1635.

MIDDELBURG, a Town on a Mount or Vluchtberg

The town is located on Walcheren, a former island in Zealand between the Easter and Wester Scheldt. The town originated on a constructed hill where two natural gully ridges converged. The Dutch word for such a place is *Vluchtberg*, literally a hill to flee to, higher ground to escape from floods. Constructed hills as the origins for settlement are very common in the Low Countries. In Friesland these dwelling mounts are called *terps* and can be found along much of the North Sea coast up to Denmark, where they are called *værft*. At Middelburg, the Count of Flanders enlarged the hill and fortified the place in AD 1103 (Lambert, 1985, p. 139). However, as a settlement, the hill at Middelburg probably originated in the 9th century not only as a place to escape to during floods, but also as a place to defend oneself during Viking raids, like the recorded raid in AD 890.

On my visit to Middelburg, I cycled to the former monastery tower in the center of the town, climbed up the 207 steps to the top of *Tall Jan*, and had a clear view over the town below. The streets and their buildings form two concentric circles; they reveal the origins of the town in the shape of a fortified hill. The outer ring was the original moat up to where

172 PART III The Dutch Delta

boats could reach Middelburg from the Scheldt estuary. The harbor curves away to the northeast. There is an impressive courtyard at the site of the former Our Dear Lady Monastery, the original religious and still functioning government nucleus at the town center.

As one of the oldest towns on Walcheren, Middelburg's location was well chosen in the middle of the island, thus protected from the North Sea, yet with direct access to the sea via the sound between Walcheren and the neighboring Beveland Islands. Lambert reports that in 1435 the Sloe Channel silted up and that a wind-powered scratcher was employed. The so-called *Krabb-clar* would sail back and forth to loosen up the accumulated silt with its claw-like feet. The outgoing tide completed the task by flushing the loosened sediments out to sea (Lambert, 1985, p. 140).

When Middelburg received city rights in 1217, it was a town in the zone of influence of Bruges, Ghent and Antwerp. At that time, Flanders was one of the most prosperous regions in Europe. Cloth industries had made the Flemish cities some of the largest in Europe during the 10th and 11th centuries. As a result, long-distance trade had its base in the ports along the Scheldt (Rutte, 2014). Similarities can still be found in the design of embankments, harbor basins, fish-markets and in the design of high towers that served as markers to navigators in

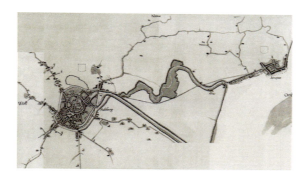

▶ Figure 3.2.14

Top: Middelburg in 1550 (approximately) by Jacob van Deventer (source: Environmental Design Library, TU Delft). Middle: the "idea of a town on a Vluchtberg connected to the sea via a slough named Sloe". Below: Middelburg in 2010 (source: Google Earth).

CHAPTER 2 An Archipelago of Cities

◀ Figure 3.2.15

Top: view from Tall Jan over the former monastic enclosure, now government center. Middle: view from Tall Jan towards the old harbor which extended into the area now used as a parking lot. Below: Tall Jan, the tower as navigational signal in the center of the town.

this horizontal landscape. In the Middle Ages, the Scheldt River ports had greater importance than others until Amsterdam took the leading role in the 16th century. But prosperity was constantly challenged by the sea. Brutal and unforgiving, the North Sea altered the shape of the islands in the Dutch Southwest Delta, especially from the late 14th century onwards, when large tracts of land with towns and villages were lost to the waves. Middelburg held on to the direct sea access well into the 18th century, but that was only possible by building a canal, first to Veere, a harbor town known for its wool trade with Scotland. The canal gave Middelburg access to the open sea via the Easter Scheldt. Later, a second canal through Walcheren connected Middelburg to Vlissingen on the Western Scheldt.

▲ Figure 3.2.16

Middelburg in the Walcheren landscape, topographic map from 1906 (source: Environmental Design Library, TU Delft).

▶ Figure 3.2.17

Delta Works at the Eastern Scheldt (source: Raymond Spekking, Wikimedia Commons).

CHAPTER 2 An Archipelago of Cities

When the Delta Works were planned in the 1950s and 1960s in response to the devastating flood of 1953, it was clear that the Western Scheldt would need to remain open to the sea with access to Antwerp, Belgium's main port. However, the proposal was to seal all other waterways, including the Eastern Scheldt, to avoid floods caused by storm surges. Granite rock, boulder clay and asphalt were used to build massive dams to close the Haringvliet and the Grevelingen. When it came time to close the Eastern Scheldt in the same manner, political opposition surfaced which pointed to the long-range ecological damage that would result by changing the saline tidal estuary into freshwater lakes. Instead an impressive battery of large sluice gates was built across the Eastern Scheldt that could be closed in the event of a tidal surge. Now, 40 years later, the foundations of these gates have proven to be not as long lasting as expected. As a result, profound discussions are taking place to evaluate alternatives to the single line of a coastal barrier. Instead, a coastal zone with a built-in redundancy of defense is contemplated. Such a zone would be wide enough to store water in the event of a tidal surge and strong enough to protect land through a sequence of parallel dikes.

KAMPEN, a Town on a River Dike

Finally, we look at Kampen in the IJssel River valley. Kampen also originated from a set of economically interdependent towns that included Deventer, Zwolle, Elburg and Harderwijk. German colonization eastward towards Poland opened a rich market in the Baltic region in the early 13th century. The harbor towns of the Low Countries benefitted greatly from this expansion. Among the Dutch towns, the lower IJssel Valley towns held an added advantage in their competition with other towns in the Low Countries: in addition to sea routes, the towns were close to established highways that connected them over land to early monasteries or episcopalian courts at Verden, Corvey and Fulda, thus land routes to Saxony and Hessen. Shared with other cities in Holland, Kampen also had the advantage of the latest sailing vessel technology (Unger, 1978). In a confluence of Portuguese shipbuilding techniques with German methods, the originally Frisian single mast square-rigged *cog* was developed further to be rigged with both square and lantern sails. These ships were built in Hoorn (Davids, 2008, p. 215), a harbor town across the Zuidersee from Kampen. By the mid 13th century, these larger sailing vessels with a more spacious cargo hold gave navigators the confidence to round the tip of Jutland and reach the Baltic countries directly (Mak, 2001, p. 33). Timber, amber, tar, pitch, linen, furs and wax reached Kampen in return for processed herring and salt from the Zuidersee; cheese and butter came from towns in Holland and Friesland. In addition, cloth from Flanders and Italy came via the Vecht from Utrecht, wine from the Rhineland and metal from the Maas Valley. By 1236, Kampen had received city rights and rivalled only Bruges for trade with the Baltic region (Lambert, 1985, p. 146).

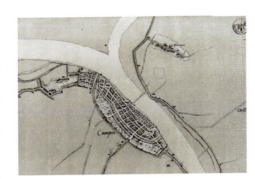
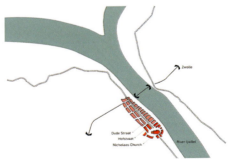

▶ Figure 3.2.18

Top: Kampen, app. 1550 by Jacob van Deventer (source: Environmental Design Library, TU Delft). Middle: the "idea of a town on a river dike". Below: Kampen in 2010 (source Google Earth).

▶ Figure 3.2.19

Top: looking down Oude Straat towards the Nicholaas Church spire.

Second frame: view of the cross nave. There is a cinematic effect. Due to the curvature of Oude Straat, the entire Church is revealed upon approach.

Third frame: the Nicholaas Church from the parallel Hof Straat.

Bottom frame: Town Hall on the Oude Straat dike with the Nicholaas Church in the distance.

CHAPTER 2 An Archipelago of Cities

▲ Figure 3.2.20

Kampen in the IJssel Delta landscape, topographic map from 1906 (source: Environmental Design Library, TU Delft).

Kampen's Early Form

At the time when city rights were granted, the IJssel at Kampen was wider (Speet, et al., 1986, p. 7). The river formed an inside bend where fluvial deposits formed a natural levee. Early Kampeners built the original settlement on a rise where St. Nicholaas Church is located, initially a small Romanesque basilica. The old church was half the length of the five-nave Gothic church that was erected in its place in the early 14th century. A topographic survey from 1818 (Lambert, 1985, p. 41), shows an elevation at the church of 3.4 meters above N.A.P.,[5] the highest point in the original layout of Kampen and apparently unchanged at the foot of the church tower. Extending from the tower, the narrow Hofstraat maintains an elevation of +2.5 m N.A.P. and runs parallel to the river toward the center to a place where the weigh house was located and where the IJssel could be forded. The street on top of the dike is called Oude Straat, the oldest street in town. Oude Straat follows the crest of the levee and curves parallel to the river towards the old town hall. The curvature of the street results in a sequence of memorable views; stepping onto Oude Straat at the center and looking towards the church, the framed view is dominated by St. Nicholaas' pointed spire, and on approach the frame shifts due to the curvature of the street and centers onto the raised choir and transept, which also provides the main entrance into the church. As a consequence of the street's curvature, the entire structure of the church is revealed to a person walking along Oude Straat in a cinematic effect.

Oude Straat is raised to function as a river dike at an elevation of +3.4 m N.A.P., the same elevation as the square around the church. The parcelization is of a very fine scale along Hofstraat and Oudestraat. According to the Historical City Atlas of the Netherlands (Speet, et al., 1986, p. 45), we are looking at the oldest core area of Kampen. An oblong-shaped moat protected the city on the land sides. During approximately 1325 to 1350, the city grew northwards along the levee. The Oude Straat and dike were extended. A second parish was added centered around Our Lady's Church. Its tower, made higher by a tall open lantern in 1453–4, became taller than St. Nicholaas' tower. The placement of the two church towers gave Kampen a dual orientation, with St. Nicholaas clearly visible to barge traffic traveling downstream on the IJssel towards Kampen, and Our Lady's Church tower tall enough to be seen by ships approaching the town from the Zuiderzee. In 1607, Our Lady's Church tower collapsed due to soil failure at the foundation. A tall municipal tower was erected in its stead near the old city hall in 1646.

In the 13th century, the riverbank was largely undeveloped, with probably beach-like moorings. Starting in 1320, the wooden ramparts were replaced by stone walls with handsome gates. The Historical City Atlas of Kampen (Speet, et al., 1986, pp. 33-34) records 21 such gates, some with dual round towers reminiscent of the Hanseatic city of Lübeck's famous Holsten Gate. A formal embankment was constructed along the IJssel Kade; it formed the landing place for river barges and for vessels going out to sea. Consequently, the area between the old linear core and the new walls were urbanized by 1350. Further to the north, a new harbor was added in the second half of the 15th century. By the end of that century, the town grew out of the confines of the old moat, the Burgel. A new moat became necessary and was completed by 1462.

Kampen is located at a place along the IJssel where the river could still be forded. Immediately to the west of the town, the river forms a delta prior to debouching into the Zuiderzee. It is its strategic location as a trans-loading port that enabled Kampen's rise to a township of importance; the city charter was the result, as are the walls that Kampen could afford to build by 1320. The protection of the bishops of Utrecht as overlords also provided permanence to Kampen's existence during its development. As a sign of strength, Kampen became a full member of the Hanseatic League in 1441, having maintained associated status long before that year. This association gave Kampen access to a large number of ports between Novgorod and Bruges. A further sign of strength, but also a sign of caution, came when Kampen received the right to place buoys and beacons in the Zuiderzee to guarantee safe shipping routes to the North Sea, a right that Kampen was forced to surrender to rivaling Amsterdam in 1527; a sign of caution, because the Zuiderzee had become too shallow in places. Sand shoals formed as river deposits accumulated. Access to the sea, or the lack thereof, contributed to Kampen's demise (Mak, 2001, p. 32). Lack of access to the North Sea would also hamper Amsterdam. Already by 1480, the deltaic channels of the IJssel had become choked with silt. Two channels were dammed to concentrate river discharge into a main channel; a groyne was built on the opposite IJssel shore to deflect the river flow towards Kampen's embankment. During the winter months, ice flows produced severe flooding of the town when snowmelt sat upstream in Germany, but colder temperatures kept the river frozen at Kampen. The town's importance waned as navigation on the IJssel became constricted, potentially caused by the Little Ice Age (generally dated from 1560 to 1720), but more likely by reduced Rhine River discharge through the IJssel in favor of the Waal.

The Zuiderzee near Kampen had become too shallow for the ever-larger ships. Only in the 19th century did technology became available to build new channels and so avoid the Zuiderzee altogether. The North Holland Canal was dug in the 1820s, but soon proved

▲ Figure 3.2.21

Afsluitdijk from 1932, or Closure Dam (source: Chet Smolski, open source, Rhode Island College).

to be too narrow; a second canal was dug from the IJ directly through the barrier dunes to the North Sea. This 24 kilometer North Sea Canal was completed between 1865 and 1876. The canal benefitted Amsterdam and its port but not Kampen. Modern large ships could no longer reach the city. Of diminished use for navigation, the Zuidersee still exposed Kampen to storm surges in 1825, 1855, and 1906, which made the water rise to 3.3 meters above NAP (Van de Ven, 1993, p. 238). With navigation through the Zuiderzee severely impeded, plans to reclaim the large body of water started to be discussed. As early as 1667, Hendric Stevin had proposed to turn the Zuiderzee into farmland, but such a proposal was impossible to achieve with the available technology (Van Veen, 1948, p. 105). Then, after a severe storm surge in 1916, the Dutch parliament passed an act in 1918 to close off the Zuiderzee and partially reclaim the water body as polders. The Netherlands had stayed neutral during WWI, but suffered severely from food shortages because of its dependence on foreign supplies. The potential of 220,000 hectares of additional agricultural land and the promise of permanent protection from storm surges made the 1918 decision to build a 34-kilometer long separation dam almost unanimous. The dam, called Afsluitdijk in Dutch, completed in 1932 is 89.5 meters wide, designed for a storm surge of 3.5 meters with a dam crest at +7 meters. The Northeast Polder and the Eastern Flevoland Polder flanked the mouth of the IJssel and "moved" Kampen, by 30 kilometers, from a town at the open sea to an inland town.

Initially the separation dam produced an ecological regime change for an estuary rich in fish and plant life that depended on brackish water and tidal movement. Cautionary arguments in favor of ecological preservation did not cause the frequent delays in implementing the plan to close off the Zuiderzee, nor was it the concern for the fishing industry that many towns depended on; arguments about the cost weighed more heavily. Decisions were made during economically challenging times. Would land sales and agricultural production on the four planned large polders (three were built) offset the immense cost of building a sea dike strong enough to withstand storm tides? The construction of large sluice gates was needed, designed to release excess water from the IJsselmeer during low tide into the Waddensee, the intertidal water body to the south of the barrier islands. The sluice gates were designed to control the water table of this large inland reservoir. Water storage was necessary to provide sufficient water for the largest ships to navigate through the locks along the North Sea Canal to and from Amsterdam's new harbor. In addition, dikes had to be built encircling the new polders and pumping stations were necessary to keep the below sea level polders dry and suitable for cultivation.

At the time of writing, 80 years after the construction of the enclosure dike, it has become clear that the transformation from a saline estuary produced unforeseen consequences. Marine life did not all vanish; different species thrived. We will return to ecology and shoreline conditions, water quality and salt content in the next chapter.

What to Take from History?

All five towns are well preserved, although some, like Middelburg, suffered from bombardment and destruction in WWII. All five towns have maintained substantial characteristics of their 13th to 16th century form, especially in their street layout and parcelization. Jacob van Deventer's map drawings from the 1550s can still be used to find one's way through these

▶ Figure 3.2.22

Waddensee at Tershelling at low tide when the inter-tidal mudflats are exposed; the tidal channel named Vlie was initially marked by the city of Kampen. It can be seen in the distance.

CHAPTER 2 An Archipelago of Cities

181

towns. Today they are examples of prosperous medium-sized Dutch towns. What I take from their 700 to 800-year history is the fact that all five towns had to adapt to the changing context of water, also true, in general, for the two major cities in the Netherlands, Amsterdam and Rotterdam.

It is tempting to use the word resilient to describe the five towns; the fashionable label in current usage applies no longer just to the restorative ability of living organisms and to the strength of materials under stress, but to socio-economic conditions in cities. I like to describe the context within which these towns existed as a complex system of trade relationships, central government oversight, or lack thereof, shipbuilding technology, water management technology, access to capital, and – primarily – human creativity. In the event of devastating events, mostly caused by natural disasters, the towns had no choice but to change. A resilience – as in bouncing back to an equilibrium that existed prior to such events – could not be expected and did not occur. The towns had to adapt to new conditions. This implied reorientation of towns towards deeper water, canal building, reclaiming of land or resignation to the fact that land was lost forever and that water was no longer within reach. Water, with its capricious nature, taught the Dutch to adapt, an important lesson in delta locations everywhere. As Van de Ven wrote in *Man-made Lowlands*: "In a delta area there is no final solution or permanent situation" (Van de Ven, 1993, p. 287).

Notes

1 The 1953 flood reached 3.75 meters above normal (ANP), measured in Rotterdam. It is estimated that the 1570 flood reached +3.6 meters (Nienhuis, 2008, p. 249).
2 Flevum because of its connection to Flevo Lacus (Nienhuis, 2008, p. 30).
3 "Victory started at Alkmaar." On October 8, 1573 Spanish troops were defeated at Alkmaar. The victory marked a turning point in the 80-year war with Habsburg Spain and the beginning of the independent Republic of Seven Provinces, the United Netherlands, recognized in 1648 with the Treaty of Münster, Westphalia.
4 In a conversation with Reinout Rutte about the origins of surveying and cartography in the Netherlands, a recent doctoral dissertation on the subject was mentioned (Boerefijn, 2010).
5 In the Netherlands, Normal Amsterdam Level (NAP), also known as the Amsterdam Ordnance Datum (AOD), is a horizontal plane that, more or less, co responds with average sea level and is used to indicate the height of water and land.

References

Benschop, R., De Bruijn, T. & Middag, I., 2013. *Historische Atlas van Dordrecht: stad in het water.* Nijmegen: Vantilt.

Boerefijn, W. N. A., 2010. *The foundation, planning and building of new towns in the 13th and 14th centuries in Europe: an architectural-historical research into urban form and its creation*, Amsterdam: University of Amsterdam [dissertation].

Borger, G. et al., 2011. Twelve centuries of spatial transformation in the Western Netherlands, in six maps: Landscape, habitation and infrastructure in 800, 1200, 1500, 1700, 1900 and 2000. *OverHolland*, 10(11), pp. 7–124.

Eraudel, F., 1992. *Civilization and Capitalism, 15th–18th Century, Vol. I The Structures of Everyday Life*, Berkeley: University of California Press.

Davids, K. A., 2008. *The Rise and Decline of Dutch Technological Leadership: Technology, Economy and Culture in the Netherlands 1350–1800*. Leiden: Koninglijke Brill.

Halsall, P., 1997. *Medieval Sourcebook: Annals of Xanten*. [Online] Available at: www.fordham.edu/halsall/source/xanten1.html [Accessed 27 February 2017].

Lambert, A., 1985. *The Making of the Dutch Landscape: an Historical Geography of the Netherlands*. London and New York: Academic Press.

Mak, G., 2001. *Amsterdam: A Brief Life of the City*. London: Vintage.

Nienhuis, A. & Stalenberg, B., 2005. River atlas. In: F. Hooimeijer, A. Nienhuis & H. Meyer, eds, *Atlas of Dutch Water Cities*. Delft: Uitgeverij SUN, p. 134.

Nienhuis, P., 2008. *Environmental History of the Rhine–Meuse Delta: An Ecological Story on Evolving Human–environmental Relations coping with Climate Change and Sea-level Rise*. Dordrecht: Springer Netherlands.

Rutte, R., 2014. Four hundred years of urban development in the Scheldt estuary: Spatial patterns and trade flows in the south-western delta. *OverHolland*, Volume 12/13, pp. 99–127.

Rykwert, J., 1976. *The Idea of a Town: The Anthropology of Urban Form in Rome, Italy and the Ancient World*. London: Faber & Faber.

Speet, B. et al., 1986. *Historische stedenatlas van Nederland. Aflevering 4. Kampen*. Delft: Delftse Universitaire Pers.

Unger, R. W., 1978. *Dutch Shipbuilding before 1800: Ships and Guilds*. Assen: Van Gorcum.

Van de Ven, G.P., ed., 1993. *Man-Made Lowlands, History of Water Management and Land Reclamation in the Netherlands*. Utrecht: Uitgeverij Matrijs.

Van Veen, J., 1948. *Dredge, Drain, Reclaim: the Art of a Nation*. The Hague: Uitgeverij Martinus Nijhoff.

Zweerink, K., 2011. The spatial maturity of Dutch towns (1200–1450): A comparative analysis of the emergence of the outlines of the Randstad, with reference to town maps. *OverHolland*, Volume 10/11.

Chapter 3

Contemporary Examples and Strategies for the Future

The three large-scale interventions of the 20th century, the Zuiderzee closure dike, Delta Works, and the policy to make room for rivers, responded to disasters or near disasters that threatened human life. In the view of some authors, the worst case scenario for the future of the Netherlands is complacency. As Van de Ven (1993, p. 289) wonders, what would happen if disasters like the combined river floods and storm surges of 1916 and 1953, and the near disastrous river floods of 1993 and 1995 did not reoccur for one or two generations? De Ven is not alone in registering a concern of complacency; the events mentioned stayed in people's memories and triggered public support for major expenditures and resulted in economic transformations, painful for some, but beneficial for most sectors of Dutch society.

What De Ven and others acknowledge are suggestions that have been made repeatedly by individuals and organizations to surrender certain parts of the Low Countries to the sea and to river estuaries in order to partly restore natural processes, but these suggestions have never been realized because of opposition from the inhabitants, who did not want to make sacrifices for the benefit of future generations.

In the light of climate change and an expected acceleration in sea level rise, there is wide agreement that a long-range view is required. Indeed, a long-range view would acknowledge that raising levees, strengthening dams and dune barriers, and building more powerful pumping stations has never been robust enough in the long run. The 1970s Delta Works are in need of new foundations on the sea floor. The 1932 IJsselmeer enclosure dam needs to be strengthened, as do the river dikes along the IJssel and the two great rivers, Rhine and Maas, with their many distributaries. The future of the Low Countries is made more precarious by the inescapable fact that all land on peat formation continues to subside. That accounts for much of the northern and western parts of the Netherlands.

The Netherlands' hydrological society published a graph in 1998 (Huisman, et al., 1998) that indicates the counteracting processes of irreversible land subsidence and sea level rise from the year 900 to the present. The two curves crossed in AD 1450. Since that time, sea level has continued to rise gradually and is now expected to rise more sharply, while land subsidence continues to drop notably.

The Dutch are faced with a dichotomy in their response to water: robustness or redundancy. Conceptually, robustness has relied on a single, very strong primary line of defense; redundancy would depend on a zone of defense, where land would be surrendered to store water when needed during floods and storm surges; these layers of defense within a zone are expected to provide the same, if not greater, safety for human life. While much can be explained with the robustness and redundancy response models, to be fair to proponents and opponents of one or the other strategy, the discussion is complex and full of technical considerations. Those arguing in favor of greater redundancy are convinced that their approach guarantees greater adaptability to future uncertainties. The proponents of the

▶ Figure 3.3.1

Land subject to subsidence (source: Ministry of Infrastructure and the Environment, Rijkswaterstaat 2011).

▶ Figure 3.3.2

Sea level rise and land subsidence in the Netherlands (source: Netherlands Hydrological Society, 1998, Delft).

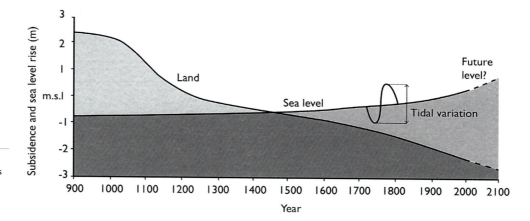

CHAPTER 3 Contemporary Examples and Strategies

robust defense optimistically declare that super-dikes along rivers and coastal defenses are necessary, can be built and maintained with current technology.

The opponents to strengthening the current form of defenses acknowledge the fact that 100-meter wide and twice as high super-dikes could indeed be a temporary fix, but point to the fact that such dikes would cause havoc in the cultural landscape, especially in traditional towns that lie in their way. The following quotations sketch out the depth of the disagreement.

Piet H. Nienhuis, Professor Emeritus, Department of Environmental Science, Institute of Wetland and Water Research, Radboud University, Nijmegen writes:

> . . . the sea level will continue to rise, and future flooding events should be anticipated. The Delta tragedy is that water management per definition is not sustainable, because the steps to be taken are inescapable and for the greater parts not reversible. Notwithstanding the great schemes and long-term visions to diminish the risk of flooding, short-term defensive measures are the only solutions conceivable in a process of an unavoidably subsiding delta threatened by sea level rise and climate change, and consequently disappearing under water.
>
> Nienhuis, 2008, p. 567

Marcel Stive, Professor of Coastal Engineering at the Technical University of Delft and a member of the Second Delta Commission, called for safety standards to be raised by a factor of ten. His colleague, Han Vrijling, Professor of Hydraulic Engineering said:

> . . . the dikes have to be brought up to par before we indulge in what is a trendy approach by the new water builders with their *terps* and the romantic call for more room for the water.
>
> Metz & Van Den Heuvel, 2012, p. 284

The Ministry of Infrastructure and the Environment for Water Management in the Netherlands (Rijkswaterstaat) admitted (Rijkswaterstaat, 2011, p. 16):

> Many of the interventions, however, have a downside which we only started to understand in retrospect such as, for example, the ecological consequences of the Delta Project. This understanding was incorporated into the integrated water management policy launched in the 1980s. Meanwhile, all these interventions caused us to forget that the sea actually intended to continue shifting our coastline further eastwards. Where it would have ended up by now is difficult to say.

[The reader will have noticed that a modern-day government agency in its official language reassigned animate qualities to the sea.]

Tracy Metz, journalist, member of the Delta Commission, Director, John Adams Institute, Amsterdam:

> The Netherlands is taking a new approach. Faith in engineering is no longer boundless. For the last ten years or so the policy has been "building with nature, living with water." That means a less defensive attitude towards water, taking the pressure off it. Water is being let in—carefully controlled—in the great water

expanses along the coast and in the delta, in areas along the major rivers, and even in residential areas. This can produce a more beautiful, more natural landscape, along with more awareness of the water, as well as reduce the risk of flooding.

Metz & Van Den Heuvel, 2012

In the context of these selected quotations we will examine some of the most important design proposals, starting with those that address the rivers, moving to lakes and estuaries, ending up with coastal defense.

More Room for Rivers

The Royal Netherlands' Meteorological Institute climate modeling indicated that all temperature increase scenarios will result in higher Rhine River discharge during the winter months (+12%) and considerable lower discharge rates (-23%) during the summer months. The explanation for the change in summer discharge of the Rhine River is related to snowmelt in the Alps that in the past has produced high summer discharge, but in future the Rhine will perform less as a snowmelt river due to the melting of glaciers. The Meuse will also have some increase (+5%) in winter discharge and a significant lower discharge (-20%) in the summer (Rijkswaterstaat, 2011, p. 69).

The meteorologists also predict more frequent periods of extreme precipitation, which will be longer in the winter and shorter but more intense in the summer. The greater variability in water supply downstream leads the water managers to increase the storage capacity of rivers and former estuaries. Similar to the way traffic engineers deal with design speeds and traffic volume in their modeling of roadways, water engineers deal with design discharge rates. Current normative discharge rates for the Rhine (16,000m3/sec) and the Meuse (3,800m3/sec) have already been exceeded. It is expected that a Rhine discharge of 18,000m3/sec will be crossed sometime between 2040 and 2045. The modeling had the consequence of a widening of riverbeds. In the low-lying areas where natural landform does not define riverbeds, the maximum cross-section of a river is defined as the space between winter dikes.

As so frequently in Dutch history, changes in policy were triggered by disasters, in this case near disasters in the winters of 1993 and 1995. In January–February of 1995, 250,000 residents near the Rhine River basin were evacuated. In April of the same year the *Delta Act Large River* passed parliament. As a result, roughly 450 kilometers of river dikes were reinforced and heightened from a safety level of 1 in 50 or 1 in 500 years to a common safety level of 1 in 1,250 years (Nienhuis, 2008, p. 568). Then in 2006, after much discussion, a policy shift took place. Instead of periodically raising river dikes, parliament approved the "Room for the River", which resulted in returning lost flood plains back to the rivers. A total of 37 projects were identified, which included the repositioning of river dikes, digging river bypasses, removing or lowering of groynes at the riverbanks, and even returning polders back to the rivers Waal and Merwede, a process called depoldering. Along the IJssel River, the excavation of flood plains includes the removal of fluvial deposits. The large volumes of excavated sediments will be used to construct artificial dwelling mounts; the "return of the *terp*," as some call it. In the context of these major undertakings there is a "nature development" component that some authors view with much skepticism because it is the creation of another cultural landscape according to standards set by present-day nature managers.

CHAPTER 3 Contemporary Examples and Strategies

187

▲ Figure 3.3.3

Waterplan 2 Rotterdam 2030. A plan that will result in more water surfaces for storage (source: www.rotterdam.nl/gw/document/waterloket/wat).

▲ Figure 3.3.4

The future Waal flood plain at Nijmegen (source: City of Nijmegen).

The Rhine of today is a fundamentally different riparian habitat from the river of the early 1800s. The old riverbank vegetation is all but gone, as are most of the old-growth forests and all the salmon runs. They live today only in paintings and maps on museum walls and in the collective memory of poetry and song. More faunal changes have occurred in the Rhine basin in the last 150 years, than in the previous 10,000 years.[1]

The use of the words "nature" and "natural" is full of controversy in many societies, especially in the Netherlands, where one is hard pressed to find nature in unaltered form; every square inch of surface area has been turned over and is constructed in one way or another. For the context of a book on urban form, the "Room for the River" policy in the city of Rotterdam is exemplary. The city has adopted Waterplan 2 Rotterdam (Jacob, et al., 2007), an ambitious plan with a target year of 2030 to provide more retention space for water. Even more than today, water will have a presence in the fabric of the city. Such measures will enhance the city's character, but these measures are born out of necessity. More surfaces areas have to be found to store water after rainfall before discharge is possible.

At Nijmegen, the Waal River, the Rhine's most important distributary, makes an almost 90 degree bend. On the inside bend, across from the historic city, a new urban extension with the name Waalsprong was planned. After the 1995 river flood, it became clear that

CHAPTER 3 Contemporary Examples and Strategies

the remaining flood plains needed protection and should be designed to store water during flooding events. The environmental permit for Waalsprong was denied and the City of Nijmegen commissioned new plans that moved the river dike in the community of Lent further north to widen the flood plain of the Waal in the flood-prone bend of the river. An auxiliary channel was constructed in 2015 that runs parallel to the river and created an island. Initially the island was envisioned as a place to live. This would have partly offset the significant expenditure for building such a high quality flood defense, but the cost for housing on top of a flood defense proved prohibitive.

The Large Inland Lakes as Former Estuaries

The hydro-morphological and ecological changes that occur when an estuary is modified are still poorly understood. This observation is true for all the former estuaries in the Netherlands. The sequence of four maps made by the War Ministry of the Biesboch area from 1699 to 1856 show the fluvial morphology of a delta formed by the Rhine and Maas at a time when the technology did not permit a fundamental restructuring of river flows. The time window of the four frames is very brief within a 10,000-year history, when the delta building process

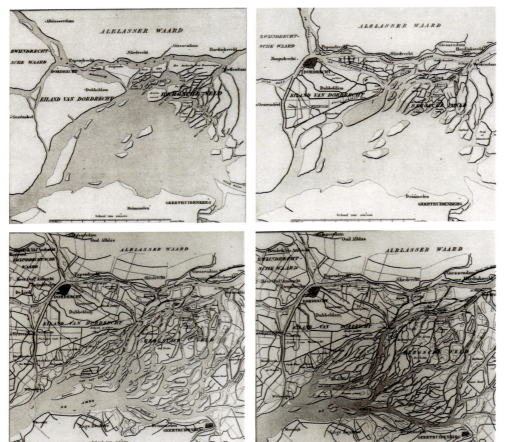

◀ Figure 3.3.5

Biesboch from 1699 to 1856, a set of maps made by the military that shows the confluence of the Rhine, and Maas river system to the south east of Dordrecht up to the mid 19th century, when technology made possible the channeling of the combined water discharge. (Source: Environmental Design Library, TU Delft.)

190   PART III The Dutch Delta

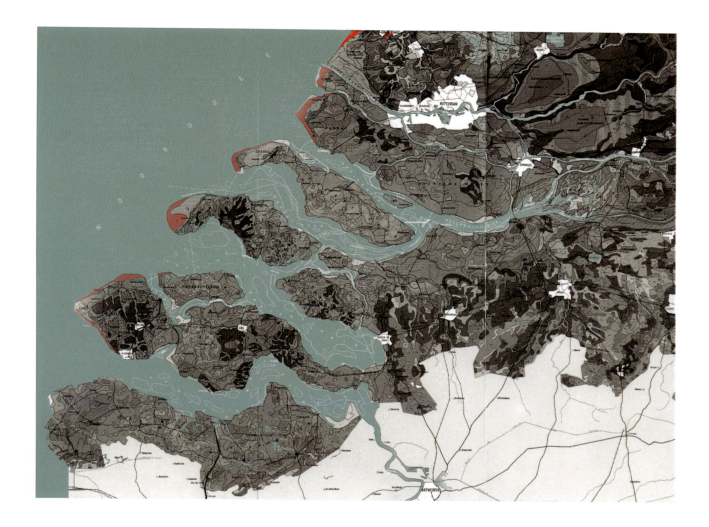

▲ Figure 3.3.6

Soil map of South Holland and Zeeland. Red: old dunes; shaded red: new dunes; grey: marine and riverine clay; dark grey: peat (source: Alterra, Wageningen-UR, NL).

started. But an overlay of historic maps for a much larger time window makes it difficult to accurately depict the transformation at a detailed graphic scale.

During the ice age, the North Sea formed a lowland plain at sea level lowstands. The great northern European Rivers moved northward through this plain. At sea level highstands the melting of the ice shield caused sea level to rise and brought the shoreline further south. A large pond formed in the southern portion of the North Sea blocked from draining by the ice shields of Britain and Norway and a 30-kilometer wide land barrier across the British channel, the so-called Weald Artois rock barrier.

New research (Gupta, et al., 2017) explains the re-routing of north-west European river drainage patters and of meltwater to the North Atlantic. Around 450,000 years ago, spillover breached the land barrier that connected Britain with continental Europe and created a flood of major proportion. The process repeated itself 160,000 years ago and created the Strait of Dover. This led to a separation of the British Isles from the Euro-Asian continent, and provided a lower drainage path for Rhine River water. The river responded to gravity by changing its course gradually away from the northerly direction through the glacial valleys. The OerIJ, in its roughly south to north course, is believed to have functioned as one such drainage channel.

CHAPTER 3 Contemporary Examples and Strategies

Then in pre-historic times, the Rhine still debouched near today's Leiden, but started to silt up during the Roman era. Gradually the main Rhine River discharge moved south-west and formed a confluence with the Waal and Maas near the Biesboch to form the Southwest Delta. Following the flow of the combined rivers, the delta is followed by estuaries that were continuously shaped by riverine deposits, tidal flow, by a third river, the Scheldt, and of course, by storm events.

Thus far in this long history, the delta forming process ended with the Delta Works that started in 1957 and was completed, with all but one estuary closed, in the 1970s and 1980s. Only the Western Scheldt was kept in its then present condition. An operable storm surge barrier was installed at the mouth of the Eastern Scheldt. Likewise, an operable barrier, the Maeslant Barrier, was completed in the late 20th century. It is capable of closing the New Waterway at Hoek Van Holland.

It would be an illusion to call the present condition of this process of many thousands of years a final state. Even if we cannot expect quite as dramatic changes as in the past, in a delta landscape, as de Ven so fittingly pointed out, there is no final state.

▼ Figure 3.3.7

Cross-sections demonstrating coastal redundancies (source: Han Meyer, Job van Berg, Arnold Bregt, Robert Broesi, Ed Dammers, Jurian Edelenbos, Lodewijk van Nieuwenhuijze, Leo Pols, Gerda Roeleveld, 2013. *New Perspectives for a Sustainable Delta*. Delft: IPDDcahier).

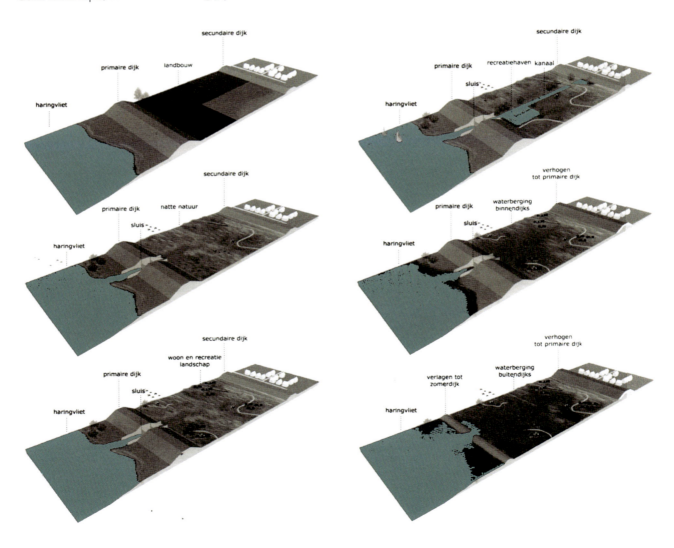

PART III The Dutch Delta

The period up to the 1970s, when the Delta Works closed the estuaries, was also a time that coincided with the greatest river pollution in the history of the Rhine and Maas. As a result, the former estuaries of Haringvliet and Grevelingen Meer have a layer of contaminated sludge at their bottom that is now covered by a layer of river silt. The water quality of the Rhine and Maas has improved drastically since the 1970s, but the sludge will remain there because a lack of fluidity prevents it from draining out to sea where it would be diluted. There is debate whether such a flushing of contaminants can be managed safely.

What can be deducted from the current literature is that ecological values have become more influential in the 30-year debate about the delta's future. The understanding has grown that estuaries with their tidal rhythm and their gradients from saline to freshwater, are ecologically much healthier than the separated and isolated water bodies. The particular ills of these former estuaries are addressed by Nienhuis (2008, p. 282) in a chapter on human interventions in the Southwest Delta; they include an abundance of algae, bacteria and toxins.

Similar to the concept of Room for Rivers, proposals are made to use the redundancy model to protect the coastline in and around the Dutch Delta. Strengthening existing dikes on the islands of the Southwest Delta would make room for the fluctuating tides, without sacrificing the safety of residents in coastal areas. Clearly, some residents would have to move, because what is envisioned is not a single line of primary defense but a zone that will experience flooding in the event of storms, though it could be used the majority of the time for agriculture and recreation.

Thus far these strategies are still in discussion (Meyer, et al., 2013). If widely accepted as a valid approach, new possibilities for urban form could open up that take advantage of the redundancy that would need to be designed into such a system from the outset. The expenditures for such a coastal defense are significant, and the expectation is that this zone of defense should be long lasting. For economic reasons, the uses such defenses will protect might have a much shorter life span, thus alternative use options are necessary. Whatever is placed inside such a zone would also need to be easy to repair if damaged.

IJBURG

No longer on the drawing board, but lived on, is a set of islands in the IJsselmeer, to be exact in the IJmeer portion of this large inland lake. Plans to build urbanized polders near Amsterdam were drawn up by the architects Van den Broek and Bakema in the 1930s (NAI, 1965), but never built. What has been built since the turn of the century is not a polder that would have residents live on the drained bed of the lake floor behind 5 meter high dikes. Instead IJburg was built as islands in the "pancake" method. Specially built ships with their holds full of sand are equipped to gradually distribute the sand through the ship's bottom. Using this method, layers of sand are spread over the bed of the lake in a highly controlled manner. The layers of sand are relatively thin at first, but build up like a stack of pancakes until the top layer forms close to the water surface. The shape of the island becomes visible when more sand is pumped on top of the last layer. The advantage of this method is an edge design that slopes gradually at an angle to the bottom of the lake, and not abruptly as a vertical edge that a steel sheet wall would create. On the sloping angle of the edge, plants will establish themselves from the bottom upwards and, in a constructed manner, first reeds than other species can be planted from the top downwards. Thus the edge is stabilized over time. Only edges exposed to strong winds need to be enforced with rocks. The result is a geometric form that responds to the exposure of the islands to surface wind and neighboring shoreline conditions.

▲ Figure 3.3.8

A green tunnel between two islands as seen in 2014. Right: a sketch that envisions the gradual buildup of vegetation, including trees that would indeed produce such a tunnel as soil conditions improve from decomposed plant matter over time.

The form also responds to underwater conditions. In this section of the IJmeer, the water is generally up to 3 meters deep, but on the floor of the IJmeer a trace of a glacial valley was found. A gully from the ice age in the shape of a large curved indenture could be mapped there; the Dutch word for this prehistoric gully is *Oergeul*. This gully is believed to have transported Rhine River water below the ice shield as mentioned earlier. To fill the gully with sand would have been possible, but that was not done; instead the underwater gully shaped the western island's curved edge. Respect for a form derived through natural processes from millennia ago? This was not the only reason. Water depth also relates to different habitat conditions because of subtle differences in currents and temperatures; the reasons that gave shape to the islands followed mainly ecological reasoning. Frits Palmboom, a leading member of the design team of IJburg wrote: "The design for IJburg lies in the respect for and the enjoyment of the wide expanse of water: an escape to infinity in a fully allotted country" (Palmboom, 2010, p. 67).

The enjoyment of a wide expanse of water is surprisingly rare for the Dutch living close to the North Sea coast. The Dutch live in cities behind dikes or dunes, rarely with a view of water:

> While the composition of the archipelago as a whole displays certain capriciousness – like ice flows on the water – the islands themselves have a simple geometric structure. The public space is shaped by a simple street plan. The IJburg-Laan with its tram and boulevard along the bay are the mainstay of the structure. A number of cross streets visually link between the weather side and the lee side of the islands.
>
> Palmboom, 2010, p. 67

Not all six islands have been built. A fourth island is under construction. It is not likely at the time of writing this book that the fifth and sixth islands will be built. The entire program called for 18,000 dwellings, 100,000m^2 of office space and 30,000m^2 of commercial space. Critics say IJburg is too far from the city of Amsterdam. Although connected by tram and metro, living at IJburg encourages an automobile-centered lifestyle. It is true that the connection to Amsterdam for cyclists across the somewhat elevated Diemer Dike and a former garbage heap is spectacular in the summer months, but on windy rainy winter days the trip

▲ Figure 3.3.9

Design for IJburg (source: Frits Palmboom, 2010).

is long and arduous. For whatever it is worth in a country with a stagnant population growth, demographers point to the fact that significantly more children have been born on IJborg during its less than ten years of existence than the Netherlands average.

Before we go on to discuss strategies for the coastline, we should briefly discuss salt intrusion into the water bodies of the Netherlands. Saltwater intrusion is a valid concern for agriculture in a country that is subsiding and that has a high saltwater content in the ground below the fresh groundwater table.

CHAPTER 3 Contemporary Examples and Strategies

195

◀ Figure 3.3.10

Oergeul, a glacial gulch in the IJmeer (source: City of Amsterdam).

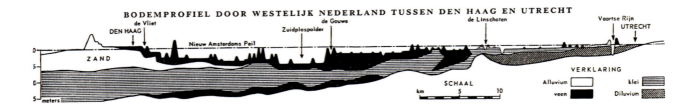

The water system in the Netherlands is designed to prevent saltwater intrusion into rivers and former estuaries, but prevention depends on river water discharge and sea level rise. With average tide and average river discharge, saltwater from the North Sea can only reach upstream along the New Waterway up to the Willams Bridge, east of downtown Rotterdam. As long as there is a minimum flow of 1,500m³/sec. at Hoek van Holland, where the New Waterway meets the North Sea, salinization is not a problem. But the minimum discharge rate cannot be guaranteed. During the autumns of 2003 and 2005, the river discharge rate was very low and storm surges produced higher than normal tides, which reduced the capability to bring salinization under control.

A separate problem is internal salinization. It is caused by deep brackish groundwater that seeps upwards due to pumping actions into very low-lying polders. This produces a problem that is virtually irreversible (Rijkswaterstaat, 2011, p. 55).

▲ Figure 3.3.11

Cross-section explaining how brackish groundwater seeps upwards into surface waters below reclaimed land and polders (source: Rijkswaterstaat, 2011).

The Coastal Dunes

The single line coastal flood defense strategy, comprising of dunes and massive seawalls, appears to be vulnerable and an inadequate strategy for the future. Since the Middle Ages the Dutch coastline has been receding eastwards at a rate of one meter per year. The reason for receding coastlines was the diminished down-river flow of sediments that tides and currents used to distribute along the shoreline. The tides and currents still function, but rivers and their distributaries no longer transport sediment to the coast, thus the material available for distribution is missing. Thus, after much fighting of coastal erosion over the ages through the building of seawalls and various other means, coastal management has experimented with depositing a very significant amount of sand – 20 million cubic meters – at a strategic location on the coast. The expectation is that currents and wind will distribute the material along the coastline. Thus far the experiment has been judged positively. The prevailing winds along the coast point eastward, the currents run towards the north-east. This form of sediment transport expects landwards-directed winds to blow sand into the dunes, thus nourishing their contours. In the Netherlands, this method of sediment transport is called a "sand engine."

In a situation of layered dunes, layers close to the sea have been opened to encourage sand nourishment of the entire depth of a dune landscape. While the use of the dynamics of wind, tide and sand can be relied upon to produce a dynamic equilibrium, a second strategy of shoreline adaptation is proposed and realized in places. Sea level rise will make the raising and reinforcing of the hard defenses unavoidable. Under this strategy, existing structures such as shoreline esplanades, boardwalks, boulevards or buildings in rows facing the sea are modified to resist storm surges. This has happened in the harbor town of Vlissingen, where former ground-level uses have moved upwards inside buildings, but remain oriented towards the sea. Related is the strategy to create new usable space inside the coastal defense. We encountered such an example in Katwijk near Leiden. A large garage was under construction that is disguised as a dune. I find this strategy questionable: first, because the new structure will not look and feel like a dune. Deprived of the dynamics that are associated with dunes, the true structure will reveal itself over time. Second, why is a large concentrated amount of parking at the seashore even desirable in a place like Katwijk? Those who argued in favor are motivated by use options that generate revenues, and options that would open up current parking lots for more intensive uses, meaning more land can be developed for resort-like functions.

I was interested in a fourth strategy that would create barrier islands offshore. Islands several kilometers in front of the existing shoreline would dampen the brunt of a storm surge by introducing a coastal redundancy in response to sea level rise. While proposals for such barrier islands were drawn up, they are currently experiencing a loss of momentum. The pursuit of such vanguard dikes in front of the existing shoreline might resurface in the future.

Port activities are quintessential for the Netherlands. Historically, the form of delta cities was shaped by the loading and trans-loading of goods onto ships. The hinterland for the ports, much of central Europe, remains unchanged. What has changed are the dimensions of harbor operations. With the widening of the Panama Canal, ever larger ships will need to be accommodated. The main ports of the Low Countries, Antwerp and Rotterdam, need direct access to the open sea. Rotterdam's port has moved to reclaimed land in the North Sea, off the historic shoreline. Antwerp, because of Belgium's national borders, is confined to a location further inland, but depends on a deepened Western Scheldt for access. Port activities will continue to drive spatial planning. For urban designers, challenges and opportunities exist in transforming former port areas that have become obsolete.

◀ Figure 3.3.12 (opposite)

The so-called "Sand Engine". Large amounts of North Sea sand is dredged up and deposited on the beach in order to be distributed by westerly wind to replenish the dunes. (Source: Ministry of Infrastructure and the Environment, Rijkswaterstaat.)

▶ Figure 3.3.13

Barrier islands along Dutch coast (source: TNO and West 8 Urban Design & Landscape Architecture).

Adaptations to city form require a long-range view. It exists in the Netherlands, where the long history of towns and their relationship to water has forced upon the Dutch the need for deliberation prior to taking action. It has been important to adjust incrementally and to recognize that mistakes will be made, thus repairs must be anticipated. This important lesson can be applied to the design of coastal cities in low-lying areas everywhere. Designers need to anticipate a greater emphasis on our collective ability to adapt to ever-changing conditions.

Note

1 In this direct quote Nienhuis (2008) cites M. Cioc (2002) and R. Kinzelbach (1995).

References

Cioc, M., 2002. *The Rhine: an Eco-biography, 1815–2000.* Seattle: University of Washington Press.

Gupta, S. et al., 2017. The Two-stage Opening of the Dover Strait and the Origins of the Island of Britain. *Nature Communications*, 8.

Huisman, P. et al., 1998. *Water in the Netherlands.* Delft: Netherlands Hydrological Society.

Jacob, J., De Greef, P., Bosscher, C. & Haasnoot, B., 2007. *Waterplan Rotterdam 2: Working on Water for an Attractive City.* Rotterdam: Municipality of Rotterdam.

Kinzelbach, R., 1995. Neozans in European waters: Exemplifying the worldwide process of invasion and species mixing. *Experientia*, 51, pp. 526–538.

Metz, T. & Van Den Heuvel, M., 2012. *Sweet & Salt: Water and the Dutch.* Rotterdam: NAi .

Meyer, H. et al., 2013. *Nieuwe Perspectieven voor een Verstedelijkte Delta, Technical University Delft.* [Online] Available at: http://urd.verdus.nl/upload/documents/IPDD-Cahier.pdf [Accessed 27 February 2017].

NAI, 1965. *Pampus Plan.* [Online] Available at: schatkamer.nai.nl/en/projects/uitbreidingsplan-pampus [Accessed 23 April 2017].

Nienhuis, P., 2008. *Environmental History of the Rhine-Meuse Delta: An Ecological Story on Evolving Human–environmental Relations coping with Climate Change and Sea-level Rise.* Dordrecht: Springer Netherlands.

Palmboom, F., 2010. *Drawing the Ground – Landscape Urbanism Today.* Basel: Birkhäuser.

Rijkswaterstaat, 2011. *Water Management in the Netherlands.* Den Haag: Ministry of Infrastructure and the Environment & Rijkswaterstaat.

Van de Ven, G.P., ed., 1993. *Man-Made Lowlands, History of Water Management and Land Reclamation in the Netherlands.* Utrecht: Uitgeverij Matrijs.

Conclusion

In each of the three regions covered by this book we have reached back into the history of settlement form with the expectation of finding guidance for the future. In history, settlements in all three low-lying areas were shaped by natural processes, chiefly water, landform and climate. We now understand that the same processes have taken on a new importance in the response to climate change.

Water

The belief in mastery over natural processes such as water is still strongly with us. We have the technology and we will use it to sustain our cities. While examples of significant public works projects that protect cities from inundation are still few in number, their use is increasing. The Thames Barrier in London, operational since 1982, protects the boroughs of Greater London from floods. In its first two decades of existence, the barrier closed for maintenance but rarely to prevent the effect of tidal surges on London. Closure events have now increased and take place not only to prevent flooding at spring tides, but more frequently to control combined tidal and fluvial events (Environmental Agency, 2014). This was especially true in the 2013/14 flood season, when the barrier closed 41 times for combined tidal/fluvial events and an additional nine times for solely tidal events.

The Italian Mose Project at the Lido will protect the Venetian Lagoon from aqua alta when it is expected to start operating in 2020 (Consorzio Venezia Nuova, n.d.). High water in the Venetian Lagoon has occurred regularly during winter months and generally lasts for two and a half hours. The three inlets that connect the lagoon to the Adriatic Sea are expected to close during each high water event.

The Maeslant Barrier at Hoek van Holland, near Rotterdam, with its two gigantic arms capable of closing New Waterway, the main Rhine/Maas River's discharge channel, began operation in 1997, but only closed for the first time on 8 November 2007 to prevent a more than 3-meter rise due to a storm surge (Stichting Deltawerken, 2004).

These substantial engineering projects are still recent; it is likely that others will be built in the future, especially in locations where inland ports need to remain accessible to navigation. The timing of barrier closures is predictable ahead of storm or flood events. The re-opening of such barriers is also predictable and necessitated by river discharge.

Landform

Climate change has influenced the discussion on how our defenses should be designed. Each shoreline consists of water to land transition zones. At the seashore this transition takes the form of beaches, cliffs or dunes and inter-tidal mud flats. Rivers form banks with sediments;

they form flood plains with marshes and ponds. Around estuaries, tidal flats and tidal marshes transition from water to land. At San Francisco Bay, the estuary formed an estuarine to terrestrial transition zone of over 250,000 acres or 110,000 hectares. This large area is referred to as the baylands (The San Francisco Wetlands Ecosystem Goals Project, 2015). Prior to urbanization this transition zone was primarily made up of tidal marshes and tidal mud flats. The use of the baylands changed greatly in the 200 years of urbanization. In the year 2000, only 60,000 acres of tidal marshes and tidal flats remained. The point is that the baylands, in their changed condition but roughly at the same low elevations, still exist. Baylands have actually grown to a slightly larger size. It is this transition zone that is most precious as society confronts sea level rise. Here design decisions have to be made. Some designs include tidal marsh restoration that also protects upland conditions from sea level rise. These restorations are referred to as soft edge solutions. Approximately 34,000 acres of restored tidal marshes have been added since 2009. In other areas, decisions still have to be made with a current emphasis on restoring the transition zone. That leaves around 84,000 acres where urbanization has occupied baylands up to the water's edge and where hard edge solutions will be necessary. For the landscape ecologist, these 84,000 acres are degraded ecosystems or patches. For an urban designer, the design of such patches needs to include human activities, sometimes intensely human, allowing people, and many of them, right up to the water's edge. It is the design of such places that is most challenging. Living near water, overlooking water, stepping down to water, sensing water on approach to the edge – these are profound human experiences that sustain life in cities.

The discussion about the design of the transition zone between water and land is broadly on the public mind in the Netherlands; that discussion is in the beginning stages in the San Francisco Bay Area, and only somewhat discussed in China. The design of the transition zone requires a greater balance between the engineering solutions that protect communities and commerce and the repair or reconstruction of ecological systems that have been engineered out of existence. Coastal cities are starting a new cycle of adaptations with built-in redundancies. Along rivers in the Netherlands, multiple and overlapping designs create redundancy in the defense against flooding. Redundancy as a concept is now competing with a single line of defense. The same redundancy is now also considered for the transition zone of coastal estuaries and the seashore. Redundancy increases safety in the long run. The danger is that the maps showing projected inundations of the transition zone by some date in the distant and not so distant future will scare society into making major mistakes that would never have been considered if the scare did not exist. I would consider it a mistake if, for example, infrastructure funding to improve bridges and highways would make large coastal engineering protection measures feasible without examining more benign interventions. A moveable barrier attached to the Golden Gate between San Francisco and Marin County would be such a mistake. Mistakes will be made; an approach to design is necessary that is incremental and allows us to repair our mistakes. Much more frequently than in the past designers will need to ask, how do we repair our designs if they fail?

Climate

Climate change has made the human and the natural worlds more strongly interdependent. In interpreting the choices for the future, Ian McHarg's (1971) writings certainly need to be remembered; McHarg reflected early on the causes and consequences of climate change by re-examining the human versus nature paradigm. When it comes to repairing the causes of climate change, designers play a more limited but still important role. Urban transportation is the largest source of carbon emissions in the Dutch Delta and the San Francisco Bay Area; in the Pearl River Delta, industrial emissions still contribute significantly to carbon emissions, together with the ever increasing emissions from urban transportation. In all three regions covered in this book, the evolution of urban form is inseparable from urban transportation. The spatial structure in the three regions differs greatly, but the low density sprawl of single family homes and dispersed workplace concentrations or the sprawl of high-rise clusters, as in China, produces the same results. Dispersed settlement forms require mobility over large distances. We frequently referred to an adaptation of settlement form designed to reduce carbon emissions. It is obvious how far we are from realizing such a goal when driving on the expressways in each of the three regions covered by this book. Unfortunately, San Francisco Bay Area cities remain among the world leaders in carbon emissions per capita, 20 tons of carbon dioxide emissions per year from private automobiles and small trucks. Half that amount would bring the Bay Area region on par with the Netherlands. Do not misunderstand, expressways for high mobility will continue to exist in the future; but urban design's over-reaching objective remains access to work opportunities, services and amenities within closer proximity rather than mobility over larger distances.

Social Equity

Social consequences of urbanization have provided major challenges. When walking the streets in the inner city areas of San Francisco and Guangzhou, and in the cities of the Dutch Randstad, we witness the growing attractiveness of living in urban settings: this return to the city from suburban settings is a positive trend fueled primarily by young professionals, especially the greater number of women who have joined the workforce. These and other trends have been identified that make living close to jobs and amenities more attractive than suburban living. But the urban way of life has become expensive and out of reach for many. Displacement of less affluent groups resulted and they were forced to move to the metro-politan edge.

Both discussions, the one on the consequences and the one on the causes of climate change give rise to concerns for social equity. Climate change has and will affect urban form at interrelated social and physical levels. In the Pearl River Delta, one quarter of the population lives in informal settlements. The term applies to former villages and traditional forms of settlement that were converted from agricultural homesteads to multistory dormitories for low-income residents and members of the rural population who migrated to the Pearl River Delta in search of work. To demonstrate an incremental repair of villages in the Pearl River Delta has been a major focus of the work in part II.

The Metropolitan Landscape

In all three settings, we stressed the form of the region and not only the form of the inner city, for good reason. In regions with population growth, a design focus only on the inner city cannot suffice. All three regions discussed in this book have a polycentric conurbation, urban agglomeration, or mega city form, whatever terminology might apply at a given time. How many new towns, how many satellite cities were actually needed in the past? How could a region limit their proliferation? Once built, the critiques of these satellites remained harsh. Aging modernism can be found in all three regions. Now aging post-modernism has been added. The problem is not of style, but is with placement, scale and distances between developments. Let's face it: the list of large projects that failed is long. Whether government sponsored as in Europe and China, or developed by the private sector as in the US, the pitfalls are the same. To get the job done in designing a large planned community, repetition of elements rules the work and sameness results. The economic imperatives dominate. With large planned projects the question will always remain: how do we reach the larger objectives? The goals remain for good integration of workplaces and places to live, and for a sufficient ridership to support public transportation, for compact urban patterns that support interactions, thus life in cities; an urban form that meets the threshold values of urbanity.

An alternative approach to large-scale planned developments is the incremental repair of existing settlement form. The structures of the past are there and in most cases can be adapted through infill and redesign. Early on in her fight against large-scale redevelopment in lower Manhattan, Jane Jacobs defined the importance of context as a guiding principle in urban design. When designers repair through reuse or infill they are doing so in a context that already exists. Trained as a journalist, Jacobs focused on social context as well as physical context; because context has a way of defining what is possible, and the range of options open for consideration. The result is incremental change. Incremental change does not create large profits for those few developers who bid on large planned communities. Incremental change and repair attract a much larger group of smaller developers, simply because the risk is not as high. Greater variety results because of multiple creative processes. Frequently, higher monetary value can be achieved over time with incremental repair than with large planned developments.

In today's metropolitan landscape much context exists. We currently might label much of the regional context as ugly, certainly fragmented – a constructed wilderness, cacophony or dystopia. The fact remains that a landscape of patches exists. Adaptation is the creative process that examines such patches for future viability.

The work presented in this book originated in an educational setting. It included design concepts developed by young professionals over roughly 10 years from 2007 to 2017. Students who came to the Master of Urban Design Program at Berkeley generally held professional degrees in architecture; fewer came with a landscape architecture background and very few came from urban planning. The subjects discussed here require an interdisciplinary approach. For urban designers of the future, an understanding of hydrology is essential, and of climatology and environmental engineering. Yet designers bring to the task a special skill, the ability to communicate what an experience of future urban form can be like. Cities in low-lying delta regions will out of necessity resemble more closely the historic cities that were shaped by water. Numerous towns in China (Feng, 2009) provide examples, with Suzhou as the most famous; so do many cities of the Low Countries from Bruges to Kampen or the Venetian Lagoon from Torcello to Chioggia. To contemporize urban form with an eye on water, climate and landform will be a wonderful challenge for the remainder of the 21st century and beyond.

References

Consorzio Venezia Nuova, n.d. *Mose: Per la difesa di Venezia e della laguna dalle acque alte.* [Online] Available at: www.mosevenezia.eu/?lang=en [Accessed 4 March 2017].

Environmental Agency, 2014. *The Thames Barrier.* [Online] Available at: www.gov.uk/guidance/the-thames-barrier [Accessed 27 February 2017].

Feng, L., 2009. *Canal Towns South of the Yangtze.* Shanghai: Jiao Tong University Press.

McHarg, I., 1971. *Design with Nature.* New York: Published for the American Museum of Natural History.

Stichting Deltawerken, 2004. *Deltawerken: Maeslant barrier.* [Online] Available at: www.deltawerken. com/maeslant-barrier/330.html [Accessed 4 March 2017].

The San Francisco Wetlands Ecosystem Goals Project, 2015. *The Baylands and Climate Change: Baylands Ecosystem Habitat Goals*, Oakland: California State Coastal Conservatory.

Index

Note: Page locators in *italics* refer to captions

adaptation by design in the San Francisco Bay Area 67–71
Afsluitdijk dam 180, *180*
air quality 43, 62, 95, 116
Alkmaar 151, *153*, 168–172; canals, laying out of 170–171; dike building 168; dune barrier 168; landscape around *171*; North Holland Canal 169, 179–180; onion dome designs *170*; peat extraction 168, 171; peat extraction reclamation schemes 171, *172*; River Rhine 168; water discharge 168
Allies, Bob 29–30
Alviso Archipelago *70*
Amsterdam 152, 154; 16th century water management *155*; aerial perspective in 1538 *155*, 156; dam typology *154*; lack of access to North Sea 179; transport links with IJburg 194–195; urban blocks 30, *33*
Anthonisz, Cornelis *155*, 156
Antwerp 24, 197
apartment blocks, sun angles and separation of 129, *132*
Asia Games 2010 132–133

backyards, access to 25
barrier island proposal, Dutch coast 168, 197, *199*
Bay Conservation and Development Commission 10, 63
Bei Jiang 76
Bloomsbury Block, London *30*
Braudel, Fernand 2, 23, 57, 73, 145, 158
business district extension *see* Pazhou Island

California State: greenhouse gas emission targets 48; incentives to reduce vehicular travel 43; Senate Bill 375 48–49
Canton 73
car: California state incentives to reduce usage 43; compact urban form 43; automobile dependency in dispersed city form 3, 39, 46, 48
carbon dioxide emissions 1, 4n1, 11, 43, 48, 203
cartography 156

Chevron 38–39, *40*, 41
CIAM 29
climate change: and building of flood protection barriers 201; causes of 1; consequences of 1, 4; current and future strategies in the Dutch Delta 184–200; designs in the San Francisco Bay Area to address causes of 64–67; designs in the San Francisco Bay Area to address consequences of 67–71; future strategies in the Pearl River Delta 137–142; future strategies in the San Francisco Bay Area 62–63; high density design in response to 24–25, 30, 43; influencing discussion on design of defenses 201–202; move to more compact urban form 13, 17, 129; predictions for the Dutch Delta 187; social equity concerns 11, 203; urban transportation and causes of 202–203
comb structure, village 97–99, *98*, *117*, *118*
community, sense of: in Dadun 99, *100*; designs for the San Francisco Bay Area with 66–67, *66*, *67*; infrastructure for *65*; Xinxi affordable housing project with 119–121, *120*
commute patterns, San Francisco Bay area 39, *42*, 48
compact urban form: climate change necessitating move to 13, 17, 129; Pazhou Island, proposals for 132, 134, *135*; popularity with young professionals 203; in proximity to waterways 3, 4; in San Francisco Bay Area cities 43; social equity concerns 203; warehousing portion of Xinxi, proposal for 116–117, *117 see also* Jiangmen historic center
constructed hills (*terps*), Low Countries 154, 165, *165*, *172*, 187
Crockett-Velona 12, *15*

Dadun 88–107; alternative future for 91, *91*, 94–95, *95–97*, 100–104; ancestral halls 93, *93*, *94*, 97, *98*; ancient settlement pattern *98*, 99; building heights 90, 91, 102, 104; building inventory 2010 *102*; canals 90, *92*, 93, 95–96, 97, 100, *102*; comb structure of village 97–99, *98*; decision to maintain collective ownership over land use and building 94–95; designing for future 94–95; distinguishing village from surrounding urban center 100, *103*; Dong Ping River *89*, 90, 105; fertilizers 90; floods 88; implications of policy tested through design 100–104; increased powers in Shunde district government and impact on 105; Jiefangzhong Road integrated project 104; land use rights 5, 91, 94–95, 104; livelihoods 90; micro-climate 88, 95, 97, *102*; migrant workers in 91, 92–93, *92*, 103; new building construction 102–103, *103*; plans for new city center for Foshan *87*, 90, 105, 106; public life 99–100; response to design proposals for 104–105; sewage system 90, 95–96, *97*, 100, *101*, 105; silkworm cultivation 90; social structure 94; typical water village 88–90; water quality 90, 95, *96*, 100, 105, *105*; Yandu River *89*

de Klerk blocks, Amsterdam 30, *33*

Delta Works 164, *175*, 176, 184, 192

density: building heights in Dadun to increase 91; call for a redefinition of 24; designs to counteract feelings of being crowded 25–29; forms acceptable to residents 24; high density designs in response to climate change 24–25, 30, 43; measuring 27–28; models and affordability 116–117; proposed changes to Dougherty Valley 56–57, *58*; residential footprints 30, *30*, *33*, *35*; threshold values of urbanity 2–3, 23–24, 43, 57–61, 67

depoldering 187

developers: bids for new development in San Francisco 64, *64*, 66; large and small 63, 66, 204; power equation between local government and 63, 66; preferred builds of large 66; reluctance to take on mixed function projects 63

Deventer, Jacob van *154*, 156, *159*, *161*, *165*, 168, *169*, *173*, 176–181, *176*, 181

dispersed city form 2, 179, 203; car dependency in 3, 39, 46, 48; critique of North America's vision for 39–40; San Francisco Bay Area *see* San Francisco Bay Area, dispersed metropolis

Dixon 12, *14*

Dong Ping River *89*, 90, 105

Dordrecht 160–165; changing river landscape 162, *162*; dikes *163*, 164; floods 164; Great Church 160, *161*, 164; harbor 160, *162*; Maas River 160, *162*, *163*, 164; Merwede River 162, *162*, *163*, 164; peat extraction 162, 164; urban form *161*, 164–165; water management *163*, 164–165

Dougherty Valley 43–47, *45*, *47*, 56; commute distances 48; gaining land from "rights of way" 56–57, *58*; likely opposition to adapted designs for 61–62; planners objections to 46, 47; road width 44–46; size of homes and separation by value 46; urban hybrids 57, 59–61, *59*, *60*; water system 46–47

Downs, Anthony 39–40, 48

Drusus, Claudius 152

dunes: at Alkmaar 168; at Katwijk *167*, 168; North Sea Canal through 180; old and new *167*, *191*; strategies for 197–199, *197*, *198*

Dutch Delta 4, 145–200; adaptability of towns 158, 160, 164, 182, 199; Alkmaar 151, *153*, 168–172; barrier islands offshore proposals 168, 197, *199*; cartography 156; catchment area *146*; climate change predictions 187; compact urban forms 4; contemporary examples and strategies for future 184–200; dam typology *154*; defenses in need of repair 4, 176, 184; definitions 145, 148; Delta Works 164, *175*, 176, 184, 192; depoldering 187; development of towns and settlements 153–156, *153*, *155*; Dordrecht 160–165; dunes *167*, 168, 180, *191*, 197–199, *199*; Eastern Scheldt storm barrier 176, 192; ecological damage concerns 176, 180, 181, 193; great rivers 149–151, *150*; IJburg 193–196, *194*, *195*; internal salinization 196, *196*; Kampen 152, 176–181; land subsidence 154, 158, 164, 168, 184, *185*; large inland lakes as former estuaries 190–193; Leiden 165–168; Maeslant Barrier 192, 201; making of 149–157; Middelburg 172–176; modifications of existing structures to resist storm surges 197; mountain routes leading to 145; Netherlands from satellite *147*; North Holland Canal 169, 179–180; peat extraction 162, 164, 168, 171; peat extraction, reclamation schemes for lakes formed by 171, *172*; peat moors 150, 153–154; polders 165, 171–172, *172*, 180; policy changes triggered by disasters 187; port activities 197; Randstad 148, 168; receding coastline 197; redundancy models to protect coastline 176, *192*, 193, 197, 202; robustness vs. redundancy models, 4, 184–187; Roman occupation 152; Room for Rivers 187–190, *188*; saltwater intrusion 195–196, *196*; sea level rises 150–151, 154, 158, 184, *185*; sequence of maps of delta formed by Rhine and Maas 190, *190*; shoreline along North Sea 151–153, *152*; soil maps *167*, 168, *191*; survey methods 156,

206   INDEX

171; *terps* 154, 165, *165*, 172, 187; towns that drowned 151, 174; Waal flood plain at Nijmegen 189–190, *189*; water boards 154; Waterplan 2 Rotterdam 2030 *188, 189*; Western Scheldt 176, 192, 197

East San Rafael *70*
Eastern Scheldt storm barrier 176, 192
ecological damage concerns 176, 180, 181, 193, 202
Economist 117–118
Embarcadero, San Francisco *71*

Feng, Jiang 81, 99
Feng Shui 79, 119, 132
Foshan *87*, 90, 105, 106

Geddes, Patrick 50–51
Gerckens, L. C. 43
Golden Gate 8, *8*, 21, 202
Golden Gate Bridge 8, 12
greenery 25–26
greenhouse gas emissions, Californian targets on 48
Gropius, Walter 129, *132*
Guangzhou 73, 76, *77*, 81; drainage system map *82*; housing costs *115*; landscape *74*; new central business district *see* Pazhou Island; road patterns 108, 110; transects 108–110, *109, 110*; watercourse systems map *78*

Haight Ashbury perimeter blocks 24–29, *26*, 30, *33*
Half Moon Bay 12, *15*
handshake buildings, Shenzen 118
height of buildings: Dadun 90, 91, 102, 104; San Francisco Bay Area 24; wood construction 24
Heuvel, M. van den 186, 187
historic centre, repairing and upgrading *see* Jiangmen historic center
housing: affordability 24, 30; affordability, San Francisco 24–25; affordable housing project for Xinxi 114–119, *117, 118*; costs in Guangzhou *115*; integration of workspace and 66–67, *66, 67*, 104, 132, 134, *135*; not-for-profit concept 119; perimeter blocks 23–24; perimeter blocks in history 29–35, *30, 33, 35*; perimeter blocks, living inside 24–29, *26, 27, 28*; urban blocks, San Francisco Bay Area *20*, 21–23, 25–29, *26*, 30, 33; urban hybrids 57, 59–61, *59, 60*
Humboldt, Alexander von 49, *49*, 50, *50*, 54n10

Humen *111*
Hunters View, San Francisco *35*

IJburg 193–196, *194, 195*; transport links to Amsterdam 194–195
IJmeer 149, 193, 194, *196*
IJssel River 149; at Kampen 178, 179; removal of fluvial deposits 187; Rhine discharge into 151, 179
IJsselmeer 149, 151, *152*, 181, 184, 193
incremental approach to design and development 71, *71*, 204 *see also* Dadun; Jiangmen historic center; Whampoa Harbor
internal salinization 196, *196*
island: barrier proposal for Dutch coast 168, 197, *199*; building, IJburg 193–196, *194, 195*
Isleton 12, *14*

Jacobs, Jane 204
Jiangmen historic center 123–132; challenges of upgrading 126–129, *126, 128*; decision to preserve and upgrade 123; designing infill projects 126–128, *126*; four-minute walk *130–131*; housing on city outskirts 129; land ownership patterns 124–125, *125*; natural history shaping cultural landscape 123, *124*; residents moving to outskirts 128, 129; social justice issues 128–129

Kampen *152*; Afsluitdijk dam 180, *180*; closing off Zuiderzee 180–181; early form 178–181; IJssel River 178, 179; lack of access to North Sea 179; land routes 176; latest sailing vessel technology 176; St. Nicholaas Church *177*, 178, 179
Katwijk: barrier islands *167*, 168; garage disguised as a dune 168, 197
Kostof, Spiro 87

lakes as former estuaries, large inland 190–193
Lambert, Audrey 2, *152*, 172, 173, 176, 178
land: California's attempts to bring about better use of 43; control in Dadun over use 5, 91, 94–95, 104; development at urban edge 43–47, *45, 47*; Dougherty Valley designs for more density in use of 56–57, *58*; low intensity of use in the San Francisco Bay area 43, *52*, 53; overseas Chinese and ownership of 124–125; ownership patterns, Jiangmen 124–125, *125*; Pearl River Delta controls over 81; practices for better integration of 63; reclaimed San Francisco Bay 10–11, *20*, 22–23, *70, 71*; reforms under Mao Zedong

91; subsidence, Dutch Delta 154, 158, 164, 168, 184, *185*; undesignated use in space around tower blocks 129, 134; use as a form of capital 4
landform 53, 201–202
large-scale planned projects: alternative approach of incremental repair 204; power dynamics 63
"Law of the Indies" 22
Leiden 165–168, *165*, *166*; constructed mount 165, *165*; Rhine River 165, *165*, 166, 168; water discharge 165, 166, 168

Maas (Meuse) River: age of 145; catchment area *146*; climate change scenarios and discharge rates 187; Dordrecht 160, *162*, *163*, 164; increasing discharge rates 187; seasonal discharge 149; sequence of maps of delta formed by Rhine River and 190, *190*; water quality 193
Macao 73
Maeslant Barrier 192, 201
Mahr, A. C. 11
Marks, Robert B. 76, 78, *79*, 90, 114
Martinez 69
Merwede River 162, *162*, *163*, 164
metropolitan landscapes 2, 203–204
Metz, Tracy 186, 187
Meuse River *see* Maas (Meuse) River
Middelburg 172–176, *173*, *174*; canals 174; constructed hill 172; Eastern Scheldt 176; maintaining access to sea 173, 174, 176
migrant workers 81; affordable housing project for Xinxi villagers and 114–119, *117*, *118*; in Dadun 91, 92–93, *92*; "handshake" buildings for 118; new model of housing needed in China for 118–119, *118*; in Whampoa Harbor 115, 116
Ministry of Infrastructure and the Environment for Water Management in the Netherlands 186
Monroe Doctrine 1823 12
Mosaica *35*
Mose Project, Venetian Lagoon 201

Nienhuis, Piet H. 145, 151, 153, 164, 186, 187, 193
Nijmegen, Waal flood plain at 189–190, *189*
North Holland Canal 169, 179–180
North Sea: Dutch shoreline along 151–153; during Ice Age 191
North Sea Canal 180, 181
not-for-profit concept 119

Oergeul gully 194, *196*
O'Farrell, Jasper *20*, 21, 22–23, 29

office parks: San Francisco Bay area 38–41, *40*, 48; unsustainable nature of 41
office space: downtown San Francisco 38, *39*, 41, 47–48; Pahzou Island 134
Old Maas River 149, 160, 164
orientations, block 28–29, *28*, *132*

Palmboom, Frits 194, *195*
Panerai, Philippe 29
parking 30, 33, 46; disguised as a dune 168, *197*; ratios 35
Pazhou Island 132–144; aerial view *133*, *140*; demolition and relocation of village 133; development 132–134, *133*; former brewery site 133, 134, *134*; integration of workspace and housing 132, 134, *135*; morphology *134*; new media centre 133, *134*; proposals for adaptation to a new form of urbanity 134–137, *135*, *136*; road grid discouraging pedestrians 134; undesignated open land 134; water management 134–135, *136*, *137*; water management, future strategies 137–140, *138*
Pearl River Delta 4, 73–143; agricultural production 77–78; Bei Jiang 76; Dong Ping River 89, 90, 105; drainage basins 76; floods 78; formation 76, 137; future water strategies 137–140; geological subsidence 138; industry 73–74, 82; land use controls 81; population increases 74; project locations *84*; retaining historic identity of places in 123; rivers 76; sea level rises 138, *142*; shaped by human intervention throughout recorded history 77–78; Shi Pai, former agricultural village *83*; storm surges 138; topography *141*, *142*; urban form 79–84, *79*, *83*; urbanization 74, *75*, *141*; urbanization, slowing pace of 81–82; water management practices 80, *80*, *82*; Xi Jiang 76 *see also* Dadun; Jiangmen historic center; Pazhou Island
peat moors 150, 153–154; extraction 162, 164, 168, 171; reclamation schemes for lakes formed by extraction 171, *172*
perimeter blocks 23–24; in history 29–35, *30*, *33*, *35*; living inside 24–29, *26*, *27*, *28*
Plan Bay Area: 2013 48, 62; 2040 64
plazas 22
polders 165, 171–172, *172*, 180
polycentric regions 39, 41, 61; Randstad form 74, 148
Pompeii, urban blocks *30*
Potato Rows, Copenhagen 30, *33*
power to manage development 63, 66

208   INDEX

privacy concerns 26–27
private developments, scale and power of 63
public spaces for strangers or extended family 99

redundancy model 71, 202; to protect Dutch
coastline 176, *192*, 193, 197, 202; vs.
robustness model 184–187
registration system, China 116
repair: approach of incremental development
and 1, 40, 71, 123, 204; of defenses in Dutch
Delta 4, 176, 184; of housing infrastructure on
city outskirts 129 *see also* Dadun; Jiangmen
historic center; Whampoa Harbor
residential footprint 30, *30, 33, 35*
Rhine River: age of 145; at Alkmaar 168; between
Arnhem and Nijmegen 149; catchment area
146; climate change scenarios and discharge
rates 187; control of water distribution 151;
different riparian habitat from early 1800s
189; discharge into IJssel 151, 179; discharge
into Waal 151, 179; discharge via Waal–
Merwede 162; evidence of natural form of
mouth 168; *Flevum* discharge basin 151, 168;
increasing discharge rates 187; at Leiden 165,
165, 166, 168; from Leiden to Katwijk 166,
168; Oer-IJ branch discharge in Ice Age 151,
168; in prehistoric times 151, 168, 191–192,
194; re-routing of drainage pattern 191–192;
seasonal discharge 149; sequence of maps
of delta formed by Maas and 190, *190*; water
quality 193
Richardson, William A. 19, *20*, 21
Rio Vista 12, *14*
roads: changing practices of building 63;
gaining land from "rights of way" 56–57, *58*;
Guangzhou patterns of 108, 110; width and
impact on forms of travel 44–46, 134
Rogers, Richard 129
roofs, capturing rainwater 59, *59*
Room for Rivers 187–190, *188*
Rotterdam: port 197; Waterplan 2 *188*, 189
Rykwert, Joseph 158, *159*

Sacramento River 8, 9
sailing vessel technology 176
saltwater intrusion 195–196
San Francisco Bay Area 3, 7–71; 125,000 years
ago 8, 9; baylands transition zone 202;
bayshore transects 67, *69*; bridge building
12; campaign to prevent additional land
reclamation 10; carbon dioxide emissions
203; contested landscape 9; critique of
vision for North American metropolitan

areas 39–40; designs to address causes of
climate change 64–67; designs to address
consequences of climate change 67–71;
developers' approach to new build projects
64, *64*, 66; flooding 9, 11, 12–13; flooding
projections *10*, 11, 69; future strategies
on climate change 62–63; Haight Ashbury
perimeter blocks 24–29, *26*, 30, *33*; height
of buildings 24; housing affordability 24–25;
Market Street 23; natural history of estuary
and inland delta 8–9, *8, 9*; Plan Bay Area
2013 62; Plan Bay Area 2040 63; Plaza 22;
population increases *15*, 22; reclaimed land
10–11, *20*, 22–23, *70, 71*; Russian presence
11; Sacramento River 8, 9; San Joachim River
8, 9; sea level rises 11, *16*; size and power
of private developments 63; social justice
issues 11; space limitations 12–13, 17; stream
regulation 8–9; tectonic movement 8, *8*;
transects 51–53, *51, 52*, 67, 69; urban blocks
20, 21–23, 25–29, *26*, 30, *33*; urban form,
origins of 19–21, *19, 20*; urbanization 11–17;
water quality 10; water table 8, 11; wetlands
restoration, South Bay 10–11
San Francisco Bay Area, dispersed metropolis
38–55; commute patterns 39, *42*, 48; compact
urban forms 43; forces of large industrialized
development complex 47–49; low intensity
of land use 43, *52*, 53; office parks on urban
edge 38–41, *40*, 48; offices, downtown 38,
39, 41, 47–48; polycentric form *41*; transects
51–53, *51, 52*, 67, 69; urban infill projects 33,
43 *see also* Dougherty Valley
San Joachim River 8, 9
sand engine, Netherlands 197, *199*
Sausalito 12, *13*
scale of private developments 63
sea level rises: adaptation by design in San
Francisco Bay Area to address consequences
of 67–71; complacency over 138; Dutch Delta
150–151, 154, 158, 184, *185*; not addressed
in Plan Bay Area 2040 63; predictions for
Pearl Delta 138, *142*; San Francisco Bay Area
11, *16*
Secchi, Bernardo 2
sediment transport, Netherlands 197, *199*
Senate Bill 375 48–49
separation of apartment blocks 129, *132*
sewage system, Dadun 90, 95–96, *97*, 100, *101*,
105
Shi Pai *83*
Sieverts, Thomas 2
Silicon Valley, California 11, 33, 48, 134

size of developments 63, 66, 204
social justice: climate change and 11, 203; issues in Jiangmen 128–129
Sonoma 12, *14*
Spanish colonial towns, laying out of 22
Stive, Marcel 186
suburban settings: displacement of less affluent city groups to 203; move away from 203; on outskirts of Jiangmen 128, 129 *see also* Dougherty Valley
sun angles and separation of apartment blocks 129, *132*
sunlight in perimeter block flats 29
survey methods 156, 171
synoecism 87; example of Dadun 95; Whampoa Harbor village 114

terps 154, 165, *165*, 172, 187
Thames Barrier, London 201
threshold values of urbanity 2–3, 57–61, 67; urban blocks and 23–24
transects 108; Guangzhou 108–110, *109, 110*; in natural sciences 49–50, *49, 50*; San Francisco Bay Area 51–53, *51, 52*, 67, *69*; in urban context 50–51, *52*
transportation, urban 202–203; California state incentives to reduce vehicle usage 43; car dependency in dispersed city form 3, 39, 46, 48; compact urban forms and lower use of 33, 43; linking IJburg and Amsterdam 194–195
trees 24
typhoons 138

Ungers, O. M. 60
urban blocks: attracting new residents 30, 33; in history 29–35; living inside perimeter 24–29; San Francisco *20*, 21–23, 25–29, *26*, 30, *33*; and threshold values of urbanity 23–24
urban edge, living at 43–47, *45, 47*; in China 128, 129 *see also* suburban settings
urban hybrids 57, 59–61, *59, 60*
urban infill projects: Jiangmen historic center 126–128, *126*; San Francisco 33, 43

Van Veen, Johan 154, 180
Vioget, Jean Jacques *20*, 22
Vlissingen 197

Waal River 149, 152, 162, 164, 192; flood plain at Nijmegen 189–190, *189*
water: adaptation by design in Bay Area to respond to rising levels of 67–71; Dougherty Valley 46–47; future strategies in Pearl River Delta 137–142; management practices in Chinese city design 80, *80*; politics, Dutch 154; Room for Rivers, Dutch Delta 187–190, *188*; storage, Pearl River Delta 97, 111, 134–135, *136, 137*, 140; system repairs 95, 100, 119, 121, *121*
water engineering projects 201; Delta Works 164, 164–165, *175*, 176, 184, 192; Eastern Scheldt storm barrier 176, 192; Maeslant Barrier 192, 201
water quality: Dadun 90, 95, *96*, 100, 105, *105*; Rhine and Maas rivers 193; San Francisco Bay 10
water table: Pearl River Delta 134, *137*; saltwater intrusion 195–196, *196*; San Francisco Bay 8, 11
water villages, Pearl River Delta *see* Dadun
Waterplan 2 Rotterdam 2030 *188*, 189
West Harbour, Malmø 30, *35*
Western Scheldt 176, 192, 197
wetlands: proposal for construction of Whampoa Harbor 119, 121, *121*; redesigning ground near Dadun canals to include 95, *97*; restoration of South Bay wetlands 10–11
Whampoa Harbor 108–122; affordable housing project for Xinxi 114–119, *117, 118*; canals 111–112; comb structure, village *117, 118*; designing for future of Xinxi 119–122, *120*; economy 114; environmental regulations 115–116; floods 121; housing costs in Guangzhou *115*; integration of water villages into new developments 114; land use 114, 115; lending agreements 119; migrants 115, 116; new harbor designs 110–114, *113*; not-for-profit concept 119; public space, designs for *120*; registration system 116; road patterns 108, 110; transects, Ghangzhou 108–110, *109, 110*; water system 111–112, *112*, 119, 121, *121*
windows, views from 25–26
Wirth, Louis 99
wood construction 24
workspace: downtown office space 38, *39*, 41, 47–48; integration of housing and 66–67, *66, 67*, 104, 132, 134, *135*; office parks 38–41, *40*, 48

Xinxi: affordable housing project 114–119, *117, 118*; migrant population 115, 116
Xintiandi, Shanghai 105–106

Yandu River *89*

Zuiderzee 151–152, 179; closing off 180–181